A2 Level for **Edexcel**

Travel & Tourism

Gillian Dale

Endorsed by Edexcel

www.heinemann.co.uk
✓ Free online support
✓ Useful weblinks
✓ 24 hour online ordering

01865 888058

Inspiring generations

Heinemann Educational Publishers
Halley Court, Jordan Hill, Oxford OX2 8EJ
Part of Harcourt Education

Heinemann is the registered trademark of Harcourt Education Limited

© Gillian Dale, 2006

First published 2006

10 09 08 07 06
10 9 8 7 6 5 4 3 2 1

British Library Cataloguing in Publication Data is available
from the British Library on request.

10-digit ISBN: 0 435 46354 3
13-digit ISBN: 978 0 435463 54 0

Edited by Alistair Nunn
Typeset and illustrated by Tek-Art
Original illustrations © Harcourt Education Limited, 2006
Cover design by Peter Stratton
Printed in the UK by Bath Press
Cover photo: © Getty
Picture research by Chrissie Martin & Sally Cole

Endorsement
This high quality material is endorsed by Edexcel and has been through a rigorous quality
assurance programme to ensure that it is a suitable companion to the specification for both
lecturers and teachers. This does not mean that its contents will be used verbatim when
setting examinations nor is it to be read as being the official specification – a copy of which is
available at www.edexcel.org.uk

Contents

Acknowledgements

The publishers wish to thank for their kind permission to reproduce material and photographs in this book.

The Advertising Association – page 153
Association of British Travel Agents – page 205, 235
British Hospitality Association/Wordsmith & Company – page 230, 231
Burleigh Travel – page 170
CAA UK Online Statistics – page 222
Caterer & Hotelkeeper Magazine – page 231
Center Parcs Ltd – page 162
Centre for European Regional and Transport Economics – page 55
David Browne – page 50, 54
easyJet – page 134
Eurotunnel – page 226
Explore Worldwide Ltd – page 185
First Choice – page 20, 218, 219
First Choice Tropical Brochure (April 2005) – page 30
GoWest – page 220
Hays Travel – page 207
Hertz – page 227
Holland America Line – page 191
The Internet Advertising Bureau – page 156
IRN – page 178
Kwik Travel – page 84
Leeds Metropolitan University – page 95
London City Airport – page 139
Marketing Manchester – page 213
Marriott Hotels International Limited – page 56
Mintel – page 217, 223, 223, 224
MORI – page 5
Novotel – page 56
Ofcom – page 154
Orient Express – page 180
P & O Ferries – page 225
Personnel Today – page 59–60
Teamtechnology.co.uk – page 101, 102
Tourism Ireland – page 133, 134, 138, 152
Travel Corporation – page 188
Travel Trade Gazette – page 17, 48, 52, 69, 129, 131, 137–8, 157, 158, 173, 177, 188, 206, 224, 228, 240
Travel Weekly – page 104, 128
Travelmole – page 26, 51, 52, 53, 54, 67, 137, 209, 209, 221, 237
TribesTravel – page 3
Vienna Tourist Board – page 181
VisitBritain – page 210
VisitLondon – page 55, 211
Wanderlust – page 176
West Oxfordshire District Council – page 97
Winchester City Council – pages 81, 81–2
Working Abroad – page 174
World Tourism organisation – pages 4–5, 15

www.auc.org.uk – page 236
www.flybmi.co.uk – page 89
www.haworth-village.org – page 13
www.headwater.com – page 177, 193, 194
www.iberostarfriends.org – page 92
www.iknow-yorkshire.co.uk – page 168
www.kuoni.com – page 133, 163
www.oasisoverland.co.uk – page 181–2
www.opodo.co.uk – page 150
www.ryanair.com – page 144
www.salsafever.co.uk/www.key2cuba.com – page 192
www.thomson.co.uk – page 86, 102, 143
www.thetravelfoundation.org – page 12
www.tourismconcern.org.uk – page 5
www.tourismsoutheast.com – page 211
www.tourism.it – page 59
www.tribes.co.uk – page 34
www.tourismconcern.org.uk – page 5, 13
Yorkshire Forward – page 10

Crown copyright material is reproduced with the permission of the Controller of HMSO – pages 9–10, 16, 19, 32, 79, 197

Photo Acknowledgements

Lonely Planet/Richard I'Anson – page 1
Almay/Doug Pearson – page 17
Alamy/Maria grazia Casella – page 18
Corbis/G. Rossenbach – page 31
Alamy/Justin Case – page 34
Art Directors & Trip – page 36
Corbis/Reuters – page 39
Alamy/Werner Dieterich – page 56
Getty Images/Photodisc – page 70, 135, 199
Corbis/Jon Feingersh – page 71
Corbis/Jose Pelaez – page 74
Alamy/Jochem Wijnands – page 77
Virgin – page 88
Alamy/Imagestate – page 99
Getty/Sean Justice – page 105
Corbis/J & C Hans Withoos – page 117
Rex Features/Dennis Stone – page 123
Corbis – page 136, 137, 165
Getty/Michael Prince – page 147
Harcourt Education Ltd/Debbie Rowe – page 158, 203
Getty/Robert Harding – page 169
Corbis/Joe MacDonald – page 175
Alamy/Randy Bishop – page 180
Alamy/Bill Bachmann – page 200
Corbis/Derek Croucher – page 210
Art Directors & trip/S. Samuels – page 213
Alamy/E.Simonsen – page 223
Getty/J.L. Sauer – page 242

Introduction

This book is designed to meet the requirements of the GCE A2 Advanced Level Travel and Tourism qualification. If you are studying for this qualification you have probably been successful in achieving the AS Level and already have a good grounding in travel and tourism. I hope you are looking forward to learning about the industry in greater depth and that you are ready to carry out your own research for the units 'Current Issues in Travel and Tourism' and 'Travel Organisations'.

The book follows the Edexcel specification very closely so that you can easily find relevant information and see where you are up to in your studies.

There are lots of case studies and activities to help your understanding of the different units and bring theory to life by setting it in context. In addition there are assessment practice activities which will help you to put together assessment evidence for your portfolio.

The units covered in this book are:

Unit 7 Responsible Tourism
Unit 8 Current Issues in Travel and Tourism
Unit 9 Working in Travel and Tourism
Unit 10 Promotion and Sales in Travel and Tourism
Unit 11 Special Interest Holidays
Unit 12 Travel Organisations

Features of the book

Key term

✱ REMEMBER!

Key terms and Remember!

These help you check your knowledge or remind you of key concepts that you have met in previous units. They are also useful as a quick reference tool.

Theory into practice

Theory into practice

These are short practical activities that allow you to apply theoretical knowledge to travel and tourism tasks or research.

CASE STUDY

Case studies

These give real examples of travel and tourism issues or organisations. They will show you how the topics you study affect real people and businesses. They always have questions to help you explore the relevant issues. Extension questions are often provided for those who are aiming for higher grades.

Knowledge check

Knowledge check

At the end of each unit a set of questions is provided to test your knowledge of the information given in that unit.

Assessment practice

Assessment practice

These are provided for each unit that is assessed within your centre. These are:

Unit 8 Current Issues in Travel and Tourism
Unit 9 Working in Travel and Tourism
Unit 11 Special Interest Holidays
Unit 12 Travel Organisations

You can use these as practice for your eventual assessment activities, which may be set by your school or college.

Assessment guidance

Assessment guidance

This features guidance from Edexcel and is reproduced alongside each activity so that you can see what has to be done to achieve each mark band.

Unit 7 Responsible Tourism and Unit 10, Promotion and Sales in Travel and Tourism are externally assessed by Edexcel, so do not include these last two features.

I hope that you enjoy your course and find this book supports you in achieving success in your qualification!

Gillian Dale

Responsible tourism

This unit covers the following sections:

In this unit we will discover what is meant by responsible tourism. We will examine the development of tourism and the different agents involved. You will study the Tourism Area Life Cycle (TALC) model and consider how potential positive and negative impacts of tourism can be managed in a responsible or sustainable way.

During your study you will be introduced to a range of examples of responsible tourism in different destinations. These will include destinations from the less economically developed world (LEDW) and the more economically developed world (MEDW).

How you will be assessed

This unit is externally assessed. You will undertake a test set and marked by Edexcel. This test will consist of a series of short and long answer questions.

A variety of activities and case studies are provided in this unit to help you understand all aspects of responsible tourism and to help you prepare for the assessment.

The external assessment will require evidence of:

* the ability to demonstrate knowledge skills and understanding of responsible tourism, and of related skills in a travel and tourism context

* the ability to apply your knowledge, skills and understanding of responsible tourism and related skills in a travel and tourism context

* the ability to use appropriate research techniques to obtain and analyse information relevant to responsible tourism

* the ability to evaluate information and reach reasoned judgements, draw conclusions and make recommendations based on knowledge of responsible tourism.

7.1 Responsible tourism

Responsible tourism is a term that can be used to describe many different kinds of tourism, for example; fair trade tourism, green tourism, sustainable tourism, ecotourism and alternative tourism.

> ### Key term
>
> *Responsible tourism* Tourism that recognises the impacts of tourism on a destination and seeks to maximise the positive impacts and minimise the negative impacts.

Responsible tourism has many forms and many different stakeholders, such as developers, tour operators, tourists and environmental groups, have different priorities and different understandings of the term. Some tourists consider that they are behaving responsibly if they buy local crafts and if they are aware of their impact on the destination visited. Others appreciate that there is a whole range of behaviours that create a responsible tourist. Some tour operators have responded to demand for responsible tourism by producing policies for responsible tourism. In addition there are several pressure groups which work towards responsible tourism. Examples include the travel agent responsibletravel.com and Tourism Concern, an organisation which campaigns for fair trade in tourism.

We will look at some different terms used to describe forms of responsible tourism.

Fair trade holidays

A fair trade holiday is one where the local community benefits from tourism so that local people gain employment, local restaurants and bars gain custom and the money spent remains in the local economy.

> ### Key term
>
> *New tourism* is a general term used to describe all kinds of responsible tourism – as if it were a new idea. Specifically, it is a term used by the World Travel and Tourism Council to denote partnerships between tourism stakeholders in the public and private sector who work together to develop tourism policies which are of benefit to local communities. You can find out more in their 'Blueprint for new tourism' document.

Ecotourism

The International Ecotourism Society defines Ecotourism as 'Responsible travel to natural areas

---

CASE STUDY
Tribes Travel

This extract from www.tribestravel.com explains how the company views fair trade.

Fair Trade Travel is not just about the obvious – paying people a **fair wage** for the services that they provide, although this is of course an important factor. What matters to us is that nothing which our company does abroad or at home compromises the environment or exploits the local people. In fact we would prefer that our activities actually have a **positive impact**, so that the money generated by tourism is helping with sustainable development of underdeveloped areas as well as promoting conservation of the environment and the rich cultural heritage of the areas we visit.

1. **Do you consider that this is responsible tourism? Why?**
2. **Think about the last holiday you went on – in what ways did you have a positive impact on the destination? In what ways did you have a negative impact?**

that conserves the environment and improves the well being of local people.' Note again how the concept of responsibility occurs.

Sustainable tourism

Sustainable tourism means developing and managing tourism in such a way that the positive economic and socio-cultural benefits to the environment, the host community and the visitor are maximised without exhausting or abusing precious natural or cultural resources.

Green tourism

This is another term that describes responsible tourism, usually referring to rural tourism. However there are several 'green tourism' schemes that businesses can sign up to, to reassure their customers that they have good environmental policies.

What all these types of tourism have in common is that they do not encompass mass tourism. Mass tourism is generally perceived as being more irresponsible than other forms of tourism. This is not always the case as many tour operators have made efforts to become more responsible in their approach to local communities and we will examine some examples later.

All the terms discussed so far have the same general principles – responsible tourism occurs where tourism development:

* minimises negative economic, environmental and socio-cultural impacts

* creates economic benefits for local people and improves their quality of life

* promotes the conservation of natural and cultural heritage

* promotes respect between tourists and local people.

Key term

Greenwashing This means that an organisation adopts responsible tourism policies in order to reassure customers and gain favourable publicity. However, these policies are often superficial and do not fully adhere to the principles of responsible tourism.

Think it over...

How do you find out if a company is greenwashing or practising responsible tourism? Here are some clues to look for:

* Does the company have a written policy regarding its practice towards the environment and local communities?

* Can they give examples of specific projects where they have benefited a local community?

* Do they have a system of measuring their contribution to the local community?

* Are local people employed in the hotels they use – and in management?

* Do they work with local charities?

* Do they provide information to tourists about local culture?

* How is sewage treated from their hotels?

* How is water conserved?

* Do they employ local guides at their destinations?

These principles are derived from a series of initiatives over the last decade involving governments and pressure groups working towards the promotion of responsible tourism.

In 1992 an Earth Summit on Environment and Development took place in Rio. It produced a programme of action to sustain the future of our planet. This programme is known as Agenda 21 and was endorsed by 182 governments.

In 1996, the World Travel and Tourism Council (WTTC), the World Tourism Organization and the Earth Council worked together to develop an action plan entitled Agenda 21 for the Travel and Tourism Industry: Towards Sustainable Development. From these beginnings the principles of responsible tourism have grown and been adopted by our own government and by many private sector organisations.

The World Tourism Organisation says that sustainable tourism should:

* **Make optimal use of environmental resources** that constitute a key element in tourism

development, maintaining essential ecological processes and helping to conserve natural heritage and biodiversity.

* **Respect the socio-cultural authenticity of host communities**, conserve their built and living cultural heritage and traditional values, and contribute to inter-cultural understanding and tolerance.

* Ensure viable, long-term economic operations, **providing socio-economic benefits to all stakeholders** that are fairly distributed, including stable employment and income-earning opportunities and social services to host communities, and contributing to poverty alleviation.

Source www.world-tourism.org

Tourism Concern

Tourism Concern is a registered charity which encourages sustainable tourism in destination countries by working with communities and trying to find ways of reducing the social and environmental problems connected to tourism and increasing local benefits.

Tourism Concern's 10 Principles for Sustainable Tourism were produced to coincide with the Rio Earth Summit and aim to influence the policies and programmes adopted by the travel and tourism industry worldwide:

* **Using resources sustainably** – The conservation and sustainable use of resources – natural, social and cultural – is crucial and makes long-term business sense.

* **Reducing over-consumption and waste** – reduction of over-consumption and waste avoids the costs of restoring long-term damage and contributes to the quality of tourism.

* **Maintaining diversity** – maintaining and promoting natural, social and cultural diversity is essential for long-term sustainable tourism, and creates a resilient base for the industry.

* **Integrating tourism into planning** – tourism development which is integrated into a national and local strategic planning framework undertakes environmental impact

assessments and increases the long-term viability of tourism.

* **Supporting local economies** – Tourism that supports a wide range of local economic activities and which takes environmental costs and values into account, both protects those economies and avoids environmental damage.

* **Involving local communities** – The full involvement of local communities in the tourism sector not only benefits them and the environment in general but also improves the quality of the tourism experience.

* **Consulting stakeholders and the public** – consultation between the tourism industry and local communities, organisations and institutions is essential if they are to work alongside each other and resolve potential conflicts of interest.

* **Training staff** – staff training which integrates sustainable tourism into work practices, along with recruitment of local personnel at all levels, improves the quality of the tourism product.

* **Marketing tourism responsibly** – marketing that provides tourists with full and responsible information increases respect for the natural, social and cultural environments of destination areas and enhances customer satisfaction.

* **Undertaking research** – on-going research and monitoring by the industry using effective data collection and analysis is essential to help solve problems and to bring benefits to destinations, the industry and consumers.

Source: wwwtourismconcern.org.uk phone no. 020 7133 3330

Think it over...

Consumer research carried out by MORI in 2002 showed that:

* 76% want their holiday to benefit local people

* 87% feel it important that their holiday does not damage the environment

* 81% want their holiday to include visits to experience local culture and foods

* 81% say they will pay at least 1% more.

Source ABTA/MORI package consumer research

7.2 Agents involved in tourism development

In this part of the unit you will learn about the many different kinds of organisations and agencies involved in tourism development. You will learn about their role and their reasons for being involved in tourism development. These organisations represent the public, private and voluntary sectors. They are sometimes described as **stakeholders**.

Key terms

Public sector Public sector organisations are owned by the state and receive their funds from local or central government and usually aim to provide a service. Their policy will be directed by national or local government.

Private sector Owned by shareholders or individuals rather than the state – they are commercial companies and usually aim to make a profit.

Voluntary sector Voluntary organisations are often charities or pressure groups. They do not always make a profit but put funds into the company activities, for example, conservation.

Private Sector Agents

Landowners

Landowners and owners of stately homes are not always cash rich and seek to develop their properties and land to benefit from tourism. Their main role is in the provision of land for development. Others may develop their properties and homes for tourism. Most British stately homes are open to visitors for some part of the year. Many welcome film crews to their parks and houses and then benefit from increased tourism as the films gain publicity.

In developing countries, land owned by local people is often bought up cheaply by developers. If local authorities are powerful enough they can prevent this happening and ensure that local people are involved in development. Where locals own the land they can make money from tourism and stop the advent of large hotel chains. In Tobago there are very few large hotels as local people own the land – and want to keep it. They welcome tourists and cater for them with local produce.

Some of the hotels are all inclusive and these are not always as beneficial to the economy as tourists have all their needs catered for in the hotel.

Developers and accommodation providers

Developers can be anyone from individuals who decide to open a hotel to major international companies responsible for developing whole resorts. Developers are in business to make money out of their development and are often

Texas Parks

Many landowners in Texas currently derive substantial income from wildlife-associated recreation in the form of hunting and fishing on their private lands. The 2001 Survey of Fishing, Hunting, and Wildlife-associated Recreation showed that fishing contributed $2.0 billion to the state's economy, while hunting contributed $1.5 billion, and wildlife watching $1.3 billion. Interest in nature-based tourism is rooted in a growing understanding among landowners that providing recreational opportunities for emerging markets of experiential tourists is another important way to derive economic benefit from the natural resources found on private lands. Activities such as birdwatching, photography, backpacking, horseback riding, mountain biking, wildlife viewing and canoeing are increasingly popular as urban residents and visitors strive to connect with the outdoors.

Texas Parks and Wildlife Department (TPWD) is actively involved in nature tourism development on the private landowner level through the work of the nature tourism coordinator. Through presentations at landowner workshops, TPWD also provides assistance to landowners statewide by answering questions, helping to locate available resources and meeting landowners throughout the state.

Source: Texas Parks and Wildlife Department, 4200 Smith School Road, Austin, TX 78744

1. **Explain the role landowners have in attracting tourists to Texas.**
2. **What reasons do landowners have for getting involved in tourism?**
3. **What sector does Texas Parks and Wildlife Department belong to?**
4. **What is the department's role in developing tourism?**

Extension task: Carry out research and find a similar example of a landowner working with another tourism developer within the UK. Describe and explain the roles of both parties and the reasons for their involvement.

in conflict with host communities who do not want to lose their land or see over-development. The public sector has to take responsibility for overseeing development and ensuring that community needs are met and that development is sustainable. The Bahamas provides a good example. The government policy is to extend the economic benefits derived from tourism and to have a hotel sector that is private sector led. In the UK it is the norm for hotels to be privately owned but in 1992 in the Bahamas 20% of hotels were government owned. In the last 10 years or so, most of these have been privatised. Many hotels were bought and refurbished by international investors and developers. New hotels have also been built and redevelopment of resorts has taken place. A consortium of American, British and South African investors recently bought four hotels on Paradise Island and redeveloped them at a cost of over $250 million. The government gave exemptions from property tax and customs duty for companies investing in hotel and resort development. The purpose was to inject capital investment from the private sector into development, rather than the government provide the capital from taxes.

Consultancies

These are companies and individuals who provide specialist advice. They may be advising governments on policies, advising on new products or helping tour operators restructure their business. Consultants work in all industries but examples in tourism are Equinus, a technology consultant and PA Consulting Group who provide services to private tourism companies, international tourism development organisations and government agencies.

Here is an example of a travel and tourism consultant:

CASE STUDY

Luton Airport

In October 2005, Luton Airport unveiled plans for a new runway and terminal planned to be operational in time for the London Olympics in 2012.

The proposed development came as both Stansted and Heathrow, both owned by the British Airports Authority, are in the process of planning new runways and Stansted is only 25 miles from Luton. All the proposals follow the Government White Paper on Air Transport which supported regional airport development. The development at Luton will cost £1.5 billion and will triple the passenger capacity of the airport from nine million to thirty million passengers by 2030. The airport is owned by Luton Borough Council but is on lease to Abertis, a Spanish tollroad operator. The Council supports the expansion as Luton needs to create jobs locally following the closure of Vauxhall car factory.

Summarise the roles in airport development of:

* the government

* Luton Borough Council

* BAA

* Abertis.

What are the objectives of each stakeholder in the development?

Extension task: Describe and explain how the objectives of these organisations might conflict. See page 15 for information on objectives.

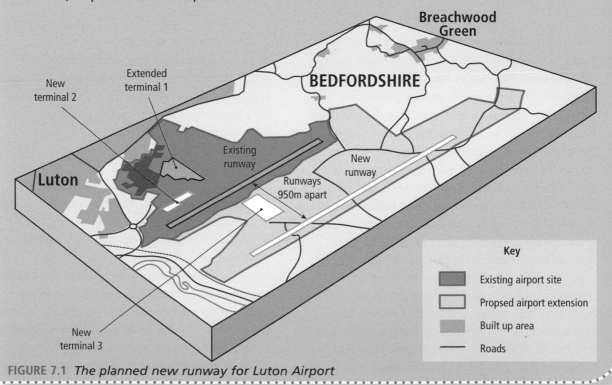

FIGURE 7.1 *The planned new runway for Luton Airport*

An example of one of SQW's projects is a development plan for the conservation of Kinloch Castle in Scotland undertaken for Scottish National Heritage.

Travel organisations

Travel and tourism organisations have a part to play in tourism development. Airlines and tour operators often instigate development by introducing services and package holidays to a destination. They are also represented by their industry bodies allowing them to have a voice in government policy decisions.

Leisure and entertainment organisations

These companies usually enter into a development in the later stages and choose a location where they will benefit from the advent of tourism. Examples include cinemas, casinos and leisure centres. In the Bahamas the Paradise Island development we discussed earlier is operated by the world's largest leisure company, Sunhill International Corporation. They operate the hotels but also casinos.

Think it over...

Think about the last holiday you went on. What were the leisure and entertainment centres in your resort? What was their role in terms of tourism development?

Think it over...

Why do you think private sector organisations want to get involved in tourism developments? The obvious answer is to make money from commercial development but increasingly there are companies who combine commercial practice with concern for the environment or regeneration of urban environments.

Public sector agents

The public sector role is of utmost importance as it is responsible for setting policy on tourism and for putting in place the legislation needed to implement policy. In a developed country like the UK the public sector structure is well established and works in harmony with the private sector to develop and monitor tourism. In countries where the tourism industry is in its infancy, the government may have less control over development than private enterprises and has to begin the process of establishing national tourism organisation networks.

National regional and local organisations

In the UK the structure of the public sector is shown in the diagram below.

The Department for Culture, Media and Sport (DCMS) set down its strategies for tourism in the UK in 1999 in 'Tomorrow's Tourism'. Fifteen action points were at the core of this document:

* A blueprint for the sustainable development of tourism.

* Initiatives to widen access to tourism.

* More money for a more focused and aggressive overseas promotion programme.

* New Internet systems to deliver more worldwide tourist bookings for Britain.

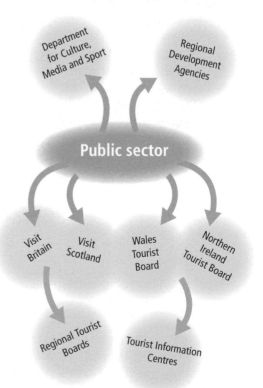

FIGURE 7.2 *The structure of the public sector of the tourism industry*

- New computerised booking and information services.

- A major careers festival and image campaign.

- A hospitality industry programme to sign up 500 employees to work towards Investors in People standard.

- A new strategic national body for England.

- A new grading scheme for all hotels and guest houses.

- New targets for hotel development in London and a further £4.5 million for marketing.

- More integrated promotion of our wonderful cultural, heritage and countryside attractions.

- The development of innovative niche markets, such as film tourism and sports tourism.

- Encouraging the regeneration of traditional resorts.

- More central government support for the regions.

- A high profile Tourism Summit bringing together industry and government.

Source: 'Tomorrow's Tourism' 1999

These targets are still valid but in July 2004, an update, 'Tomorrow's Tourism Today', was published reporting on progress and establishing further targets under categories of marketing and e-tourism, product quality, workforce skills, improved data and advocacy across Government.

CASE STUDY

Yorkshire Forward

Yorkshire Forward is the regional development agency that has responsibility for regional tourism policy and strategy in Yorkshire. This is part of its role in regeneration and economic growth. It is funded directly by the government. Yorkshire Tourism is a new regional tourism organisation which will be responsible, with Yorkshire Forward, for developing and monitoring the Strategic Tourism Agenda. Yorkshire Tourism will also be responsible for the regional marketing tourism plan, research and intelligence, skills and training, quality assurance and a destination management system. In addition there will be four destination management organisations; one for each of the following sub-regions:

- South Yorkshire

- The Humber

- West Yorkshire

- North Yorkshire

The destination management organisations will be responsible for product development, visitor management, business support services and co-ordination of local and sub-regional promotions. Some funding for Yorkshire Tourism and the destination management organisations will come from Yorkshire Forward. The destination management organisations will be subscription organisations. Subscribers will be tourism businesses of all types and sizes. By joining their relevant destination management organisation, tourism businesses will have access to the full range of services offered.

Source: www.yorkshire-forward.com

1. Draw up an organisation chart illustrating the relationship between the different public sector organisations described in the extract.
2. Describe the role and objectives of each organisation in tourism development.
3. Suggest the organisations who might become members of the destination management organisations. Describe their role in tourism development.

Decide how to present your findings and then present them.

Extension task: Discuss the conflicting objectives and positions of the agents of tourism development and their impact on development in Yorkshire. See page 15 for information on objectives.

Tourist boards

Visit Britain and the other national boards are responsible for implementing government policy nationally and the regional tourist boards are responsible for implementing it in their regions alongside the regional development agencies. The regional development agencies have a remit that extends beyond tourism. The tourist boards have to promote their areas as destinations and work to influence government policies. They also advise businesses in their area about government policy.

Regional development agencies (RDA)

These agencies were set up by the government to promote sustainable economic development in England. Since 2003 they have had strategic responsibility for tourism in their regions. They work in conjunction with the tourist boards. Whilst the development agency determines policy, the tourist board is responsible for delivering it. The tourist board develops its business plans with the development agency and has them approved by the development agency board members.

Key term

QUANGO This is an acronym which stands for quasi autonomous non governmental organisation, otherwise known as non departmental public bodies. They are set up by government with government funding but they work independently of government. Examples include the regional development agencies. Can you think of others?

English Heritage

This body is sponsored by the DCMS and is an executive non departmental public body. Its official name is the Historic Buildings and Monuments Commission for England. The organisation also works with other government departments as their work also affects heritage. An example is the Department for Environment, Food and Rural Affairs (DEFRA) which takes care of policy on rural issues. The government provides funding for English Heritage but it also earns revenue from the historic properties.

The role of English Heritage is described on its website:

'English Heritage works in partnership with the central government departments, local authorities, voluntary bodies and the private sector to:

* Conserve and enhance the historic environment

* Broaden public access to the heritage

* Increase people's understanding of the past.

Source: www.english-heritage.org.uk

The organisation looks after over 400 properties for the nation and maintains registers of England's most significant historic buildings, monuments and landscapes.

Theory into practice

Find out more about the role of conservation at English Heritage. What partners does the organisation work with? How do they fund projects? You might choose a particular project to report on. Write up notes on your findings.

* REMEMBER!

Public sector organisations develop tourism to take advantage of the economic benefits to the community or region, in terms of jobs or increased revenue. Organisations like English Heritage aim to preserve our heritage and culture for all to enjoy.

Voluntary sector agents

Many voluntary sector organisations are charities and pressure groups. Probably the best known in tourism is the National Trust. There are several voluntary organisations related to tourism development and responsible tourism.

CASE STUDY

Travel Foundation

The Travel Foundation is an independent UK charity that aims to help the outbound travel industry manage tourism more sustainably.

It offers a unique resource to the tourism industry, helping to safeguard resources on which business depends and balancing the need for sustainability with profitability.

The Foundation's focus is on protecting and enhancing the environment and improving the well-being of destination communities, thereby enriching the tourism experience, now and in to the future.

The development of the Foundation helps enable a real breakthrough for sustainable tourism and is good news for consumers, companies, destination communities and policy makers.

* Consumers get greater quality and an enriched holiday experience, as well as the reassurance that their favourite destinations will be protected for generations to come.

* Businesses are better able to meet the needs of their customers, at the same time as protecting the resources on which their future depends.

* Destination communities receive greater benefit from tourism, with a boost to their local economy and conservation of the natural environment, local traditions and culture.

* Local and national governments have evidence to develop effective tourism policies and support destination communities and environments.

Source: www.thetravelfoundation.org.uk

1. **Find out three ways in which the Travel Foundation helps businesses practise sustainable tourism.**
2. **Find out how the Travel Foundation is funded.**
3. **Give examples of partners with whom the Travel Foundation works.**

You might send for the Insider Guide published by the Travel Foundation. This is a leaflet aimed at tourists and gives tips for responsible travel. It can also be downloaded at www.thetravelfoundation.org.uk/our_insider_guides.asp

Theory into practice

Voluntary organisations

Choose one of the following voluntary organisations involved in tourism development:

* Tourism Concern

* Green Hotels Association

* Wildlife Trust

* CERT (Centre for Environmentally Responsible Tourism)

* Earthwatch

* Kathmandu Environmental Education Project.

Work with a partner.

Research the chosen organisation. Prepare a presentation which covers:

* the objectives of the organisation

* an example of a current project

* how to support the organisation.

Community Groups

Community groups may be formed specifically to deal with proposed tourism developments or may have been formed for a different purpose but become involved in tourism development. Local people wish to be consulted on possible developments to protect their personal and community interests. Community groups can also act as pressure groups. Community groups may be invited to join tourism working groups so that they are included in decision making and can put the point of view of the community to officials.

The Haworth Village Trust is an example of a community group who have interests in tourism. Haworth is a major tourist attraction as it was home to the famous Bronte literary family and houses a museum about them in the old parsonage. The tourists outnumber local people and have brought traffic congestion to the village as well as increased revenue to the economy. This extract from www.haworth-village.org explains how the group is funded and its current projects:

> 'The Haworth Village Trust was formed in 2000 by a group of local people committed to the unique nature and circumstances of Haworth.
>
> The Trust is a company limited by guarantee and gained charitable status in 2003. Its membership is drawn from local villagers.
>
> The Trust has several projects in hand at any one time. To date these are the promotion of a cycle path from Oxenhope to Keighley, to reinstate the Bandstand in the park, the preservation of the old school building at Butt Lane, the redevelopment of the Community Centre, Weavers Hill car park.
>
> The Trust relies on its membership for support, and grant giving bodies for funding.'

Pressure groups

These organisations work to lobby government and change policies. Many of them are concerned with protecting the environment and wildlife. Examples include the Wildlife Trust which is a conservation charity dedicated to wildlife and Tourism Concern whose role is described in the case study on this page.

Other examples of pressure groups in tourism are The Responsible Tourism Partnership and Pro-Poor Tourism. The Responsible Tourism Partnership is a not-for-profit organisation that

CASE STUDY
Tourism Concern

Tourism Concern has been working since 1989 to raise awareness of the negative impacts of tourism, economically, culturally, environmentally and socially. Advocacy is a major part of our work and time and again, the message from our Southern (Third World) partners is the same: "We want tourists, but at the moment we don't benefit from them." Communities often find they have tourism imposed on them by governments and foreign developers and tourism businesses; that there is little linkage between tourism – especially at a mass scale – and local industry, such as agriculture; that land and natural resources are frequently co-opted, often illegally; and that their cultural traditions are appropriated and commercialised.

Our links with communities and agencies working in developing countries show that there is great concern that the trend in tourism is towards greater control by multinationals, more all-inclusive tourism which excludes local people and businesses, and greater numbers. The consequence of such a trend proving true could prove disastrous for local people.

Source: www.tourismconcern.co.uk

1. **Visit the Tourism Concern website and choose one current campaign.**
2. **What is the role of Tourism Concern in this campaign?**
3. **What other partners are involved in the campaign?**
4. **What sector does each of the partners belong to?**

Extension task: How do the objectives of Tourism Concern in your chosen campaign conflict with those of government or developers?

aims to improve destinations for local people and their visitors. The organisation works with private tourism businesses, governments and with local communities. Pro-Poor, as the name suggests, works to help poorer people in local communities benefit from tourism activities.

National Trust

The National Trust differs from English Heritage in that it is completely independent of government. It is a registered charity and therefore a voluntary organisation. It was founded in 1895 by three Victorian philanthropists who were concerned about industrialisation and set up the trust to acquire and protect threatened coastline, countryside and buildings.

This is still the role of the National Trust today. It protects over 200 historic houses and gardens and 49 industrial monuments and mills. It also owns more than 248,000 hectares of countryside and almost 600 miles of coast for people to visit and enjoy.

The Trust also has a role in managing the environment, developing best practice and acting as a source of advice on environmental issues. The National Trust has over three million members. It looks after over 300 properties and 612 acres of land. The Trust is funded by membership fees, revenue from entrance to properties and donations. It is not funded by the government.

The National Trust for Scotland is a similar organisation and cares for over 100 properties.

The Historic Houses Association (HHA) represents a group of privately owned stately homes and its aim is to help with the preservation of privately owned historic houses, their contents and their gardens.

Its mission is to 'work for a fiscal, political and economic climate in which private owners can maintain Britain's historic houses and gardens for the benefit of the nation and for future generations.'

Source: www.hha.org.uk

Theory into practice

Public, Private and Voluntary Organisations.

ORGANISATION	ROLE	PUBLIC	PRIVATE	VOLUNTARY
English Heritage				
VisitBritain				
Yorkshire Forward				
National Trust				
Hilton Hotels				
Tourism Concern				
British Airways				
Blackpool Pleasure Beach				
Thomas Cook				
DCMS				
British Airports Authority				

Complete the chart deciding whether the organisations are public, private or voluntary.

Try to summarise the role of each organisation.

The HHA has emphasised the contribution of the private sector historic owners to our economy:

✳ annual contribution to rural economy: £1.2 Billion

✳ employment in all tourism and commercial operations: over 10,000.

The Landmark Trust acquires historic properties and renovates them so that they are suitable for holiday lets.

Think it over...

Can you summarise the reasons why voluntary organisations get involved in tourism development? Consider factors such as encouraging responsible tourism, education and raising funds.

Objectives of tourism development

Key term

Tourism development can be defined as the process of providing facilities and services for visitors to a destination in order to gain economic and other benefits. Although it occurs throughout the world, it does not occur at the same rate and some countries and destinations are just beginning tourism development whilst others are highly established. Tourism development is complex as it may mean a local area opening up to visitors, the development of a specific resort or hotel or a country setting up policies and tourist board structures to promote tourism. On a national level tourism development is driven by governments setting policy for tourism and creating a structure that promotes tourism.

Economic objectives

In most cases economic objectives are the aim of tourism development. This is not surprising as world wide tourist arrivals and receipts are increasing and all countries would like a piece of the action. World Tourism Organisation figures for 2004 suggest an all time record of 760 million

international tourist arrivals. This means an increase of 69 million arrivals from 2003.

The chart below shows which areas received the new arrivals in 2004.

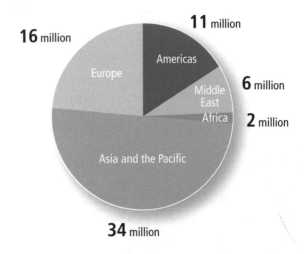

Source: World Tourism Organization (WTO)

FIGURE 7.3 *New arrivals 2004 by region (worldwide 69 million)*

In the UK inbound and domestic tourism provided over £74 billion in 2003. This represented 4% of Gross Domestic Product (GDP).

Key term

Gross Domestic Product – A measure of the market value of goods and services produced by a country within that country.

Gross National Product – As GDP but includes goods and services produced abroad and foreign investment returns.

The economic objectives of tourism development include:

✳ employment creation

✳ increasing foreign currency earnings

✳ tourist contributions to the multiplier effect.

Employment creation

In 2003 2.1 million people worked in tourism in the UK. This represented over 7% of the working population and more jobs than in construction or transport.

Employment in tourism See table 7.1) is growing at a faster rate than in other industries. Tourism is a service sector and therefore jobs can be created with low start-up costs unlike manufacturing where plant and equipment are needed.

TABLE 7.1 *Employment in tourism in the UK*

	TOTAL (MILLIONS)	TOURISM-RELATED (MILLIONS)
Total Employment	28.1	2.17
Employee Jobs	24.4	2.01
Self-employment	3.6	0.16

Source: Labour Market Statistics 2003

Direct employment occurs in hotels, airports, airlines, tour operators, travel agents and tourist offices.

Indirect employment occurs in industries and businesses that service the travel and tourism industry. For example, construction workers are needed to build the infrastructure that supports tourism such as roads and rail networks, hotels and gas and electricity services. Also local shops and services benefit from tourist business and need more employees.

Think it over...

How many people do you know who work in tourism or related industries? How would a reduction in tourists affect their job?

Increasing foreign currency earnings

Tourism generates foreign exchange earnings. Tourism is an invisible export. This means if tourists spend their money in the UK it brings the same benefit to our economy as if they are buying goods exported from the UK, in their own country. By the same token when we travel abroad we spend our money in another country and this is the same as buying imported goods in the UK. Inbound tourists spend money whilst in the UK and some also spend money on travel with UK

carriers. The more tourists who come into the UK the more the spend increases and the more revenue the economy gains. The impact on the economy of incoming and outbound tourism is recorded in the travel balance, a section of the *Balance of Payments*. Each sector of the economy is measured in terms of its imports and exports. A happy situation for our economy is where there is a surplus in the **Balance of Payments** rather than a deficit. This means more money coming in than going out.

Key term

Balance of Payments – one of the UK's key economic statistics. It measures the economic transactions between the UK and the rest of the world. It tells us the difference between spending on imports and exports.

The Balance of Payments was £18 billion in the red in 2003. The UK government hopes that increased inbound tourism will help to reduce this deficit and aims to increase the value of tourism to £100 billion by 2010.

The Multiplier Effect

Key term

The Multiplier Effect – the additional revenue created in an area as a result of tourism expenditure.

Direct tourism expenditure has a wider impact on the economy. If a tourist visits a destination and stays in a hotel, the hotel then spends money on local services and provisions to run the business and provide food and facilities for guests. Staff working at the hotel receive wages which are then used to buy further goods and services. Thus, the impact of the initial spend is 'multiplied' throughout the economy. The multiplier is expressed as a ratio. It can also be applied to jobs; the building of the hotel leads to direct employment in the hotel but also to extra employment in the construction and service industries. The World Travel and Tourism Council estimates that tourism generates an indirect spend equal to 100% of direct tourism spend.

NZ targets the big spenders

Tourism New Zealand has identified its ideal visitor – 'the interactive traveller' – as it chases a rise in tourism earnings rather than volume. Interactive travellers tend to be well-educated, travel internationally on a regular basis and have relatively high levels of discretionary income.

Tourism minister Mark Burton said: "These guests are exceptionally valuable, as they spend more, visit outlying regions and are as keen as us to interact with, and protect, the environment and heritage that have drawn them here." Wally Stone, chairman of Tourism New Zealand, added: "Tourism is New Zealand's largest export industry.

Visitor spending grew four per cent in 2003 against 2002."

New Zealand's tourism industry generated £2.19 billion in 2003 – a four per cent increase on 2002. Of this, the inbound market from Australia accounted for NZ$1 billion (£346 million) for the first time. Burton called this a 'milestone', and added: "Without these visitors, New Zealand would have to double the size of its dairy herd, add 5.3 million hectares in forest and expand the wine industry by 23 times to compensate. I am confident that the sector will continue to be an economic powerhouse."

Source: Travel Trade Gazette, June 4th 2004

1. **Do you think that interactive travellers are 'responsible'? If so, why?**
2. **Explain how tourism is an export industry.**
3. **What is meant by discretionary income?**
4. **Why are tourism earnings of more interest to New Zealand than volume of visitors?**

Extension task: Find out about the role of Tourism New Zealand. Which sector does the organisation belong to? What are its objectives?

Environmental objectives

Environmental education

Visitor centres are usually a source of information for tourists and school groups. Such education helps the tourists understand the reasons for conservation and encourages them to respect the environment. It also allows children and students to learn about the environment in a practical way. Some national parks provide information and fact sheets which schoolchildren can download from the Internet.

Preservation of wildlife habitats

National parks and other protected countryside areas are common in most countries to enhance the environment for the benefit of visitors and to protect the areas from over-development.

Environmental improvements

Investment in tourism can bring about improvements to areas which benefit local people as well as visitors. This might include cleaning buildings, providing riverside and canal walkways and getting rid of litter.

Conservation

Our precious natural habitats and heritage sites have to be conserved or they will be lost to future generations. It is often difficult to balance conservation with allowing the public to view or enjoy their heritage and parklands. National Parks are heavily protected and although people are allowed to enjoy them, there are restrictions on the types of activities that can take place. Historic buildings such as the colleges in Cambridge and Oxford are often open to the public but access is restricted by time and numbers so that too many tourists are not detrimental to the buildings' structure.

Regeneration

Revenue from tourism can be used to preserve heritage sites. Ironically, the preservation is sometimes necessary because of increased tourism. Tourists wandering around a site cause erosion and litter. Industrial regeneration is a common theme in the UK as our case study shows.

CASE STUDY
Salford

Salford is being transformed. Three new heritage walks have been introduced with maps and guides to accompany them. Chapel Street is included in the walking tour, the first street in the country to be lit by gas and the scene of one of the first battles of the Civil War. There have been walking tours for some time but the new ones incorporate Salford Quays, Worsley and Chapel Street. The council, through its marketing and tourism department aims to promote the town as a heritage town, rather than its reputation as a dirty old town. The council says that the city has 60% green space and the entire docks area has been regenerated. Salford Quays boasts modern apartments amid the remains of the old docks.

1. **Find out more about regeneration, either in Salford or in your own town if appropriate. Find out who are the stakeholders involved in regeneration projects and their role in the regeneration. How do you think the regeneration will impact on the economy?**

Present your findings to your colleagues.

Socio-cultural objectives

Promoting cultural understanding

Welcoming visitors to a country or community can promote mutual understanding. It can inspire people to learn new languages and to try new foods and experiences. On a global level such interaction can help promote peaceful societies. This works both ways. Hosts must have a positive attitude to visitors and be encouraged to welcome them and take part in community tourism initiatives. On the other hand, visitors must respect the people and the culture of the destination they are visiting.

Improving quality of life

Sometimes planning permission is only given to developers as long as they provide facilities for the host community alongside or as part of their development. Examples include leisure facilities or even schools. In addition the host community has a better standard of living because of the increased revenues from tourism.

Maintaining cultural traditions

Traditions may be lost as younger generations lose interest in them. The objective of tourism may be to preserve such traditions. In fact cultural and heritage tourism are rising in popularity.

Political objectives

Tourism is related to politics in that it is the government of a country that determines tourism

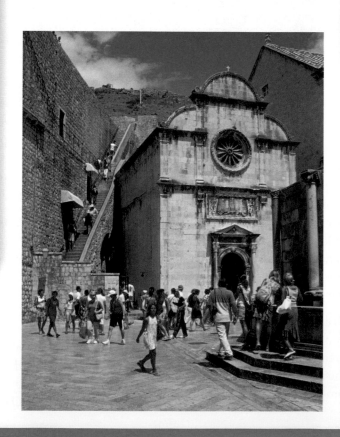

policy. The policy is often to use a national network of tourism organisations to attract greater numbers of tourists to generate revenue or to manage tourism in a sustainable way. There may be other political objectives too.

Enhancing the image of an area

How a country is perceived is often related to tourism and the perceptions of visitors. Where a country has suffered conflict and is in the stage of recovery, tourism can be a means of proving to the international community that the country is stable and safe. Croatia provides a good example. As part of the former Yugoslavia the area was a very popular tourist destination. The civil war in the 1990s meant that the tourism industry was devastated. Although a lot of Croatia was unaffected by conflict, tourists naturally stayed away. Now, tourism is an essential part of the country's regeneration.

Creating a national identity

Our national identity comes from images and experiences within our country but also from how others perceive our country.

Theory into practice

Choose three countries. Discuss your perceptions of those countries as a tourist. How do you think tourists see the British? Are these perceptions right? What gives us our national identity?

Partnership

In recent years the importance of responsible tourism has been increasingly recognised and, in developed destinations especially, an integrated approach to development is either in place or being put into place. This means that partnerships are essential in planning so that all parties are aware of the issue of responsible tourism.

Different partners may have conflicting objectives. For example, a developer aims to make a profit whilst the local authority may be interested in creating jobs and ensuring protection of the environment. Such conflict may be resolved through negotiation, regulation and planning.

For tourists to engage in responsible tourism it has to be an issue at all planning levels, from international to local, and across sectors so that planners, transport departments, marketing agencies and economic development units are all party to it.

Following Agenda 21, the Department of Culture, Media and Sport is committed to responsible tourism and seeks to promote it by working closely with other government departments such as the Department for Transport, the Office of the Deputy Prime Minister on planning issues and the Department for Environment, Food and Rural Affairs on countryside and wildlife issues.

Responsible or sustainable tourism was established as a priority for the UK in the government publication 'Tomorrow's Tourism' in 1999. The policy followed a consultation exercise with a wide range of organisations.

A strategy, 'Time for Action' was to be implemented by the English Tourism Council (now VisitBritain). The strategy had three objectives for sustainable tourism:

* to benefit the economy of tourism destinations
* to support local communities and culture
* to protect and enhance the built and natural environment.

These were then expanded into objectives and targets for the national tourist boards. Regional tourist boards and local authorities must also be aware of these objectives and incorporate them into planning.

You can see that the basis for planning exists internationally and in the UK throughout our public sector but it is essential that foreign governments also adopt the principles of responsible tourism in their planning and also that private organisations are committed to it.

Key term

Sustainable Tourism Initiative was a multi-stakeholder partnership seeking to introduce sustainable tourism practice in the UK outbound tourism industry.

The Sustainable Tourism Initiative was developed in 2003 in preparation for the World Summit on Sustainable Development. The aim was to encourage sustainable tourism practice in the UK outbound tourism industry, through acknowledging that there is a responsibility to sustainability, not just in our own country but also to the destinations we visit. The organisations subscribing to the initiative included government, tour operators and other industry members.

Its aims were to:

* raise awareness amongst the industry and the public about the issues of tourism and sustainable development via clear communications and training programmes.

* research, develop and demonstrate best practice initiatives for companies to adopt.

You can find out more at www.fco.gov.uk.

Private organisations, such as tour operators, working in destinations abroad are in a position to influence responsible tourism and there are many examples of good practice. In the UK, in line with the Sustainable Tourism Initiative, 25 different tour operators have banded together to develop 'The Tour Operator's Initiative'. The initiative is a commitment to responsible tourism by these tour operators and is open to any others to join. They have produced a report which gives examples of different actions that tour operators can take to contribute to responsible tourism.

Some tour operators, for example Thomson, support the Travel Foundation, the UK charity that claims to help protect the natural environment, traditions and culture. You read about the Travel Foundation on page 12.

First Choice is one of the tour operators keen to develop a sustainable tourism strategy. Their vision and policy is shown below.

First Choice UK & Ireland
Sustainable Tourism Vision & Policy

Vision
Enable people to explore and enjoy the world without harming it.

Policy
We recognise that the environment, the communities and cultures within which we operate and our relationships with key groups and individuals are vital to the success of our business. We therefore commit in the long term to:

* minimising the direct environmental impact of our operations and being proactively involved in activities and projects that work to protect and restore the natural environment

* working with customers, employees, shareholders, suppliers, industry partners, local communities and other relevant interested parties, to understand and respect their needs, and also supporting them in delivering our commitments

* using the collective influence of the First Choice Group responsibly to create momentum to make tourism more sustainable

* being open, honest and realistic about our environmental and social impacts, targets and achievements in the context of our business objectives.

In support of this we will work to:

* engage First Choice employees and gain their commitment to action, by raising awareness and understanding of sustainable tourism and the benefits of addressing it

* promote fair working conditions throughout our own business and our supply chain

* comply with all relevant legislation, act in advance of it where possible and keep pace with best practice

* review current business practices and ensure plans are in place to embed the company's sustainable tourism vision

* deliver long-term strategic benefits and shareholder value by maximising the synergies that sustainable development provides.

Source: First Choice – Sustainable Tourism: The Tour Operator's Contribution

Sustainable Tourism policy

In addition the tour operators should give guidance to their customers on how to behave responsibly on holiday. First Choice does this – the guidance is included in their brochures under 'Essential reading'.

Theory into practice

Just how committed to raising awareness about responsible tourism are tour operators? Carry out a survey of brochures using a selection of tour operators. Go through the brochures and find examples of tips similar to those printed by First Choice. Discuss your findings in your group.

CASE STUDY
Serengeti National Park

This case study is designed to help you prepare for your external assessment.

Serengeti National Park is located in northern Tanzania and is a UBESCO World Heritage site. It covers over 14000 square kilometres and is populated by 'the big five' that is lions, leopards, rhinos, buffalo and elephants. In addition it is famous for over a million wildebeest which roam the park. The park has a fragile ecosystem which is protected. The southern plains of Serengeti are populated by the Maasai warrior race who live in harmony with the land and the animals. Measures have been taken to protect the parks and the Maasai from tourists. It is against park regulations to take photos of the Maasai and tourists who want to vist a Maasai village must go to one of the specially developed tourist 'bomas'. These were set up so that tourists do not disturb the real villages.

The Tanzanian government has recently planned to allow a Dubai based developer to build a 120 room hotel complex inside the park. The Tanzanian National Parks Authority is divided over the project and it is expected they will carry out an environmental impact study. Wildlife conservationists say such a huge investment inside the park will disrupt conservation efforts and will degrade the fragile environment inside this famous wildlife park in Africa.

Frankfurt Zoological Society, which has been funding wildlife conservation programs in Serengeti National Park for decades, opposes the plan. The head of the group's operations in Africa, Dr. Markus Borner, told reporters he would voice his opposition to the proposed hotel project or any other permanent structures there. If the hotel is allowed it will be the biggest hotel complex inside the protected areas of East Africa.

1. **Identify the following from the text:**
   - **A private sector agent of tourism development**
   - **A public sector agent of tourism development**
   - **A voluntary sector agent of tourism development.**
2. **Explain the role of each in terms of the proposed development.**
3. **What are the objectives of the development as far as the government is concerned?**
4. **Suggest how the development might be carried out so that it meets with the principles of responsible tourism.**
5. **Explain why conflict might occur between the various parties involved in the development and how the conflict might be resolved.**

7.3 The impacts of tourism development

In this section of the unit you will learn about the different types of tourism impact. You will study destinations where planned and unplanned development has occurred and learn how to interpret information and explain the positive and negative impacts.

Economic impact

Economic impacts can be divided into positive and negative impacts.

Positive economic impacts

Increased domestic and foreign currency earnings

We have already noted that tourism development brings economic benefits in terms of increased expenditure in an economy. This may come from domestic or inbound tourism. Inbound tourism brings with it increased earnings from foreign currency exchange. In developing nations, investment from foreign companies helps build the infrastructure and the facilities needed for tourism.

The government also benefits from increased revenue as it receives taxes from businesses earning revenue from tourism and in VAT from goods and services bought by tourists.

Think it over...

What kind of businesses can you think of in your locality that earns revenue from tourism? Divide them into those which earn a direct income and those which earn indirectly.

Benefits of the multiplier effect

You saw earlier that the multiplier effect is one of the objectives of tourism. The multiplier effect means that the whole community can benefit from the initial injection of cash from tourism. Here is a simple example.

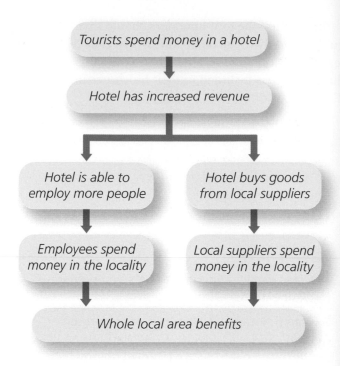

FIGURE 7.4 *The multiplier effect means a whole community can benefit from the money tourism brings.*

Increased opportunities for employment for locals

Jobs in tourism are generally desirable in developing destinations. Employees may be able to undertake professional training and improve their job prospects. The quantity and quality of training naturally varies across countries and companies. In areas of good practice, line staff may receive weekly training and support for higher education programmes.

Remember that jobs can be directly related to tourism or to support development, for example in construction.

In the UK, tourism is not a statutory duty for local authorities, meaning they don't have to spend money on it – but they do, an estimated £90 million per year. In Birmingham, they claim that their tourism business has provided 31,000 jobs and a return to the local economy of £1,013 for every 87p of council tax spent on generating tourism (Sunday Times 21 Nov 2004). Greenwich also used tourism to regenerate the area. It had very high unemployment in the 1990s as it lost traditional jobs. Now, after the programme of regeneration, 25% of jobs are provided by tourism and £327 million is generated for the local economy.

Improved infrastructure

Development may also bring about improved infrastructure which can be used by tourists and local people alike. For example, improvements in roads allow people to travel more easily or improvements in plumbing may provide clean water supplies. Developments to infrastructure create more jobs and the improvements in quality of life mean the area is more attractive to tourists.

CASE STUDY

Eurostar

In 2007, Eurostar train services will move to the newly completed St Pancras station in London instead of Waterloo. This is part of the plans for development of the new high speed line between London and the Channel Tunnel. Eurostar prefers St Pancras for its operations because it has more underground lines and direct rail links to the Midlands and the North of England and Scotland. It is hoped that these links will encourage travellers from those areas to use Eurostar and increase custom. It is even possible that direct Eurostar trains could operate from northern towns without changes in London. Two new Eurostar stations will be built in Stratford in east London and Ebbsfleet in Dartford, Kent. These two stations will serve the east and south east of London. The high speed line to the channel will cut the journey time from London to Paris to 2 hours 15 minutes and travel between Brussels and London will take under 2 hours.

1. **Discuss how these improvements in journey time and infrastructure will provide economic benefits in the UK.**
2. **Are there any negative impacts you can think of?**

Extension task: Find out what other partners are involved in this development. How will the 2012 Olympics aid the development?

Negative economic impacts

Leakage

Economic benefits can be lost if there are high imports of goods and services used in tourism, for example if food and drink for hotels are imported rather than bought locally. Similarly, if materials and workers for construction projects are imported then the local economy does not benefit.

Key term

Leakage is the term used for the amounts – taxes, money spent on imports, wages, etc. – paid outside the region and company profits, subtracted from direct tourism expenditure in an area. Tourism Concern estimates that 89% of money from holidays stays in the UK. Leakage can be prevented by sourcing local materials, using local produce, allowing people to sell crafts in resorts and employing more local people.

Think it over...

Can you think of a reason why 89% of money spent by UK residents on holidays abroad might stay in the UK?

Change from traditional employment opportunities

Traditional industry can be penalised by tourism if workers choose to leave their employment in search of jobs in the tourist industry. This often occurs in developing economies where the jobs in tourism may initially provide more pay. When tourism is regionalised in a country people may leave their homes and communities to take up jobs in tourism. More serious displacement occurs when whole communities are moved on to make room for tourism development. Economic distortion can occur when one region of a country is highly developed for tourism and other areas have none. This occurs to an extent in the UK where the South East and London receive far more tourists than other regions. It is a greater problem in countries where there is little other industry. Overdependence on tourism is a potential problem. Tourists are fickle and fashions change quickly

Seasonal employment

Jobs provided by tourism are often less than ideal. They may be seasonal, part time and low paid. In addition, international hotels often bring in management from developed countries rather than train local staff. This leaves only low paid, less skilled jobs for local people. In the UK many visitor attractions are closed in the winter leaving employees to search for alternative work or register as unemployed.

Increased living costs for the local community

When tourists arrive in an area, particularly a developing area, they can have an impact on costs in the area. Restaurateurs find that tourists are able to pay higher prices than locals and put prices up. Taxi drivers can charge tourists more. Retailers can sell more expensive goods. In the worst cases this can cause a two tier economy. When tourists buy second homes in a locality, there is often an impact on house prices which means that local people can no longer afford to buy houses in their own area.

Environmental impact

Positive environmental impacts

Environmental education

This applies to local people and tourists. Through tourism people can be made more aware of environmental issues. They may become more in touch with nature and schoolchildren may benefit from visits to attractions such as the Eden Project in Cornwall where environmental projects are undertaken.

Landscaping

Many special interest holidays allow tourists to contribute to the landscaping of the environment by taking part in a working holiday. BTCV – the conservation holiday operator, has many examples such as restoring paths in the countryside or building stone walls. In the countryside of Norfolk and Suffolk a project known as Tracks in the Sand has developed routes for visitors to use

on horses or cycles. Money has also been spent improving the landscape and on interpretation. This is all part of the Brecks Tourism Partnership.

Conservation and habitat preservation

Sites and properties are protected and preserved for the enjoyment of visitors and to conserve our heritage. Tourism contributes enormously to this conservation in several ways:

* The fact that a site is a tourist attraction means it is recognised as warranting preservation.
* National parks and other conservation bodies provide information and education for tourists helping tourists' environmental awareness.
* Revenue from entrance fees to attractions pays for conservation activities.
* Conservation holidays are a growing market sector as offered by BTCV and the National Trust.

Regeneration of derelict areas

Both the built and natural environment benefit from upgrading and regeneration when a tourist opportunity is uncovered by local and national government. Examples include the Liverpool and Salford dock areas. Salford has a theatre and museum besides new residential and shopping development.

Negative environmental impacts

Traffic congestion

Within the UK most day visitors and domestic holidaymakers travel by car causing traffic congestion and pollution at destinations and attractions. Some villages in Yorkshire and in the Lake District are now closed to traffic whilst large car parks have been built on the outskirts to accommodate coaches and cars bringing visitors.

Erosion of land

A problem in many destinations is that the influx of tourists puts pressure on scarce resources. Water is a scarce resource in many places and tourists tend to use up more than local people. Where there are golf courses and gardens even more water is used.

Land is taken for development of hotels, airports and roads causing loss of natural habitats. Soil is eroded for development changing landscapes. Forests are cleared for ski resort development.

Trampling occurs on well trodden trails spoiling the countryside that people have come to see. Walkers are encouraged to stay on paths in order to reduce the erosion.

CASE STUDY
China's Great Wall

Tourists Spell Ruin

The Great Wall of China is more than 200 years old and once stretched almost 6,500 kilometres. It is now much shorter as millions of tourists and related developments have left their mark, causing damage to entire sections of the wall. Only 2,500 kilometres of wall are left in place.

One of the most accessible and popular parts of the wall to visit is at Badaling. Here tourists clamber over the wall and any local hawkers follow them trying to sell their wares.

It is not only walkers who contribute to the damage, TV programmes have been filmed at the Wall and even rock concerts have taken place there. Some sections of the Wall have been demolished to make way for motorways. Conservationists are increasingly concerned that the Wall will suffer more and more damage unless action is taken soon.

Adapted from *The Times*, April 11th 2005

1. **Why do you think this situation has been allowed to develop?**
2. **What measures could be taken to protect the wall whilst still allowing tourists access?**
   For ideas on how to do this, research measures taken at Stonehenge in the UK.

Loss of natural habitats

Even protected areas can be lost for tourism development. A part of the Pembrokeshire coastline in Wales has national park status yet in spite of this developers have managed to get permission for the building of an all weather holiday village, complete with a snow dome. A watchdog body, the Council for National Parks is bringing a challenge to prevent the development at the High Court in London. The reasons for approving the development were the 600 permanent jobs it will create plus a further 300 jobs in the wider economy. Also its investors say they will build to the highest environmental standards.

Think it over...
What is more important – preserving the national park or creating jobs?

Think it over...

Turtle Haven?

The current trend for spa tourism will be followed soon at Cousine, a privately owned 60 acre nature reserve in the Seychelles. The spa will be run in partnership with the Caribbean based beauty company, Ligne St. Barth. Plans are for a fitness centre, yoga and gym alongside the four villas which provide accommodation to the guests. A pavilion built in French colonial style provides restaurant facilities. A mile long beach is inhabited by hawksbill turtles. There are many more turtles than visitors on the island – over 7,000 have already been hatched this year.

Staying at the spa for five nights on half board costs from £3,239 for a couple, including flights and helicopter transport.

Adapted from *The Times* July 20th 2005

What is the potential negative impact of this development on the turtles? What measures could be taken to minimise this impact?

IBIZA

"In danger of becoming a concrete jungle"

Spanish environmental campaigners have pledged to oppose plans for further tourism development in Ibiza and Majorca.

Three environmental groups from the Balearic Islands, including Friends of the Earth Ibiza, have lodged a formal complaint with the European Union's environment commission against what they claim is the planned destruction of important ecosystems.

They say changes in Balearic planning legislation will override existing legal protection for species of birds and habitats of European importance in favour of tourist developments.

"This will result in the Balearic Islands being the region with least environmental protection in the whole of Spain," a spokesman from the environmental groups claimed.

Threatened areas include Cala d'Hort in the north west of Ibiza and Llevant in Majorca.

Environmentalists claim an Ibizan wetland area, Feixes, declared by UNESCO as a World Heritage Site due to a unique irrigation system developed by the Moors, is being allowed to deteriorate to ease the way for urban development.

There are also plans to build a new larger passenger port within the limits of an internationally protected wetland site and two four-lane motorways to connect towns only 17 kilometres apart.

Friends of the Earth Ibiza spokeswoman Hazel Morgan said: "Ibiza is in danger of becoming a concrete jungle, as the government is encouraging tourist developments at any cost. We are in danger of losing our last valuable wildlife habitats. The European Commission must prevent this.

"We already face problems because natural resources are stretched to the limit: fresh water has to be produced by desalination plants; the central electrical generating plant cannot keep up with demand, so a connection to the mainland is being planned."

Source: Travelmole, December 3rd 2004

	FOREIGNERS	% CHANGE 05/04	SPANISH	% CHANGE 05/04	TOTAL	% CHANGE 05/04
Mallorca	1,114,729		215,275		1,330,003	
Menorca	146,137		67,869		214,006	
Ibiza-Formentera	276,796		81,361		358,158	
By Air	**1,537,662**	**+0.3**	**364,505**	**+22.6**	**1,902,167**	**+3.9**
Mallorca	6,347		40,210		46,557	
Menorca	1,295		16,776		18,071	
Ibiza-Formentera	3,221		56,872		60,093	
By Sea	**10,863**	**−59.0**	**113,858**	**−2.6**	**124,721**	**−13.0**
Total Illes Balears	**1,548,525**	**−0.7**	**478.363**	**+15.5**	**2,026,888**	**+2.7**

FIGURE 7.5 *Arrival of 53,000 more tourists than last year.*

Source: www.illesbalears.es

Decreasing biodiversity and pollution

Pollution can be in the form of air, water, noise or can even be visual in the case of some buildings or industrial plants. Hotel development may cause visual pollution by spoiling a natural coastline. Pollution can also arise, for example, from jet skis and motor boats in coastal resorts. Pollution may cause distress to wildlife through noise affecting their normal activities or by destroying marine life.

The disposal of sewage is a problem, particularly in developing destinations where sewage plants either do not exist or are not able to cope with the extra waste. The cruise sector is booming but cruise ships produce tonnes of waste. Sewage pollutes seas and rivers, damages wildlife and encourages the growth of algae which in turn damages coral reefs.

Coral suffers damage in many ways including trampling by snorkellers and divers, anchors from boats chipping it away and even mining for building materials.

Socio–cultural impact

Positive social impact

Preservation of traditional customs and crafts

Crafts are revived because the tourist trade makes them viable again, such as lace making in Malta. In some destinations hotels have now adopted a policy of inviting local people into their complex on a particular evening each week in order for them to access the tourist market in the hotel to sell their local crafts. The EUROTEX project, funded by the European Commission aims to develop textile-related cultural tourism in disadvantaged areas of Europe. The aim is to encourage tourists to buy local textile crafts to preserve the crafts themselves but also to strengthen the local economy. The pilot regions for this project were Alto Minho in Portugal, Lapland and Crete.

Revival of festivals and ceremonies

In the same way that crafts are preserved, sometimes festivals and events are kept going because of tourist interest. Traditional dances and ceremonies may be staged for the benefit of tourists but also preserve local culture.

Think it over...

The noise around our airports is in excess of World Health Organisation limits. Air pollution is a problem aggravating asthma and contributing to poor lung function and lung disease. Increases in flying capacity will bring about more noise pollution and greater air pollution. The Campaign to Protect Rural England (CPRE) argues that the effect of flying is to 'reduce and erode the quality of life of people who live around airports, and people who live in or enjoy the countryside'. If the airline industry continues to grow as expected then its contribution to greenhouse gas production will rise to 75% by 2050, according to the Royal Commission on Environmental Pollution (RCEP).

Discuss the impact of the airline industry on the environment.

Provision of community facilities and public services

Improved roads and rail networks may be introduced to cater for tourists but are also of benefit to locals. Sport and leisure facilities may also be introduced. This means the standard of living for the host community may generally improve.

Improved infrastructure for local community

This was mentioned earlier as it has both economic and social benefits. Having clean water, effective sewage systems and road and rail networks improves quality of life for locals as well as conditions for tourists.

Negative social impact

Conflicts with and influence on local community

Western tourists visiting developing countries represent an entirely different and sometimes unknown society. Members of the host community may try to copy western behaviour or dress resulting in changes to their traditional way of life or causing conflict between the hosts and the visitors. Tourists sometimes fail to respect the customs and traditions of the host country causing irritation. The host population may feel resentful about the wealth of the incoming tourists. Even though the tourists may not be wealthy in western terms they have a lot more disposable income than the people in the developing destination. This resentment can lead to crime.

Crime

Increases in tourism numbers are often accompanied by a rise in levels of crime. Tourists may carry expensive cameras and wear expensive clothes and jewellery so they become targets for criminals. Resorts may be built in enclaves next to poor areas. The problem perpetuates as tourists become afraid to leave the resort for fear of crime and the host population becomes more resentful about people who do not mix with their society and spend their money in the resort and not in the community.

Prostitution

Tourism has encouraged the growth of prostitution in destinations as young women are willing or persuaded to sell their bodies to get an income. There is even an industry defined as 'sex tourism'. There are also several organisations that are fighting against sex tourism. One is ECPAT (End Child Prostitution, Child Pornography and Trafficking of Children for Sexual Purposes) is a network of organisations and individuals working together to eliminate the commercial sexual exploitation of children. In 1998 they produced a code of practice for endorsement by tour operators and other travel organisations. The code aims to prevent sexual exploitation of children in tourism destinations. The code is implemented by 45 companies across the world.

Staged authenticity of festivals and events

In contrast to the view that tourism preserves national dance and ritual, critics sometimes believe that traditional events and dances are degraded by being put on specifically for the entertainment of tourists.

Loss of cultural identity

As it becomes easier, faster and cheaper to travel the world so each destination begins to look like any other. For example, McDonalds can be found almost anywhere including Eastern Europe and Africa. Some tourists want to carry on exactly as they do at home, but with sunshine; in many resorts in Spain you see English pubs and English food advertised for sale. This kind of development results in a loss of the destination's cultural identity. In the southern resorts of Tenerife, there are beautiful hotels with excellent facilities and good food but there isn't anything remotely Canarian —even the hotel workers are from mainland Spain! You have to hire a car and travel away from the purpose built resorts to find the Canarian culture.

7.4 The tourist area life cycle

Study of the destination life cycle called the tourist area life cycle (TALC) developed by Butler (1980) helps us to understand how tourist areas develop and evolve. It cannot be strictly applied to all destinations but is a useful planning guide and shows how destinations can be viewed as resources which have a finite life. Some communities become dependent on tourism and if a destination goes into decline their livelihood is at risk, as are the resources and infrastructure invested in tourism.

The figure below depicts the destination life cycle. You will note the resemblance to the product life cycle you will meet in Unit 10 (page 148).

Stage 1: Exploration

At this stage there are few tourists as awareness of the destination is very limited. In fact the few tourists there are, the more likely they are to be termed 'travellers' being the type of people who are looking for unspoilt destinations, new experiences and adventure. They will have found their own independent transport to the destination as the area will have poor or no access for mass tourism. There are few facilities and basic infrastructure. Nothing has been put in place for tourism and as there are so few tourists their impact is negligible. The local culture remains intact and the natural attractions undisturbed, adding to the attraction for the independent traveller. Attitudes of local people are likely to be positive towards visitors.

It is quite difficult to find places in the world that are untouched by mass tourism but there are a few. In China, the world's highest railway line is being prepared to accommodate passengers. The line goes from Lhasa in Tibet to Gormo in the Qinghai province of China and is being developed to develop this poor region. The line will cross the Himalayas and much of the track will run on ice. The trip is certain to appeal to adventurous travellers.

Stage 2: Involvement

The destination begins to develop, travel companies start to organise transport links and there is an increase in tourist numbers. Local people may start to take advantage of the new opportunities opening up to them and open up local facilities such as restaurants or offering accommodation in their homes. The public sector starts to investigate how tourism can be developed and to invest in facilities and infrastructure. There may be some advertising of the destination.

Stage 3: Development

The early 'explorers' will no longer visit this destination. Instead the tourists are more institutionalised and likely to arrive on organised tours. There is a rapid growth in the number of tourists. The local people start to lose control of development as private companies move in and take control. There will be marked changes in infrastructure and in the appearance of the destination. There may be massive building projects for accommodation and also of attractions. The public sector's role is very important at this stage if the resident population's interests are to be protected and if tourism is to be sustainable. A tourist season will have emerged and there is heavy advertising to market the destination.

An example of a destination in development is Oman where there is a great deal of investment in tourism by the government along with developers.

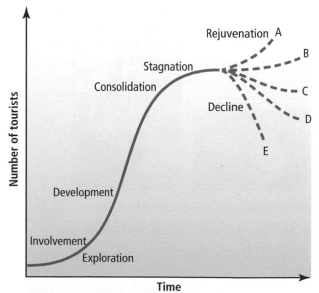

FIGURE 7.5 *The TALC model*

Source: RN Butler (1980) 'The Concept of a Tourist Area', Canadian Geographer, ed 24.1 pp 5–12

CASE STUDY

Kerala

A truly exotic retreat, perfect for adventure and relaxation. From glistening backwaters and palm-fringed beaches to colourful villages and wildlife; her tropical scenery and gentle atmosphere are ideal for unwinding with ancient Indian Ayurvedic treatments. It's easy to see why National Geographic voted this spectacular Indian state, one of its ten 'Paradise Found'.

Kovalam

Poovar

Chowara

Kovalam

Airport transfers 25 mins (approx)

Popular. Laid-back. Beautiful beaches.

Best for those seeking a relaxing holiday in a central location with many cultural attractions to explore, superb beaches and delicious cuisine.

Facilities include a coastline divided into five bays, including the popular Lighthouse Beach area with its good selection of shack-style restaurants, bazaar-style stalls, tailors and Ayurvedic centres.

Famous for its colourful local culture, fishing community and superb beach. Kerala's busiest beach resort, it still remains unspoilt by tourism, with a beautiful seafront, lined with palm trees, restaurants and stalls, perfect for leisurely strolls.

Poovar

Airport transfers 1 hr 15 mins (plus 20 min. boat transfer along backwater to hotel)

Total relaxation. Idyllic scenery. Charming retreat.

Best for a complete escape. Poovar Island is a true paradise setting, fabulous for honeymooners, couples and those seeking a tropical hideaway.

Facilities include golden sands and wonderful spa facilities offering relaxation and Ayurvedic treatments. Boats sail along the backwaters to Poovar village, with its market offering homegrown produce, fish and spices, while taxis run to busier Kovalam, just 20km away.

Famous for its spectacular setting, both on Kerala's famous backwaters and along a shore of golden sand, washed by the Arabian Sea. With its superb wildlife and traditional fishing communities, Poovar offers a fascinating glimpse into Kerala's rural charms.

Chowara

Airport transfers 45 mins (approx)

Stunning beach. Unspoilt. Beautiful scenery.

Best for those seeking peace, tranquillity and stunning scenery, within close proximity of the busier resort of Kovalam.

Facilities include an unspoilt shore of golden sands, a scattering of restaurants, traditional Ayurvedic treatments and a simple, easy-going nature.

Famous for its vast stretch of golden sand and swaying palms, virtually untouched, except by local fishermen whose boats line the shore. A spectacular church lies almost hidden by tropical forest and the area is alive with colourful flora and fauna.

196 🌸 **First Choice** click **firstchoice.co.uk** call **0870 750 0001** visit **shops nationwide**

Explain why Kerala in India is in the involvement stage of tourism.

Visit www.wttc.org and search for a paper on Kerala entitled 'Impact on jobs and the economy'. Read this paper and discuss the issues raised in your group.

Source: First Choice Tropical Brochure (April 2005)

The main areas for development are the Muscat metropolitan area and coastal towns. The Ministry of National Heritage and Culture is restoring historical sites at Muscat and in the coastal towns. Oman has seven international hotels, the majority located in the Muscat metropolitan area.

Think it over...

What kind of tourist would Oman appeal to? Would you consider a visit there?

Stage 4: Consolidation

Tourist numbers are still growing but not so rapidly. The host population has reached the state of resentment to tourists rather than expressing an interest in their visitors. There is extensive marketing to try to extend the season and attract yet more visitors. Many destinations are at this stage at any one time, including most popular package holiday destinations. At this stage, the strain on the environment is growing.

Stage 5: Stagnation

This is the stage of mass tourism. Peak numbers have been reached and the types of tourists are those who are looking for much the same experience as at home, possibly with a better climate. The natural environment may have been spoilt or hidden by the man made attractions and infrastructure in place. The problems and negative impacts of tourism are most evident. The destination is over commercialised and overcrowded.

The photo shows how the natural beauty of the coastline of Benidorm has been blighted by development.

After Stage 5 there are two potential future stages for the area.

Stage 6: Decline

Some of the tourist facilities are closed or fall into disrepair as tourist numbers decline and the tourists go elsewhere. The destination may lose tourism altogether. This sometimes happens to clubbing resorts. Clubbers are attracted to

resorts like Faliraki due to the cheap prices and good nightlife. Although at first the increase in tourism is welcomed, local people soon tire of the drunken behaviour of some of these tourists and resent them and their impact on the community. Other tourists may decide that the destination is not suitable for them due to the presence of young clubbers and go elsewhere. Once the clubbers move on to the next fashionable destination, the original resort is left with few tourists.

Stage 6: Rejuvenation

Butlins is a good example of rejuvenation. The first Butlins was set up in Skegness in 1936. It became a popular holiday camp business providing reasonably priced holidays for families who liked the 'happy camper' lifestyle with organised entertainment, games and the famous reps known as redcoats. As holidaymakers became more affluent and more sophisticated this style of holiday became outmoded. Today, accommodation is more luxurious and massive investment has allowed Butlins to take advantage of the conference market and in addition the short break market.

If action is taken destination managers can avoid the decline and the resort can be rejuvenated. This involves sometimes drastic action in redevelopment and the injection of capital as was the case with Butlins.

CASE STUDY
Destination trends

The Office of National Statistics (ONS) Travel Trends Survey showed that Spain remains the most popular country for UK residents to visit. There were 13.8 million visits to Spain in 2003. France is the second most popular country, with 12 million visits in 2003. According to the ONS, Londoners were more likely to visit France than Spain.

Since 1999, Finland showed the highest (8.6%) annual growth amongst countries in EU Europe. This was followed by Italy which showed an average annual growth of 8.3%. There were a number of countries outside EU Europe showing a significant increase in UK visitors since 1999. Visits to South Africa showed an average annual growth of 16.1% since 1999, the former Yugoslavia and New Zealand both showed a significant increase since 1999 (21.5% and 8.6% respectively). Iceland also showed a significant average annual increase since 1999 of 14%. According to the ONS there has been a 4.1% average annual increase in UK

Source: ABTA Trends 2005

1. Copy or draw the Tourist Area Life Cycle.
2. Locate the destinations mentioned in the extract from ABTA Trends on the TALC chart.
3. Add notes explaining why you think they belong in that stage of TALC.

CASE STUDY

Malta

This case study is designed to prepare you for your external assessment.

Tourism is vital to Malta's economy. It accounts for one third of employment and a quarter of the gross national product. 6% of the population is directly employed in tourism. Tourism was first introduced in 1959 and at that time there were 12,583 visitors.

In the early 80s most arrivals to Malta were British. They were attracted by the beauty of the island, the climate, the fact that there was no language barrier and easy air access.

In a bid to attract more tourists there was substantial development of tourist areas like St Pauls Bay, Mellieha and St Julians. Much of this development was directly on the seafront taking up valuable coastal space and preventing locals from using the areas for recreation. Sensitive rural areas have also been developed. Hotels and other facilities were encouraged to reduce prices at this time to attract more tourists. Unfortunately this strategy, whilst providing a short term increase in tourist numbers, does not attract high spending visitors and also leaves hoteliers with insufficient funds for refurbishment.

By the 90s other markets had developed and the island was popular with Germans and Italians. This is important as it means tourism is not dependent on one market. However, it has resulted in mass tourism and it is feared that tourist numbers will decline in the long term as they are currently doing in Spain. The island has also suffered negative impacts including pressures on infrastructure because of the numbers of visitors (1.1 million in 2003), impaired quality of the environment and poorer tourist experience. By 1999 it was apparent that the sea and sun package offered by Malta was in decline. An evaluation of the product was carried out and it was decided to pursue a policy of offering niche products based on experiencing Malta and its culture. Special interest holidays could also be developed.

In 2005 Malta acceded into the EU. This gives Malta a wider market and the tourism authority aims to maximise the potential of the conference and incentive market. Refurbishment of tourist areas is taking place and hotel development is concentrated on the luxury end. There are now two dozen 4 and 5 star hotels. Many have conference centres.

The tourist authority is also mindful of developing tourism in a sustainable way.

1. **What stage of TALC was Malta at in 1959? What were the positive impacts of tourism at this stage?**
2. **What stage had been reached in the early 80s? Explain the characteristics of this stage in relation to Malta.**
3. **What stage had been reached by 1999? Explain why you think this. What were the negative impacts of tourism by this stage?**
4. **Give examples of how the principles of responsible tourism can be followed in future developments in Malta.**
5. **Explain how the Malta Tourism Authority can minimise the negative impacts of tourism and maximise the positive impacts.**

You should expect to carry out further research to help you with this case study. There are several websites about Malta and holiday brochures will be useful.

7.5 The management of responsible tourism in destinations

The impacts of tourism must be managed to support the principles of responsible tourism. Different strategies are used to maximise the positive impacts of tourism and minimise the negative impacts. In this section of the unit we will examine some of these strategies.

Maximising positive impacts

Retention of visitor spending

Where tourist facilities are owned by local people, more of the income from tourism is retained in the community. This can be achieved in various ways:

* Regulation on ownership of hotels so that they cannot be entirely foreign owned.

* Encouraging the development of small businesses.

* Encouraging partnerships between local people.

Hotels should be encouraged to buy produce locally wherever possible rather than importing. This may mean that support has to be given to local producers to help them meet the needs of large hotels. Hotels or local government may supply seeds and agrochemicals on credit to producers to help them set up. In some cases hotels have participated in 'adopt a farmer' projects, where the hotel agrees to use that farmer's produce.

Where tourism takes place in particular geographic regions, tours should be set up to other areas to allow other communities to benefit from tourism. A good example of this is **agro tourism**

where local people turn their farmhouses into tourist accommodation or restaurants. The restaurants provide meals serving traditional local delicacies. This helps keep tourist money in the local economy. The aim of these projects is to help local people benefit from tourism, especially when they are no longer able to make their living from agriculture.

Think it over...

Tribes Travel (www.tribes.co.uk) ensures that 75% of the cost of its holidays remains within the destinations. Here is one example of how they achieve that:

'We work in cooperation with local communities as far as possible. We offer **fairly-traded revenue** and use **locally owned and run services** such as hotels. Because of this you should find that your hosts are welcoming and open in their invitations to show you their region and cultures. We try to ensure that the local people are happy to receive tourists in their home region, and are informed of the possible impact. We will avoid travelling to any areas where we know tourism is not welcome.'

Visit their website to find out more.

Widening access to facilities

There are many examples of good practice where the proceeds of tourism are used to bring improved facilities and a better standard of living to local people. Turtle Island is a privately owned resort in Fiji. It has Green Globe status and it has implemented projects to aid local people. There was no school on the island but the resort owners initiated a project to provide a school, which was completed in 2002. A high school project for 100 pupils is also underway. Healthcare in the islands of Yasawa was also basic. There was no resident doctor and a lack of equipment in nursing stations. For one week in January each year the resort is closed to guests in order to provide eye clinics. At these clinics local people can be issued with glasses, get cataract operations and even corneal transplants. The resort also sponsors other medical clinics throughout the year but the ultimate goal is for a state of the art medical centre on the island.

Staff training and development

The benefits of training staff include a more satisfied staff who are more likely to remain in their job. This leads to lower staff turnover and costs. If the staff are satisfied with their work this will lead to better customer relations and in turn customers will be more likely to remain loyal. Training may take many forms from induction to specific job training.

Investment of tourism income in community projects

Income from tourism should be reinvested in social and public projects. Tourism taxes are often in place for such purposes. In the Gambia tourists are subjected to a £5 tax on arrival. This money is earmarked for improving the infrastructure of the country and for training local people to enable them to work in tourism. Of course this is not always the case. In 2005 a controversial tax on car hire to tourists was proposed in the Balearics. Visitors will be charged up to 5 euros a day to raise about 12 million euros in local taxes. The fear amongst tour operators is that this tax will deter visitors to the islands. The tax is designated to decrease the annual overspend on health services.

Training and employment of local people and tourism education

First Choice, the tour operator, whose sustainable policy you noted on page 20, claim to employ local people where possible. Their company, Paradise Management, in the Specialist Holidays sector in Egypt employs 98% of its staff from the local area. Also Sunsail in Dominica use 100% local suppliers for their holiday boat clubs.

Hotels should also employ local people wherever possible. Where local people lack the necessary skills, training programmes should be implemented. Some large hotel groups have a good record of doing this. An example is Sandals in the Caribbean who claim to have obligatory training for 120 hours per year for line staff in their hotels.

CASE STUDY

Sandals

All Sandals & Beaches Resorts have been awarded the coveted Green Globe Award for environmental stewardship. From recycling to conserving, ecological responsiveness is a Sandals commitment. Because at the 'resorts made for love', loving the environment has become second nature.

* **All our resorts are Green Globe Certified** – Our mission is to offer the ultimate Caribbean vacation experience by innovatively, reliably and consistently providing the safest and highest quality services and facilities to guests, while attaching a premium to our human resources and being among the most environmentally responsible and community friendly groups in the hospitality industry.

* **Staff awareness** – Team members, participation in workshops and seminars conducted by the environmental committee, local government organizations, and also by non-governmental environmental organizations.

* **Water Conservation program** – Monitoring of total water use on property (pools, guestrooms, kitchens, dining room and garden areas).

* **Energy Management program** – Use of timers on electrical equipment such as Jacuzzi blowers, steam rooms at the Spa,

outdoor lighting for walkways, refrigeration equipment in the kitchens, etc.

* **Waste Management program** – Waste disposal practices and procedures at the hotel such as recycle of linen and bed spreads, food, office paper, and packages.

* **Control of hazardous substances** – Hotel determines suitability of product before any purchase is made and provides full training for staff whenever new chemicals or equipment are purchased for use in the hotel.

* **Social and cultural development and interaction** – Promoting and selling local tours and attractions with special recognition of 'Green tours' at the tour desks.
Inviting local craft vendors to the hotel at least once per week to display and sell their craft items.

Source: Unique Vacation Ltd

1. **What is the 'Green Globe' Award? (www. greenglobe21.com)**
2. **What is the Green Globe based on?**
3. **Find an example of another company awarded a Green Globe and suggest why they were awarded it.**

Minimising negative impacts

Visitor and traffic management

It should not always be assumed that the objective of tourism is to maximise visitors. Where resources and space are limited then the aim is to manage visitors and prevent negative impacts which occur through erosion of paths, buildings and over-development. Examples of such visitor management occur in many historic towns and at historic sites such as Stonehenge.

Think it over...

How many tourists are too many? Some small islands in the Mediterranean have begun to try and reduce tourist numbers in order to minimise the negative effects of tourism. How do you think they still make profits from tourism?

Planning control

Restrictions on the quantity and type of building help prevent a destination becoming overdeveloped. In Majorca tourism has become the most important source of revenue to the economy. Parts of the island became over developed due to mass tourism. Eventually action had to be taken to try and reverse the decline in the island's image as a cheap destination for low spending, heavy drinking tourists. Building restrictions were imposed on hotels throughout the island and the capital, Palma was restored.

Visitor management is needed to stop locations being flooded with tourists.

Change as a result of environmental impact assessment and environmental audits

Environmental auditing should begin with analysis of the environmental resources in the area. Careful planning in advance can help ensure that environmental resources are protected and conserved during development. Green building helps decrease the negative impact of tourism on the environment.

Examples of environmental auditing include several programmes which aim to protect coral reefs throughout the world. These include monitoring the state of the reefs and education programmes to help conserve them.

CASE STUDY

Friends of the Lake District

The **Friends of the Lake District** is a registered charity, established in 1934, and currently supported by nearly 7000 members and 50 affiliated organisations. FLD's objectives are:

> "to promote and organise concerted action for the protection and conservation of the landscape and natural beauty of the **Lake District** and the County of Cumbria as a whole and co-operate with other bodies having similar objects or interests".

FLD cover the **Lake District** National Park, but also represent the Council for the Protection of Rural England (CPRE) in Cumbria.

The following statements are extracted from the FLD's tourism policy. The whole document can be found at www.fld.org.uk.

The statements can be viewed as a wish list from the FLD to tourism businesses.

* Adopt a long term perspective, via a business plan and the adoption of an Environmental Management System.

* Support the local economy and traditional skills by using local employees and local firms, and participate in local recruitment initiatives.

* Supply information on activities which further the quiet enjoyment of the area.

* Purchase products and services locally and encourage guests to do likewise.

* Create menus featuring local dishes and foods.

* Adopt an environmental policy, annual environmental audit and adopt the Green Audit Kit.

* Offer environmental and management training to staff and encourage them to work towards your environmental policy goals.

Tourism operators, and organisations promoting environmental management should prepare an environmental policy and commit to an annual environmental audit with the sustainability indicators serving as a set of 'benchmarks'.

1. **Explain what would be included in an environmental audit.**
2. **Explain how tourism in the Lake District can have negative impacts on the region.**
3. **Explain how the measures suggested in the FLD tourism policy would benefit the local community**

Extension task: Suggest further ways in which the positive impacts of tourism in the Lake District could be maximised and the negative impacts minimised.

Knowledge check

1. What is a fair trade holiday?

2. What is greenwashing?

3. What is Agenda 21?

4. What is meant by the public sector?

5. Give examples of two public sector organisations.

6. To which sector do developers usually belong?

7. What is the DCMS?

8. What are the key points of the 'Tomorrow's Tourism Today report?

9. Describe the role of a regional development agency.

10. Outline the differences between English Heritage and the National Trust.

11. How does the Travel Foundation help businesses?

12. Give two examples of tourism pressure groups.

13. Describe two economic objectives of tourism.

14. Describe one socio-cultural objective of tourism.

15. What is meant by Balance of Payments?

16. What is TALC?

17. Describe the characteristics of the exploration stage of TALC.

18. What might happen after the stagnation stage?

19. Give two examples of how the positive impact of tourism might be maximised.

20. Give two examples of how the negative impacts of tourism might be minimised.

Current issues in travel and tourism

This unit covers the following sections:

8.1 Issues in travel and tourism

8.2 Travel and tourism research project

Introduction

The travel and tourism industry is always affected by current events and issues that arise either within the industry or in the external environment. Travel and tourism companies have to continually react to changes and issues and it is vital that managers have a high level of awareness of the issues impacting on the industry. In this unit you will have the opportunity to develop knowledge and understanding of an issue that is currently affecting travel and tourism. In so doing you will develop your research skills and be able to make links with other units that you have covered on your programme. You will be introduced to useful information sources to help you with your research and you will be taken step by step through the planning and research process.

How you will be assessed

This unit is internally assessed by your tutor and externally moderated by Edexcel. A variety of activities and case studies is provided in this unit to help you complete your research project and prepare for assessment.

Your work must include evidence of:

* a research proposal that includes a description of the issue and a plan that shows the project aims and the research methodology adopted, including timescales and planned sources of reference

* how you worked independently and followed your reseach plan to meet the project aims and timescales

* how you dealt with changes to your plan

* research undertaken as indicated in the plan for the project and an analysis of the issue and its effect on the travel and tourism industry or one of its component sectors

* an evaluation of the project and the research methodology with recommendations for approaches to be adopted for future projects.

The research project must be based on a travel and tourism related issue. It may be an issue that you are already interested in, or it may be something that you meet for the first time in this unit.

8.1 Issues in travel and tourism

In this section you will be introduced to a number of current issues affecting the travel and tourism industry. You may find one of these is of particular interest to you and then decide to study it in greater depth. Remember that, if you wish, you can choose a different issue which interests you, as long as it is current and relates to travel and tourism. However remember this must cover a *current* issue in travel and tourism – many of the issues in this chapter may not remain current. This unit is about *issues* not events.

PEST analysis

One way of deciding which issues currently affect travel and tourism is to carry out a PEST analysis.

> **Key term**
>
> *PEST* A PEST analysis is when an organisation takes stock of the external factors affecting its business, identifying political, economic, social and technological factors. You will be introduced to this concept in Unit 10.

People 1st carried out a market assessment report of the travel and tourism industries in February 2005 and below are the PEST factors which they highlighted. They do acknowledge that there are many more.

> ✱ **REMEMBER!**
>
> People 1st is the Sector Skills Council licensed by government in the UK for the hospitality, leisure, travel and tourism industries. This is what they aim to do:
>
> ✱ Be the voice of industry on skills matters and encourage best practice
>
> ✱ Help direct funds for skills where they're needed most
>
> ✱ Ensure qualifications are developed that are fit for the purpose
>
> ✱ Produce the information employers need on skills training
>
> ✱ Help people find the training and the provider that fits their training needs.

Here is a PEST analysis extracted from their Travel and Tourism Services Industry Report.

POLITICAL	ECONOMIC
Transport system London's tourism threatened by poor transport system in the South East.[1] **Congestion Charge** Since its introduction in 2003, it has been blamed for loss of business.[2] However given the success of the scheme to reduce traffic in central London, proposals have been drawn up to extend the zone and increase the charge to £6.[3] **Disability Discrimination Act** The Disability Discrimination Act came into force in 2004 meaning that service providers and businesses must take reasonable steps to allow for disabled access.[4]	**Travel Numbers** Overseas visitors rose by 12% to 3.09 million in 2004 when compared with 2003. This is following the dramatic falls in numbers following foot and mouth and 9/11. British tourism is growing strongly.[5] **Olympics** London is bidding to host the 2012 Olympic Games. If successful the games will boost tourism revenues owing to increased visitor numbers. Following the Athens Olympics where hoteliers put their prices up and so discouraged visitors, London hoteliers have agreed to provide 40,000 affordable rooms for London 2012.[6]

SOCIAL	TECHNOLOGICAL
Holiday destinations The seaside is still an important bank holiday destination in the UK despite the poor weather.[7]	**Direct Booking/Internet Online companies** Internet sites are out pricing hoteliers because they fail to manage their bedroom Inventories.[8] **E-commerce** Travel & tourism accounts for the highest overall value of ecommerce sales.[9] **Low Cost Airlines** Some take 90% of their bookings on the internet.[10]

1 Travel and Tourism Gazette 2004
2 Congestion charge eats into restaurant profits – Cater online 13th July 2004
3 London gets ready for new fight on congestion charge – Caterer & Hotelkeeper 22-28 April 2004
4 Leisure Industry welcomes introduction of DDA – Leisure Opportunities October 2004
5 Strong growth for British tourism – caterer Online 8th October 2004
6 London hoteliers back Olympic bid with 40,000 rooms – Caterer Online 9th September 2004
7 One third of Brits plan visit to the seaside this weekend – Caterer Online 27th August 2004
8 Online Companies beat hotels on price too often – Caterer & hotelkeeper 18-24 March 2004
9 Key Notes Travel & Tourism Report 2002
10 Travel and Tourism Key Note Report 2002

Source: The Travel and Tourism Service Industries: Industry Report February 2005

Points to note on the People 1st PEST

1. Any PEST represents a particular point in time. Remember that this PEST was published in February 2005 and it is already out of date. Consider the following:

   * The congestion charge is now £8 per day.

   * London won its Olympics bid in July 2005.

   You can see, therefore, that any PEST analysis must be constantly updated.

2. Each point in the PEST analysis is referenced and can be traced back to a reliable source such as a trade magazine or market research report. This is important as it shows that the points made in the PEST are not conjecture but are based on fact.

3. It is not always easy to categorise factors impacting on the industry into the four PEST areas. Some of the technological factors are also social – people book on the internet because they have computers at home and are becoming more familiar with using technology. The congestion charge has been put into the political area as it was introduced by local government but is also an economic factor as it is a cost which may deter people from driving into London.

4. The PEST cannot cover every possible factor which impacts on travel and tourism. Whoever does the PEST has to be selective and choose the factors which have greatest impact and which can be responded to.

Theory into practice

In order to understand PEST you need to be aware of what is happening in the world and how it affects travel and tourism. For this activity you will need all of one day's newspapers. Sunday newspapers are ideal as they report on a whole week.

Work in small groups and go through one of the papers and find examples of natural incidents/ political change/interest rates rising, etc. Mark up each article with a few notes on how you think it impacts on travel and tourism.

When you are ready present your articles and discuss with your group. You may have found an issue that you would like to explore further.

CASE STUDY

People 1st PEST for the hotel sector

POLITICAL

Disability Discrimination Act
The Disability Discrimination Act came into force in 2004 meaning that service providers and businesses must take reasonable steps to allow for disabled access.[1] This particularly affects small business and may have some serious implications for the leisure and tourism industries.

Olympics
London is bidding to host the 2012 Olympic Games. If successful the games will boost tourism revenues owing to increased visitor numbers. Following the Athens Olympics where hoteliers put their prices up and so discouraged visitors, London hoteliers have agreed to provide 40,000 affordable rooms for London 2012.[2]

Gambling Bill
The changes to the gambling laws will allow for large Las Vegas style casino resorts but the focus of the bill is on social responsibility rather than on casinos.[3] These resorts could have a positive impact on hotel demand in the area.[4]

London Congestion Charge
Since its introduction in 2003, it has been blamed for loss of business.[5] However, given the success of the scheme to reduce traffic in central London, proposals have been drawn up to extend the zone and increase the charge to £6.[6]

ECONOMIC

Outsourcing
Outsourcing in hotels will increase in the future as this allows management to concentrate on revenue building.[7]

Productivity
A study from Deloitte shows that the hotel industry has experienced a decline in productivity over the last four years.[8]

Euro
Following the government indecision on the euro, hotels are split on their opinion for joining the single currency; 52% of hoteliers were against adopting a single currency.[9]

Household expenditure
Weekly UK household expenditure on Restaurants and Hotels is £35.40, the total expenditure per household is £406.60.[10]

Minimum wage
Trade unions are fighting to raise the minimum wage from £4.85 per hour to at least £5.35.[11]

Staff hours
A report by Tourism Concern calls for social responsibility regarding working conditions within the tourism industry where conditions are unacceptably low and pay unpredictable.[12]

Migrant Workers
As more countries join the EU, workers from the new countries could help ease staff shortages.[13]

SOCIOLOGICAL	TECHNOLOGICAL
Weather Good weather and sport can provide a boost to sales in hotels, restaurants and pubs.[14] However a poor summer can produce slumps profits across the nation.[15]	**Booking and ordering** Maximisation of resources by using automated scheduling[16] and integrated suites which co-ordinate front office, sales and catering. These increase profitability through staff scheduling and time and attendance planning. **Optimisation** Software is now available to help managers to react quickly to lower room rates and improve room occupancy, maintaining the in profitability of the business.[17] **Direct Booking/Internet** Online companies are out pricing hoteliers because they fail to manage their bedroom inventories.[18] **Business Facilities** A survey by American Express has shown that hoteliers are getting better at providing technology and business facilities.[19]

1 Leisure Industry welcomes introduction of DDA – *Leisure Opportunities* October 2004
2 London hoteliers back Olympic bid with 40,000 rooms – *Caterer Online* 9th September 2004
3 Minister urges industry to see the bigger picture – *Coinslot* November 26–December 2 2004
4 Traditional industry must not be left behind – *Coinslot* April 30–May 6 2004 p3
5 Congestion charge eats into restaurant profits – *Cater Online* 13th July 2004
6 London gets ready for new fight on congestion charge – *Caterer & Hotelkeeper* 22-28 April 2004
7 The future lies in outsourcing, says GM – *Caterer Online* 8th December 2002
8 Hotels market shows productivity dip – *Caterer & Hotelkeeper* 18-24 March 2004
9 UK hotels split over Euro – *Caterer Online* 6th August 2003
10 Social Trends 2004 Edition No. 34 UK p98
11 Unions start fight to raise minimum wage – *Caterer Online* 18th November 2004
12 Tourism Concern calls for action on staff abuse in hospitality – *Caterer & Hotelkeeper* May 2004
13 Bigger Europe will ease staff shortages – *Caterer & Hotelkeeper* May 2004
14 Summer forecast is good – as weather and sport provide sales boost – *Publican Online* 7th July 2004
15 Wet summer weather dampens pubs profits – *Publican Online* 24th July 2004
16 Say 'hi' to high tech – *Caterer Online* 1st March 2003
17 The numbers game – *Caterer Online* 30th September 2004
18 Online Companies beat hotels on price too often – *Caterer & Hotelkeeper* 18–24 March 2004
19 In-room technology gets good marks in survey – *Caterer & Hotelkeeper* 6–12 May 2004

1. **Decide whether the PEST factors are in the correct categories and whether some could be included in more than one area.**
2. **Comment on the PEST analysis and its accuracy.**
3. **Add some more points to this PEST** according to your knowledge of current issues affecting the hotel business.

Extension task: Follow up at least three of the sources given for this PEST and add further information to the PEST analysis resulting from your research.

Selecting a Research Topic

When you select an issue for a project you must be certain that sufficient data is available for you to research your topic in depth and reach an appropriate level of analysis. This means you have to do some initial research to check on sources and find out exactly what kinds of information are available.

To help you with this initial research and to get ideas on a range of topics you should use some or all of these resources. This particular list consists of resources which report on news and events related to travel and tourism. Later we will look at other useful sources for statistics, facts and figures.

News sources

Online news information sites include:

* www.travelmole.com – a news and resource centre for the travel industry

* www.thisistravel.com – published by Associated New Media, the publishers of the Mail newspapers. It is aimed at consumers but is a useful source of news.

* www.e-tid.com – e-tid.com is a business travel news digest covering all sectors of the travel industry, from aviation and tour operating to hotel and cruise.

* www.travelwirenews.com – home of E-turbo news whose aim is to present a fair and balanced coverage of the on-going issues that concerns the travel trade. This is an international newsletter and has subscribers in 230 countries.

You can subscribe to all of these news websites at no cost. Subscription means that you will be emailed regularly with travel and tourism news items. You will also be able to access the archives of information and past features on the websites.

Trade magazines

These are an excellent source of news. The magazines can be subscribed to in hard copy or you can access them online. Your library may have some of them. If you access them online you

will have to register but registration is free. Titles include:

* Travel Trade Gazette (ttglive.com)

* Travel Weekly (travelweekly.com)

* Caterer & Hotelkeeper (catereronline.com)

* Leisure Opportunities (leisuropportunities.co.uk)

* Attractions Management (attractionsmanagement.com)

* Leisure Management (leisuremanagement.co.uk)

Newspapers

Read a quality newspaper regularly. Although the travel sections are important, you should be reading all of a newspaper, as many international and national news events impact on travel and tourism. For example, any incidences of terrorism affect tourism in an area.

All the Sunday newspapers have travel supplements. Newspapers can be accessed online but some of them charge if you want to search the archives. You do not have to pay to search recent editions. Guardian Unlimited is a particularly useful source of travel features and it is free to register.

Theory into practice

Choose three of the news sources mentioned above. Access each of them and find a breaking news story related to travel and tourism. Describe the story and then compare the reporting of the story from each source. Comment on similarities and differences. Discuss your conclusions with your group. Keep any useful stories for further research.

Once you have regular access to these news sources – and read the bulletins – you will find that your topical knowledge of travel and tourism improves immensely. You will find that some news stories develop over days and weeks and have an even greater impact on the industry. You will find it easier to choose an issue for your research project with your increased knowledge.

With a range of newspapers, your topical knowledge of Travel and tourism will increase.

It is a good idea to select two or three initial ideas for your project as it may be that further information, particularly statistical information, is not easy to access. There isn't room here to list all possible sources for all types of travel and tourism issues so we will examine some general sources of information and in the case studies later in the unit you will find some examples of sources of information for specific issues.

You will have come across many of these sources before and indeed you will have used many of them.

Theory into practice

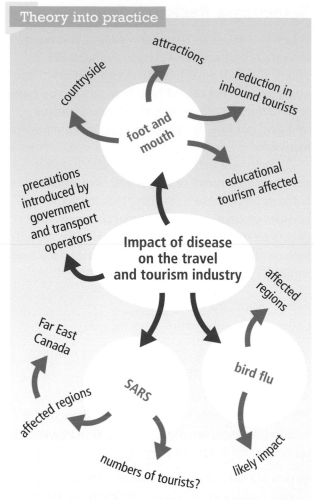

FIGURE 8.1 *A mind map*

Produce a mind map for a potential research issue of your choice. The example above is a mind-map covering the effect of disease on tourism. Once you have done it, discuss it with a colleague and see if they have any ideas to add to it. Decide if the issue has potential for a full research project.

Theory into practice

Research activity

The Virtual Training Suite on the Internet has a package which introduces you to travel and tourism resources on the web. Visit www.vts.rdn/tutorial/travel to go through a 'teach yourself' tutorial which will allow you to practise your Internet information skills. On your way round you will be able to collect sites of interest and keep them for future reference.

You might begin by brainstorming a whole list of possible research topics and then selecting two or three for further exploration. Some researchers find mind mapping is a useful starting point to determine whether a research topic has further potential. All you need is a piece of paper with your potential topic written in the middle. From this you write notes indicating all the possible approaches and sub topics arising from this issue.

General travel and tourism sources

Information about tourism in Britain – a useful introduction	www.visitbritain.com
Information about tourism in Britain – a useful introduction including statistics	www.staruk.org.uk
Department for Culture Media and Sport	www.culture.gov.uk
World Tourism Organisation	www.world-tourism.org
Customer comments about service on airlines and in airports	www.airlinequality.com
Columbus on line world travel guide	www.wtg-online.com
Locations and addresses of tourist offices worldwide	www.tourist-offices.org.uk
Spanish Tourist Office	www.spaintour.com
French Government Tourist Office	www.franceguide.com
News about visitor attractions from the British Association of Leisure Parks, Piers and Attractions (BALPPA)	www.balppaorg.uk
Tour operator – My Travel website	www.mytravel.com
Company website for the Thomas Cook group – also has a history section	www.thomascook.co.uk
Website for the First Choice group of tour operators	www.firstchoice.co.uk
Group website for Tui – parent company of Thomson – the tour operator	www.tui.com
Website for the organisation representing the Association of Independent Tour Operators	www.aito.co.uk
Website for the Association of British Travel Agents	www.abta.com
UK Foreign Office travel advice	www.fco.gov.uk
Information on technology in marketing travel and tourism	www.eyefortravel.com
Information on GDS systems	www.galileo.com www.sabre.com www.datam.co.uk
International Civil Aviation Organisation (ICAO)	www.icao.int
Civil Aviation Authority (CAA)	www.caa.co.uk
Official site of Scotland's national tourist board	www.visitscotland.com
Official site of Northern Ireland's national tourist board	www.discovernorthernireland.com
Official site of Wales's national tourist board	www.walestouristboard.com
Cruise information service	www.cruiseinformationservice.co.uk
British Airports Authority	www.baa.co.uk

Travel and tourism services on the Internet

Possible research topics

Are package holiday sales in decline?

This topic might have been brought to your attention by a news item or feature in one of your news sources. Our example comes from the hard edition of the Travel Trade Gazette.

On first view it looks like a suitable topic for further research. Why?

1. It gives a good overview of the topic including:
   - Destinations in decline
   - Reasons for the decline
2. Statistics to interpret and analyse.
3. Clues about where to look for further information.

> ### ✱ REMEMBER!
>
> At this stage you have not chosen your topic – you are considering different topics as potential research issues. You still need to find out if more information about the chosen issue is accessible.

Package decline hits traditional hot spots

The market for package holidays to traditional western Mediterranean destinations suffered heavily this summer, the latest sales figures reveal.

Package passenger numbers to Spain and Portugal for this summer up to the end of August fell by 13% compared with last year, according to AC Neilsen, the travel market research specialist.

Florida and Greece also performed badly, while Morocco, Bulgaria and Croatia saw the biggest increases, with Morocco nearly doubling its figures.

The package market to France has also suffered, with numbers dropping 19%.

Libra sales and marketing director Paul Riches said these shifts were largely due to the rise of no-frills carriers, the increasing number of Brits with holiday homes in Spain, and the growth of independent travel.

"But people still want to have package holidays to places like Egypt", he said.

Julia Slater, head of the retail sales group at Cendant Vacation Rental Group – whose brands include French Life – said factors such as droughts and fashion were affecting package sales.

She said customers were also making their own packages using the internet.

Tony Hopkins, director of product and publishing for Thomas Cook, added: "The state of the euro versus the pound has meant the cost of accommodation in the euro area has increased. As a result, the price of package holidays has gone up. But 2006 is already showing signs of a slight recovery for Spain."

His comments were echoed by Gary David, managing director of Cadogan Holidays and chairman of the Association of Tour Operators to Portugal, who said that visitor figures for Portugal had remained high during 2005.

"The bottom line is that customers are not buying from an operator – they're buying their own package or timeshare," he said.

"Bulgaria and Croatia are selling lots because they are dirt cheap. They're taking over from the Costa Brava because they offer cheap packages and it's inexpensive to get there – it's purely to do with cost."

One of the most unexpected declines was for the Florida market, which saw a 19% drop in package bookings. Operators blame terrorism, hurricanes and rising fuel prices for the decline.

A spokesperson for Visit Florida said it was expecting the year to be flat, or possibly show a downturn, but a 19% drop was way beyond its expectations for the market. Hopkins added: "In the last two years Florida has been hit by hurricanes to the point that people are having second thoughts about going."

Sri Lanka and Thailand also showed downturns following December's tsunami. However, operators expect the market to recover given time.

A Thomson spokesman said: "The tourist boards are working hard to get things back to normal. By this time next year we will see a marked improvement."

Overall, total package and accommodation-only bookings this summer fell 3% in contrast to last summer when the office of National statistics reported a 1.4% increase in package sales compared with 2003.

Source: *Travel Trade gazette*, 14th October 2005

What next? How will you find out what further information is available on this issue?

1. Look at your other news sources and see if any of them are reporting on this trend. Print out or save relevant articles for analysis. Remember to start your bibliography by noting all sources in detail.

2. Read the text and see what clues there are for further research possibilities. List them with notes. This is what your list might look like:

> - AC Nielsen – can I access their research data?
> - Can I get stats on how many British have second homes?
> - Can I get stats on the rise of no-frills (low cost) carriers?
> - How many people use the internet to book holidays?
> - What about the increase in tailor made holidays?
> - Lots of organisations are mentioned, eg Association of Tour Operators to Portugal and the Office for National Statistics

3. Armed with your list you are ready to appraise what information is available. Be prepared for this to take an hour or two even at this stage. You will find other information later. At the moment you just want to know if there is sufficient information available for you to do a good research job on the issue.

> **✱ REMEMBER!**
> Restrict your research to Internet and readily available sources at this stage. You haven't got time to write to companies or do interviews with people before you select your research issue. If you don't know how to do Internet research, turn to page 66.

Assuming you did this initial research, this is what you might find:

> - Can't access Neilsen's data on the Internet – however the statistics in the feature are quite comprehensive.
> - Lots of other news articles are available about the increase in tailor made holidays, e.g. on Travelmole.
> - A quick Google search shows that there are several sites with information about numbers of British people with second homes. Bookmark these for revisiting later.
> - Official statistics are available online at www.statistics.gov.uk
> - Found this in a Guardian Unlimited article from January 2005, at www.technology.guardian.co.uk; according to Hitwise, a company that monitors Internet website hits, hits on travel websites went up by 14% in January 2005 from the same period in 2004. In fact one in every 20 hits is to a travel website showing how popular they are.
>
> Followed this further, for example:
>
> - Found a BBC news item with figures on low cost flights – will follow that too.

Hitwise information adapted from Guardian Unlimited, January 2005

From this initial research we can see that the decline of package holidays is a suitable issue to research further. Each branch of research leads to further possibilities and relevant statistics are available.

> **✱ REMEMBER!**
> Track your research – it is very easy to find a useful source and then lose it! Use favourites on your pc or an old fashioned notebook!

Frankfurt greets A380 Superjumbo

LONDON (eTurboNews) – The Airbus A380 super-jumbo successfully landed its first international test flight at Frankfurt main airport on Saturday.

Frankfurt was chosen for the first test landing of the aircraft outside Airbus' own runway in Toulouse, rather than Paris or London Heathrow, because those airports are not so far advanced with their preparations for the world's biggest passenger airliner. It's been undergoing a series of ground tests including boarding bridges, access for service vehicles, cargo loading and fuelling as part of rigorous procedures for licensing the new aircraft for commercial service.

"Handling operations on the ramp proceeded as expected and, together with Airbus, we are delighted about the results," said Wilhelm Bender, chairman of Fraport AG, the airport operator. Tests at Frankfurt Airport's Terminal 2 included docking a passenger bridge to the upper deck of the Airbus A380 for the first time, providing catering supplies to this section of the aircraft using special lift trucks, providing the full range of supply and disposal services as well as de-icing.

Frankfurt will be a maintenance base for the Superjumbo, and construction of the servicing facility which will be large enough to hold four A380s at any one time, is due for completion in 2007. Lufthansa, Frankfurt Airport's biggest customer, has ordered 15 double-decker A380s, the first of which are scheduled for delivery that year.

The A380 will fly to Singapore, Kuala Lumpur, Sydney, Melbourne and Brisbane in the first half of November and will then be on display at the Dubai air show later in the month. Singapore Airlines will be the first to take delivery of an A380 at the end of 2006, followed by Qantas Airways and Emirates in the second quarter of 2007.

The A380 is designed to use existing large airports, but they need some adaptation to accommodate it and to handle its payload of between 550 and 800 passengers. Airports will not need to build extra long runways for the A380, since its take-off and landing distance is shorter than the rival Boeing 747.

The A380 will be the world's first modern jet with a full-length twin-deck. Airlines have an option of a number of different configurations, depending on market demand and conditions. The standard layout recommended by Airbus provides 22 first class seats and 334 economy class seats on the main deck and 96 business class and 103 economy class seats on the upper deck.

Report by David Browne

Extracted from www.travelwirenews.com

This article tells us where the A380 is in terms of its development as well as giving some useful background information to the superjumbo.

Imagine you are considering carrying out your research project on the superjumbo.

1. List the further types of information that would be useful.
2. Suggest at least five sources for this information.
3. Carry out the initial research and determine whether this is a viable research issue.

The A380 superjumbo

The A380 has been developed by Airbus. It has the capacity to carry between 500 to 800 passengers and there has been substantial interest from airlines and several orders. However, airports which accept the aircraft have to make changes to infrastructure in order to accommodate the large plane and the large numbers of passengers boarding and disembarking.

It would be easy to trace the development of this aircraft and to find out which airlines have placed orders. It is not so easy to measure the true impact on the travel and tourism industry as the plane has not yet been introduced into service.

A research project could assess the impact so far in terms of orders placed, numbers of airports preparing for the aircraft and consumer confidence in travelling on such a large plane could be gauged.

Recovery from the tsunami

Everyone is aware of the devastating events of 26th December 2004. Besides the loss of life suffered, survivors lost their livelihood, much of it dependent on the tourism industry. It is likely that you are considering this issue or the numerous hurricanes that hit the US and Central America during the summer of 2005 as potential research issues. There are many angles that this research could take and therefore before you do your initial research you should think about what aspect of the impact you would like to cover. For example you might consider:

* The potential for rebuilding resorts in a manner that fits with the principles of sustainable tourism.

* The impact on bookings and the tourism experience in affected areas.

* The advent of new businesses specialising in tourism in affected areas.

* The impact on pricing to holidays in or near affected areas.

* The management of such a crisis by tour operators.

The following extracts give a flavour of the type of material that is available. The articles come from a variety of sources and feature reports on the impact the tsunami has had on tourism in the area. What conclusions could we reach from this?

Tourists shun tsunami-hit region

Tourists are staying away from tsunami-hit regions in their droves more than seven months after the disaster, the Pacific Asia Travel Association has said.

Figures published by Visa International Asia Pacific and PATA show arrivals to the Thai resort of Phuket are down more than 40% with spending down 30%. International arrivals to the Maldives meanwhile have fallen 46%.

Only Sri Lanka is showing a positive performance with year-on-year spending growth hovering around 10% and arrivals also on the upswing.

PATA president and chief executive Peter de Jong said it was time for travellers and the industry to rally behind the destinations.

"It is understandable that some travellers may have some concerns about travelling to destinations where many lives have been lost," he said.

"But we cannot help these communities get back on their feet by staying away. The best thing we can do is continue to inform tourists that it is appropriate and supportive to visit and that they will have a great holiday experience."

He urged airlines to ensure there was sufficient capacity and attractive prices to encourage tourists to return.

Source: www.travelmole.com
30th August 2005

Sri Lanka begs for Trade Help

SRI LANKA has appealed for trade support after it admitted the message that the country was open for tourism was not getting through.

More than 40 operators will continue to offer 20% discounts on packages for the next year.

But the UK visitor numbers will fall more than 10% this year to below 100,000, due to the perception that tourism areas remain devastated.

Sri Lanka Tourism's new UK and Ireland director, Jean-Marc Flambert, said: "The UK is furthest behind in terms of recovery and needs help."

He said the main 60-mile tourism stretch between Negombo and Bentota was "perfectly sellable."

Speaking six months after the Boxing Day disaster, Flambert said close links between the UK and Sri Lanka had meant media coverage was more intense than elsewhere.

He said: "People think the country is devastated. But it isn't."

Tim Robinson, UK chairman of the Pacific Asia Travel Association said: "If agents are not getting the messge, they are going to get it wrong. If a client asks what it is like and they have just seen the TV, they might say, 'It's a bit of a mess, why don't you try Florida?'."

Source: *Travel Trade Gazette* 24th June 2005

Tsunami-hit regions still suffering

Tourism Concern has launched a withering attack on authorities in tsunami-hit regions as communities struggle to get back on their feet.

More than nine months after the tragedy, local people remain homeless, distribution of aid remains poor and land is being grabbed by developers for inappropriate tourism projects, the body said.

The findings of Tourism Concern are included in a damning report titled: Post-tsunami reconstruction and tourism: A second disaster?

Source: www.travelmole.com 13th October 2005

Theory into practice

Visit the Tourism Concern website and find out more about their criticism of the tsunami recovery programme. From this make an assessment of whether this angle on the tsunami is a suitable research issue.

Find out what PATA is and what kind of information they provide. List the types of information. Make an assessment of the usefulness of PATA as a source.

Visit the website www.sarvodaya.org and find out about the Deshodaya project. Find sources of information on similar initiatives and assess whether community tourism in tsunami hit areas is an appropriate subject for research.

Climatic change and its impact on the travel and tourism industry

The summer of 2005 saw a series of hurricanes hit the US and Central America. The tourist industry in New Orleans collapsed as the city suffered devastating flood, following Hurricane Katrina. In Mexico, Hurricane Wilma led to tour operators laying on extra flights to repatriate tourists. Holidays to affected areas like Cancun had to be suspended. My Travel said such a suspension of service and the extra flights cost up to £4 million. Floods in Boscastle in Cornwall in 2004 took over a year to recover from.

Investigate the following sources of information to find out more about climatic change. State what kind of information is available from each source and say how it would be useful to a research project:

* www.fco.gov.uk (Foreign Office)

* www.nhc.noaa.gov (National Hurricane Center)

* www.boscastlecornwall.org.uk

Suggest five more sources of information for this issue, of climate change.

Terrorism and its impact on tourism in the UK

Terrorism has a tremendous impact on tourism. Events over the last few years have caused terror and devastation across the world in places such as New York, Bali, Egypt, Madrid and London. If you choose this research issue think very carefully about how wide to make your brief. If you research this as a general issue you will not have time or enough scope to go into depth about the impact on each destination. However if you choose, for example Madrid or Bali, find out in your initial research whether relevant statistics are available to assess impact on tourist numbers. The impact of terrorism on tourism in the UK has been chosen as a feasible issue here as it is topical and there is a lot of coverage on the issue in newspapers and trade magazines and tourism statistics are available.

Initial research for this topic begins with two of our very useful sources, websites travelwirenews and travelmole.com. A common problem is illustrated with the first two articles found. One is titled 'UK visitor arrivals hold up better than expected' and the second 'London tourism is another bomb victim' This is confusing and demonstrates the need to cross reference and validate information across several sources. We will examine this issue more closely.

CASE STUDY

London Tourism and the impact of terrorism

UK visitor arrivals hold up better than expected

The London terrorist bombings in July contributed to a 13.5% slump in overseas visitors to the UK, new figures show.

Statistics from UKinbound show that numbers dropped 9.3% in July and slumped further in August over the equivalent months last year.

However, the trade organisation described the international response to the July terrorist attacks as being "mixed" with some source markets down and others – notably North America – remaining firm.

"As expected August proved to be a difficult month for our members with London-based attractions suffering the most," a statement said.

Ukinbound, which represents 290 companies and organisations, expects full year visitor numbers and revenues to be flat at 2004 levels of 27.8 million and £13 billion respectively.

It said: "Overall, the number of overseas visitor arrivals has held up better than we initially feared and by the end of the month we could just see the first, tentative signs of recovery. Forward bookings remain weak but members are reporting improved interest in last minute deals."

The group said that high oil prices remain the biggest barrier to a swift recovery.

"We expect to see the gradual improvements in our key markets continue and would hope to be back to normal trading patterns by the end of the year," UKinbound said.

Report by Phil Davies

Source: www.travelmole.com 7th October 2005

London tourism is another bomb victim

The harsh reality of the impact of the London bombings in June is revealed in the latest tourism statistics released by Visit London. While the traditional British spirit of resilience enabled daily life in London to get back to normal very quickly after the terrorist incidents, the hard facts revealed that tourism was a victim of the attacks.

The London Visitor Index, which is a compilation of ratings from ten industry surveys, reached its lowest point for two years, despite some growth in the number of incoming visitors to the UK from overseas.

About 3.25 million foreign tourists visited Britain in August, slightly more than the same month last year, when about 3.16 million traveled to Britain. North American visitor numbers for the month rose from 461,000 to 530,000. There is evidence that other cities and tourist destinations around the country benefited, and visits to central London by British consumers were markedly down, which perhaps explains a serious drop in attendance figures at London attractions.

Overall visits to London attractions declined by almost a quarter in August, and it was the free admission and large venues, particularly museums, that felt the steepest drop in visitor numbers. Small attractions didn't do quite so badly, but it is clear that the London bombs have had a significant impact on all sectors of tourism.

London venues are still not out of the woods, four months on from the attacks. Early indications suggest that in September overall attendance levels were still below last year's figures by between 10 and 15 per cent.

Visit London is putting the best possible gloss on the news and says that whilst the decline is serious, the capital's visitor economy has not collapsed. Although the London bombings have dented activity, they say the underlying prospects remain good. The organisation says that the overseas market has held up remarkably well in the circumstances, and London's five airports reported vigorous activity throughout the summer.

Report by David Browne

Source: www.travelwirenews.com

London hotels slump confirmed in aftermath of terrorist attacks

Occupancy levels at London hotels slumped by more than 13% in August as the aftermath of July's terrorist attacks took its toll on the capital.

According to figures released by PKF (UK) LLP hotel consultancy services occupancy in London was 66.9% – down 13.2% on the same period last year – while average room rate rose 3.6% to £98.13. Rooms yield dropped 10.1% to £65.67.

Source: www.travelmole.com, 26th September 2005

The London Visitor Index

What is the London Visitor Index?
The London Visitor index is a monthly composite index of leading visitor surveys. This index gives a quick indication of current trading conditions and is based upon a basket of ten individual surveys.

How it works?
The monthly year-on-year percentage change for each indicator is given a score between 1-10, depending on the change. For example, a +10% monthly change gets 10 points, while –8% change gets 0 points. These scores are then added together to get an overall tally. Any score over 50 indicates growth.

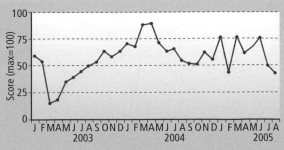

Source: *VisitLondon* http://www.visitlondon.com/corporate/faces–figures/

FIGURE 8.2 *London visitor index 2003–05*

1. Use all these source materials to draw up a list of points which can be concluded from the research so far.

2. Make a list of questions which need further clarification or research, for example, have tourist numbers in London recovered?
3. Suggest sources of information arising from these articles.
4. Suggest other sources of information that you can think of.

Extension task: produce a research plan for this issue that you could use or that you could go through with a colleague to help them get started.

✴ REMEMBER!

Websites designed to give information to tourists do not provide the hard facts you require for your research. Always look for the 'corporate' link to take you to the more useful information. The 'corporate' link contains information for other businesses looking at the website.

Eurotunnel's impact on cross channel operations

Often when you are researching an issue you will have to interpret statistics. Below is a table from a report on the impact of the Channel Tunnel on Kent, reporting on passenger numbers through the Channel. Researching this kind of data is secondary research but often gives ideas for issues to explore further with primary research.

Draw some conclusions from the statistics. Note them – you will then do further research in the form of a focus group to explore this issue further. You need to find between 6–12 people who have travelled across the Channel. Plan a discussion that you will lead and find out why they chose the particular route that they did. Consider:

✴ convenience

✴ cost

✴ timings

✴ weather.

NB: Find out how to run a focus group on page 142.

Globalisation of hotel chains

The hospitality sector of travel and tourism provides a good example of globalisation. Many national hotel chains reach a point where if they wish to continue to grow and achieve further economies of scale, they have to develop internationally. Some of these chains have developed brands which are consistent from country to country. Thus a guest in a Novotel

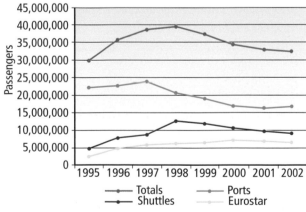

Source: KCC tables from Dover harbour board, Eurotunnel,cruise and ferry info, Hoverspeed, Port of Ramsgate (1997 figure for ports estimated, due to anomaly in the data).

Source: Centre for European Regional and Transport Economics, based on statistics published by Kent County Council (KCC) and data from the operators.

FIGURE 8.3 *Cross-channel passenger numbers*

from Africa to the UK to Sweden will receive the same type of room layout, same services and standards.

The aims of some of these organisations are described on their websites as follows.

Marriott International, Inc., is a leading worldwide hospitality company. Its heritage can be traced to a root beer stand opened in Washington DC, in 1927 by J. Willard and Alice S. Marriott. Today, Marriott International has more than 2,600 lodging properties located in the United States and 65 other countries and territories.

Source: Marriott Hotels International Limited

Novotel has more than 401 business and leisure hotels in 61 countries. In all major capitals, near business and cultural centres, by the sea or in the mountains, with easy access to transport networks (motorways, airports, railways), Novotel offers you a wide choice of destinations.

Source: Novotel

Hilton International operates over 400 hotels worldwide. Hilton International employs over 65,000 staff in over 70 countries.

Source: www.hilton.co.uk

CASE STUDY

Globalisation

There is a growing anti-globalisation movement. Globalisation protesters say that globalisation exploits the world's poor, has a detrimental impact on the environment and that individual cultures disappear and become subsumed under the US culture. Several international companies (for example McDonalds) are particular targets. An anti globalisation protest is held in London on May Day.

Here are some of the arguments against globalisation relating to tourism and the hospitality sector.

Today the tourist is a consumer. The raw material of the tourist industry is the flesh and blood of people and their cultures, thus its long-term effect on a country whose main income is derived from tourism can be devastating. Once a people or culture has been exploited and subverted to the needs of the tourist industry it can never be replaced.

– Cecil Rajendra, lawyer and human rights activist, Malaysia

"1 in 4 Brits now travel abroad on a package holiday. This is an industry that has grown from nothing not long after the Second World War. The early operators were viewed in the same light as second hand car dealers, the way the travelling public is still treated little has changed. The growth in the package holiday business has destroyed much of the Mediterranean and the tour operators are now looking further afield for places to despoil. Majorca, population 700,000, has 6 million tourists each year, 2 million of them Brits. It has brought in a lot of money and taken the local people on a journey to hell.

Tourism is having a massive global impact, not just on the global economy. Airports are seizing vast tracts of land. Residents living near airports are having their lives made a misery. Aircraft are rapidly becoming the number one global polluter, the effect is made all the more dramatic as the pollutants are emitted at high altitude where they have the maximum effect. Local cultures are being destroyed. In Tenerife local bars serve English beer and pander to English tourists, in Cyprus local Cypriot bars make way for karaoke nights and moronic English DJs. Hotels and tourist resorts need land and water. In Cyprus water is rationed to ensure a plentiful supply to hotel resorts. It is in the Third World that tourism is having the maximum impact. "

Source: www.heureka.clara.net

Corporate power

Multinational corporations are the driving force behind globalisation, and many commentators agree that they have benefited from it most. Larger than many host nations, the multinationals are often in a powerful position to dictate terms. Payment of bribes or 'commission' has fuelled corruption and secured favourable terms for multinational companies in their operations around the world.

The consequences of this growing corporate power can be seen clearly in relation to their foreign investment role. At its best, investment by a foreign company can provide jobs, stimulate economic growth and offer developing countries access to key technology and skills. At its worst, multinationals just exploit the cheap labour or natural resources which poor countries offer, and leave them nothing in return."

Source: http://pilger.carlton.com/globalisation/corporate

Task: You are aware that objectivity is essential when carrying out research. You draw conclusions from what you find out but should enter your research with an open mind. You are presented with some of the arguments against globalisation here. You are to carry out research and find some arguments for globalisation in the hotel sector of travel and tourism. Make notes on your findings and clearly reference them.

Extension task: Prepare for a debate, the motion is 'Globalisation in the hotel industry benefits local economies'. Some of the group should speak for the motion and some against. Each group member should prepare one or two points for or against in depth. You should be able to quote your sources of information. Follow the rules of formal debate.

The effect of tourism development on the culture of less economically developed countries (LEDC)

If you have studied Unit 7 on Responsible Tourism you will already have a lot of information about tourism development and will be aware of issues relating to impact on destinations. As that unit is externally assessed you may welcome the opportunity to research further into tourism development and responsible tourism by choosing this research issue. You should choose an LEDC which is of interest to you. The case study here gives you an idea of the points to include in your research.

CASE STUDY
Lithuania

Map of Lithuania

Lithuania is one of the Baltic States, formerly part of the USSR. It shares borders with Belarus, Latvia, Poland and Russia. The population is 3.4 million. The capital city is Vilnius.

In 1990 Lithuania declared its independence from Russia. However, independence was not finally achieved until 1991 as the Moscow administration turned troops on Lithuanian demonstrators.

English is widely spoken and Lithuanian is the mother tongue, although Russian and Polish are also spoken.

The country has a good transport network so it is relatively easy to get about. It has 90 kilometres of coast. There are no mountains or forests but there are hills and pleasant countryside. Art festivals are an attraction. The food tends to be heavy with meat and potatoes, pancakes, dark bread and cakes and fried cheese. The local beer is good.

The currency is the Lita.

Its industries are made up of:

Agriculture	20%
Industry, commerce and manufacturing	30%
Services	50%

Source – The World Factbook CIA 2002

Since independence more than 80% of businesses, previously state owned, have been privatised. Foreign investment is helping to boost the economy and Lithuania is forging trade links with the west. Unemployment is high at over 10%.

Tourism is seen as a means of growth to the economy and a major tourism offensive was launched in 2003 by the State Department of Tourism. Lithuania has joined the World Tourism Organisation and was the first Baltic state to do so. The country became a member state of the European Union in 2004. Many steps have already been taken to develop tourism:

* A law on tourism has been approved
* A National Tourism Development Programme up to 2006 has been prepared
* An information system on tourism in Lithuania was prepared.

A marketing plan was developed funded by state and local authorities and representatives of the tourism industry. Part of the plan concerned presenting a positive image of Lithuania. Various publications were marketed in languages such as Latvian, German, English, Polish and even Esperanto. Lithuania was represented at 19 International Fairs on Tourism.

Tourist Information Centres have been opened in Helsinki and in Warsaw.

Sightseeing tours have been arranged for journalists and travel organisers from Finland, Germany and the US.

Three hotels have been awarded the 'Green Key Award' for meeting over 70 environmental criteria in three categories including decreased power and water consumption, economic use of heating energy, waste separation and the possession of an environmental policy.

The chart shows the numbers of tourist arrivals between 1997 and 2003. Figures are in thousands.

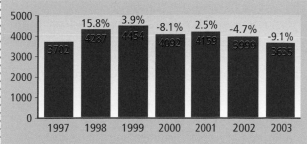

FIGURE 8.5 *Number of tourist arrivals between 1997 and 2003*

Most visitors are from neighbouring countries and they travel by car. However, numbers of visitors from Western Europe are increasing.

Useful websites for further research:

* www.tourism.lt
* www.travel.lt
* www.cia.gov
* www.neris.mii.lt
* www.lonelyplanet.com

Points for research:

1. **The objectives of tourism development in Lithuania**
2. **The agents of tourism development who are involved in Lithuania**
3. **Conflict between the agents of tourism development**
4. **Positive impacts of tourism on Lithuania (economic, environmental, social and cultural)**
5. **Negative impacts of tourism on Lithuania (economic, environmental, social and cultural)**
6. **Recommendations for good practice in tourism development in Lithuania.**

Extension task: Find examples of good practice in tourism development from other destinations which could be implemented in Lithuania.

The impact of industrial action on British Airways

Be aware that you may be looking at journals and magazines outside travel and tourism and find travel and tourism issues reported as this example from Personnel Today shows.

As this article is from Personnel Today, it explores the human relations angle of a strike. It

British Airways pays the price for putting eggs in one basket

British Airways is estimated to have lost up to £40m during recent strikes by baggage handlers and Gate Gourmet staff.

It wasn't meant to be like this. For the third consecutive summer, holidaymakers were left stranded as British Airways (BA) workers walked out yet again – this time in support of workers on a wildcat strike at troubled in-flight caterer Gate Gourmet.

The fiasco that engulfed one of the world's biggest airlines earlier this month threw 70,000 holidays and business trips into turmoil. But HR experts have said that important lessons can be learned from the way the situation was handled by all sides.

Taming the wildcat

'Companies must ensure they know their workforce and keep employees engaged if they are to avoid falling victim to a wildcat strike,' said Simon Barrow, chairman of employment brand consultancy People in Business.

That was not the case at Gate Gourmet – a firm owned by US venture capitalists Texas Pacific.

Faced with potentially crippling losses, it was desperate to cut costs, slash wage bills and reform what it claimed were outdated working practices.

But US-owned companies operating in the UK ignore the nuances of the British employment market at their peril. And the already low-paid, yet close-knit community of airport workers at Heathrow was a tinderbox waiting to ignite.

BA outsourced its catering operation to Gate Gourmet in 1997, and many BA employees knew the Gate Gourmet staff. Some were even related, so it was only natural for BA baggage handlers to support family members by joining the unofficial action.

'When you are fishing in the same labour pool – especially in a close-knit community where there is a history of employee unrest – you have to be aware of the risks and deal with things properly,' Barrow said. 'It's not just best practice – it's common sense.'

Outsourcing dangers

Companies usually outsource peripheral aspects of their business so they can cut costs and concentrate on core activities. But by outsourcing its in-flight catering operation to one company using local employees, BA left itself vulnerable.

Martyn Hart, chairman of the National Outsourcing Association, said: 'Companies should always take a business risk approach to outsourcing and must have a strategy in place to deal with any disaster.'

Putting all of its in-flight eggs in the Gate Gourmet basket was a perilous move for BA. There was no back-up plan to provide hot food should the arrangement turn sour, and passengers were left to face long-haul flights with little more than coffee for comfort.

'Outsourcing a critical aspect of a business to a single company can be very risky,' said Hart. 'There's little point in outsourcing and still taking the risk. If that's the case, it might be an idea to bring the outsourced operation back in-house.'

Dealing with illegal strikers

It is also worth noting the different ways that the two companies dealt with their errant employees. While Gate Gourmet refused to reinstate all of its staff, BA baggage handlers were soon back at work.

Under UK law, employees have no right to complain of unfair dismissal if they are sacked for taking part in unofficial strike action.

The catering staff were therefore left without a legal leg to stand on by embarking on a wildcat strike without union backing.

With its workers flouting the law, Gate Gourmet bosses were able to sack hundreds of employees without following normal procedures to protect themselves from a host of expensive unfair dismissal claims.

In contrast – and with the thousands of angry passengers camped on its doorstep – BA re-employed its baggage handlers as soon as possible, mindful perhaps that selectively re-engaging workers or sacking the lot would breed even more bad feeling.

Deborah Hely, partner and industrial relations expert at law firm Beachcroft Wansbroughs, said: 'Using shock tactics such as selective re-engagement to get rid of troublemakers often has a big impact on those who remain.'

However, BA has taken a firm line to make clear the wildcat action was unacceptable, and has said it will not pay strikers during their time of illegal absence.

Of course, the best policy is to prevent walkouts arising in the first place. 'Consultation with employees and explaining decisions in a language they understand gives any company a much better chance of avoiding disputes,' said Hely.

A contingency plan is also important, so company bosses know how - and indeed whether - they will be able to ride out the storm in the event that employees do embark on unofficial action.

Guy Lamb, partner and employment expert at law firm DLA Piper, agreed that better communication was the vital key to keeping workers on side before a situation escalates.

'If it gets to a wildcat strike situation, then you've already failed on an HR level,' he said. 'Employees walking out en masse is as fundamental a failure of managing a workforce as it's possible to get.'

Source: *Personnel Today* 23rd August 2005 www.personneltoday.com

looks at why the strike situation at Gate Gourmet occurred and how it was handled. If you decided to research the issue of strike action at British Airways you would have a number of avenues to follow having read this article as it raises a number of questions:

* It was the third consecutive summer that BA workers walked out. What happened in 2003 and 2004?

* What is the legislation regarding striking in the UK? What constitutes an illegal strike?

* Could the situation have been avoided with better employee relations?

* Terminology – what is a wildcat strike? What is meant by contingency? What is outsourcing?

* What was the impact on BA's bottom line?

How can you find the answers to these questions? You could:

* search newspaper archives to find reports on the 2003 and 2004 strikes

* find a text book about employee law and find out about strike legislation

* look up key terms

* find BA's annual report for 2005 (on the internet) and find out if they made any money and how the strike impacted on profits

* The question about employee relations is subjective and you would have to come to conclusions about this following your other research. This would lead you to make some recommendations for future practice for BA also.

Carry out the research outlined here. Make notes on your findings and as you research add other questions which occur to you about the topic to the original list.

Decide whether you want to pursue this issue for your research project.

8.2 Travel and tourism research project

In this part of the unit you will learn how to produce a research proposal, how to plan and carry out your research and how it might be presented.

Research proposal

Once you have done your initial research and selected a current issue for research you are ready to write your reseach proposal. This is completed before you start your project and provides a useful summary of what you are going to do. Your tutor will expect to see this to ensure that your chosen issue is suitable for research and that you are sufficiently prepared to begin your project.

Research proposal is an overview of and rationale for the research project.

You should also complete a research plan which will be based on the research proposal but will include timescales for each step of the project.

> **✱ REMEMBER!**
>
> You should use the research proposal to help you complete your research plan which will guide you through the project and help you track your progress.

The research proposal should contain the following elements:

* Title – this sums up what your study is about.

* Summary of the project – this gives some background to the project, explains the context (a description of events that led to this issue arising in travel and tourism) and why the issue is important.

* Aims – this covers what you hope to achieve and the limitations of the project. Limitations ensure that you do not make your project so broad that your research does not address a specific issue.

* Research Methodology – this section explains how you are going to conduct your research and the methods to be used to collect your data. The different methods that you might use for your research will be covered later in the unit. You might wish to refer to that section briefly now to help you write your research proposal.

* Sources of Information – when you did your initial research to test the suitability of your current issue, you bookmarked useful websites and you noted relevant sources of information that you wanted to revisit. List these now and include any others which have since occurred to you.

> *** REMEMBER!**
>
> Once you have completed your research proposal, you should have an opportunity to talk it through with your tutor on a one to one basis. Your tutor should give agreement to your research proposal before you continue.

Example of research proposal

Title: Are package holiday sales in decline? A study of the package holiday market and factors contributing to its decline.

Summary of the project: Several news reports in travel and tourism trade publications have indicated that sales of traditional package holidays are in decline. If this is so, the impact on the industry is of great importance as it would affect the core business of tour operators and travel agents. This research project will test whether the statement is true by looking at available data and will assess the reasons for decline, if there is one. It will also consider if and how tour operators are reacting to the issue of decline in package holidays.

Aims:

- To determine whether sales of traditional package holidays are in decline
- To determine if specific package holiday destinations are in decline
- Assess reasons for any decline
- Investigate the reactions of tour operators to any decline.

The research will be limited to sales of outbound holidays from the UK. Domestic tourism is excluded from the research project.

Research Methodology: Secondary research will be carried out using the sources of information listed in this proposal. The research will include analysis of available statistics. **Primary research methods** will include:

- A focus group with people who are intending to book holidays this year – discussion will focus on whether they will be booking a package holiday or other type of holiday
- An interview with a tour operator to find out if their data suggests package holidays are in decline and to ask what their strategies are for responding to this. This will be an informal interview with unstructured questions.

The data will be analysed and a report produced on the findings. Interview records and notes and tapes from the focus group will be available with the report.

Sources of Information:

- AC Nielsen – data given in Travel Trade Gazette article
- Statistics on package holidays taken from the Office for National Statistics
- Travelmole.com – archive search
- www.technology.guardian.co.uk
- Low cost airline websites for information on increases in passenger numbers
- www.hitwise.com for information on booking of holidays.
- ABTA Trends report available from their website
- Association of tour operators to Portugal
- Local tour operator to be approached for interview (name and address).

On page 50 you were introduced to the A380 as a potential research issue. Use the information given in the case study and the initial research you did for the A380 and produce a research proposal for this issue following the guidelines given here. Your research proposal does not have to be very long. Two sides of A4 is sufficient – you are going to add your research plan to this next.

Research plan

The research plan is going to be based on your research proposal but will include timescales. Your plan will be a working document and undoubtedly will change. This is fine as long as you write changes on the plan and they do not mean that you end up trying to do all the research at the last minute. You will need to discuss why and how your plan changed in your evaluation at the end of the research project. You will be expected to say how you dealt with problems that occurred in doing your research so make sure you note them as you go along.

It is better to get your research proposal agreed with your tutor before producing your plan and then arrange another meeting to agree the plan.

This means you do not waste time producing a plan for a research proposal which turns out to be unacceptable.

Your plan gives you a structure to work to, enabling you to make sure you have covered everything and that it is presented in a logical order.

When working out timescales allow time for writing up the project and for completing an evaluation. Include regular meetings with your tutor to allow him or her to check on your progress and discuss any problems that occur.

Research Plan: Are package holiday sales in decline?

The following timescales have been assumed for this plan. The school/college is running a semester timetable so this unit is timetabled for half a year or 15 weeks. The first three weeks have been spent introducing the unit, deciding on a research issue, completing initial research and the research proposal for the chosen issue. Week 4 is spent on one to one tutorials to assess the research proposals and allow students to write their research plan. This leaves approximately ten weeks to plan for allowing for contingencies and evaluation at the end.

WEEK	AIMS	RESEARCH METHOD	SOURCES OF INFORMATION	CHANGES TO PLAN
1	Determine if sales are in decline (initial research suggests that this is the case).	Secondary research. Analyse statistics and produce relevant graphs and notes.	TTG and Travel Weekly searches of recent archives. Neilsen statistics as given in the TTG article, Search www.statistics online. Research low cost airline websites.	
2	Determine which particular package holiday destinations are in decline.	Secondary research. Write up notes on findings – keep relevant articles/statistics for appendices.	Trade mags archives as before, ABTA Trends report.	

WEEK	AIMS	RESEARCH METHOD	SOURCES OF INFORMATION	CHANGES TO PLAN
3	Start to assess reasons for decline.	Secondary research. Categorise possible reasons and write up notes on supporting evidence.	From trade sources including Travelmole and ETid websites.	
4	Assess reasons for decline.	Add primary research plan focus group by inviting friends and family to participate – set a date for the focus group and arrange room and time. Borrow tape recorder to tape discussion.	Focus group.	
5	Assess reasons for decline.	Carry out focus group. Transcribe tape or make detailed notes from tape. Analyse findings and write up.	Focus group.	
6	Assess reactions of tour operator.	Telephone local operators to arrange interview. Prepare questions (Informal interview – primary research).	Tour operator.	
7	Assess reasons for decline.	Secondary research – find out about internet booking.	Hitwise website.	
8	Assess reactions of tour operator.	Primary research – carry out interview and analyse findings.	Tour operator.	
9		Start writing up report. Mop up research for any checks to be made.		

WEEK	AIMS	RESEARCH METHOD	SOURCES OF INFORMATION	CHANGES TO PLAN
10		Finish writing up report – check appendices and referencing, write bibliography.		
11		Evaluate the report and the methodologies used.		

Research plan

Notes on plan:

✳ All the aims from the research proposal must be covered in the plan.

✳ Each aim must link to the research methodology you are going to use to achieve that aim.

✳ The plan includes both primary and secondary research.

✳ Timescales are clear.

✳ There is scope to record changes to the plan.

Think it over...

What kinds of changes are likely to be recorded in the last column of the plan? Why would these arise? Discuss with your colleagues.

Theory into practice

At this stage you should be ready to try and produce a research plan. You could produce a research plan for one of the issues discussed in the first part of this unit or you could choose another issue that interests you. Make sure you produce the plan according to your own timescales rather than those given here in the example.

Assessment guidance

The assessment on page 66 provides evidence for Unit 8. It covers assessment objective:

1. Demonstration of knowledge, understanding and skills

   On completion of this assessment, you will be awarded a number of marks. These will contribute towards the marks for this unit. The quality of your work will determine the marks awarded. Your work will be assessed against the following criteria:

1–6 marks
There will be a research proposal that identifies and describes, with limited detail, the issue to be the focus of the research project. The plan indicates how the project aims will be met and what research methodology will be used. The plan may lack clarity, be unrealistic in parts and have some omissions.

7–9 marks
The research proposal will describe in some detail how the project aims will be met and the research methodology to be used. All parts of the plan are clear and feasible.

10–12 marks
There will be a comprehensive research proposal that clearly identifies and describes in detail the scope and range of the issue to be the focus of the project. The plan explains how the project aims will be met and the research methodology to be used. The proposal and plan reflect the project aims and include a timescale where priorities concerning the research and collection of data are acknowledged. All parts of the plan are clear, relevant, appropriate and feasible.

Research proposal and plan

The first part of your assessment is to produce a research proposal that includes a description of the issue that you have chosen to research. The research proposal will include the following elements:

* Title

* Summary of research issue

* Aims

* Research methodology

* Sources of Information.

In addition you will produce a research plan based on your research proposal. The plan will include timescales.

You should include a section in your plan where changes can be recorded.

Research methodologies

* REMEMBER!

Primary research

This is research carried out for the first time by you. It includes any surveys or interviews you do.

Secondary research

You do this first. It is called secondary research because someone else has done it and you are using their research to help you with your project.

Unit 10 has information on research methodologies including designing questionnaires and focus groups. You will find out later about the different research methods and how to decide which ones to use. Later in this section we will consider interviewing techniques and running focus groups but first we will look more closely at how to carry out secondary research in an effective manner.

During your project you are expected to carry out research independently, although this does not mean you cannot ask for guidance or check that you are on the right lines when you need to. Learning how to do research properly is very important to you as, not only does it help you find the information you need complete your project, but it gives you skills that you can apply in whatever career you choose in the future.

Secondary research involves the following:

* being clear about what you are to find out

* knowing where to search for information

* assessing the validity of the source

* cross referencing information

* being clear about what you want to find out – identifying the objective of the research.

It is worth spending some time on this preparation stage. Research is time consuming and it is easy to get side tracked so make sure you know what you are looking for. If you have completed your research proposal and plan properly, you will know what you are looking for. You will also have had an opportunity to discuss your proposal with your tutor. Ask questions and clarify anything you are unsure about. Make a list of the different things you need to find out. Write down key words to help your search.

Internet searching

When searching on the Internet remember to choose a search engine such as Google. You can search for images, news stories, using their directory or the web. The directory differs from the web in that it is human edited and sorted into categories. Be as specific as you can with your key words to narrow your search. If you want to search for an exact phrase put it in inverted commas. You might notice some of your results are termed 'sponsored results'. This means those companies have paid to be listed and may come up first. Remember that search engines provide help if you get stuck. Look for the help link on the main page.

When you are collecting information, organise it as you collect it. If you are making notes from the Internet or a book, group all the notes relating to a particular topic together. If you are photocopying or printing, highlight the relevant points immediately, and organise topics together.

Read the UKinbound article. Use a pen to highlight important points. Write a short summary of the article in your own words including at least three of the important points. Compare your summary with that of a colleague.

UKinbound attack funding snub

UKinbound has accused the government of setting ambitious growth targets for UK tourism while doing nothing to help achieve those aims.

In its monthly business barometer, chief executive Stephen Dowd said targets to grow total industry revenues from £75 billion to £100 billion – a 5% annual rise – 'already appear doomed' because of Labour's refusal to provide funds.

Hopes that new tourism minister James Purnell may play a more supportive role for UK tourism also appear dashed, he added.

'We had hoped he might have taken a more enlightened view, especially after the July bombings, but the word is that he is not inclined to support such a move,' said Dowd. "The targets of 5% growth per annum already appear doomed as the department of culture, media and sport expect this to happen without making any additional investment in tourism.

'We are told there is no budget in the department which I find reprehensible. More funds are given to culture and media than tourism even though we bring in more money.

'VisitBritain has not had an increase in funds for eight years. How are we supposed to grow when the government is not prepared to invest? We are falling behind our competitors.'

He added it was making life impossible for tourist bosses across the country.

'With government sitting on its hands, our regional tourism boards have to dream up ever more imaginative ways to raise funds for their marketing campaigns,' said Dowd.

Dowd said normal booking patterns should return by the end of the year.

But he warned a recent fall in fuel prices and improvement in exchange rates should not be taken as 'indicative of improved market conditions.'

'Fundamental economic problems in both the UK and US remain,' he said.

Visitor numbers and revenue are expected to be in line with 2004 at 27.8 million and £13 billion respectively with forecast growth in 2006 of 4%-5% for visitor numbers and 2%-3% in revenue.

Report by Steve Jones

Source: www.travelmole.com

CASE STUDY

Interpreting statistics

Look at these statistics carefully. Write five statements drawing conclusions from the statistics. For example:

* 'Nearly half of all those working in the visitor attraction industry work in elementary occupations.'

Compare your statements with those of your colleagues.

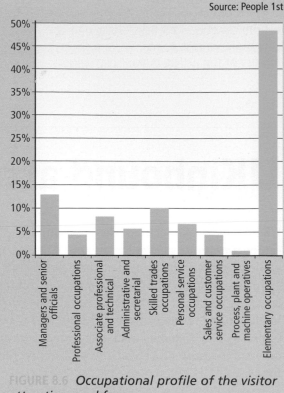

FIGURE 8.6 *Occupational profile of the visitor attraction workforce*

Assessing the validity of a source

You need to make sure that your source of information is accurate, up to date and unbiased. It is important to do this with every source but it is more difficult to assess Internet websites as anyone can set up a website and they may not always represent objective information.

Follow these criteria for deciding whether your source is valid.

* Who wrote it?

* Are they qualified to write it? – For example you can be pretty sure that a text book is written by a highly qualified person! A letter in a newspaper complaining about a package holiday may not be valid – it only represents one person's experience. Newspaper articles tend to be more trustworthy but again can reflect the paper's politics and opinions so be careful.

* What is the purpose of the information source? – If you are researching from holiday brochures or sales literature, remember the purpose is

to sell so they are biased in favour of certain products. They certainly won't tell you if there was an outbreak of food poisoning last season. A publication like 'World Travel Guide' is considered more reliable than brochures as it relies on factual information as an aid to the travel trade and is not trying to sell.

* Is the information up to date? – When was the information written? If it is a web page how often is it updated? If it isn't up to date don't use it. Of course, if you were researching a topic that does not change such as the development of tourism in the UK, then an older text book would still be useful.

* Does the author give sources of facts and figures? – You need to check this as you too need to quote sources. You may be able to go back to the quoted source and check for accuracy.

* Does the author seem to be biased in the presentation of information? – You will recognise bias when you have experience of

CASE STUDY

Assess the validity of the following pieces of information. Comment on the type of current research issue they would be useful for.

Make notes on your findings and discuss with your colleagues.

RYANAIR PASSENGER GROWTH OF 23% FOR OCTOBER 2005

TABLE 8.1 *Ryanair's passenger and Internet statistics for October 2005.*

	OCTOBER 2004	OCTOBER 2005	ROLLING 12 MONTHS ENDED 31ST OCTOBER 2005
Passengers[1]	2,462,686	3,025,080	32,180,320
Load Factor[2]	87%	85%	84%
Internet Sales Percentage[3]	97%	98%	98%

1. Represents the number of earned seats flown by Ryanair. Earned seats include seats that are flown whether or not the passenger turns up because once a flight has departed a no-show customer is not entitled to change flights or seek a refund.

2. Represents the number of passengers as a proportion of the number of seats available for passengers.

3. Represents the number of initial seat sales sold via the Ryanair Internet site as a percentage of total initial seat sales. Initial seat sales exclude changed and amended seat sales.

Source www.ryanair.com

BRITISH ARRIVALS UP BY 7%

The UK has bucked the general trend to Thailand by posting a 7% rise in the number of visitors to 251,000 between January and May, compared with the same period last year. The Tourism Authority of Thailand puts this down to strong bookings for Ko Samui, Pattaya and Hua Hin made prior to the tsunami. Worldwide arrivals to Thailand were up 0.1%.

Source: *Travel Trade Gazette* 1st July 2005

EGYPT - RED SEA RIVIERA

Whether you're looking for ancient wonders or modern marine sports, you'll find that Egypt has everything you'd hoped for . . . and more! From the tombs of the Pharaohs to the clear blue waters of the Red Sea, this matchless land will both enthral and entertain you.

For centuries the ancient sites of this amazing country have beckoned visitors from across the world. Now Nature itself is attracting the contemporary traveller, with Red Sea resorts as rich in natural treasures as Tutankhamun's tomb was rich with gold. Here the essential holiday trio of sun, sea and sand comes enhanced with crystal waters teeming with tropical fish. Sunken shipwrecks and coral gardens make exquisite snorkel and scuba grounds. Several resorts have emerged to meet increasing demand, ranging from a cluster of intimate hotels to a spread of shopping malls, golf courses, luxury complexes and a lively night scene.

EGYPT GUIDE

Source: *Airtours Far and Away 2004–2005*

---

using different sources. Initially it is difficult to recognise but you can practise by reading several newspaper accounts of the same event.

Cross referencing information

Cross referencing is a means of checking that the information is correct. It is more important if you are not absolutely certain that your original source is accurate. For example, you may have found some figures quoted on a tour operator's website and you may not be certain that they are up to date or accurate so you look for a second source of the same information to check the figures. The second source could be official statistics or other tour operators' findings.

Paris will be the destination for nearly one in ten Britons intending to take a short trip abroad in the next six months.

The attractions of the French capital will lure close on 1.4 million Brits, according to a survey for Sainsbury's Bank.

A further million will head to the canals and cafes of the Dutch capital of Amsterdam, while New York, Barcelona and Prague make up the remainder of the top five.

Londoners are the section of the population most likely to take a short trip abroad, with 40 per cent taking a short trip between now and July 2005.

They are closely followed by those in the Midlands, on 38 per cent; while those living in Wales, West and the South East or East Anglia were least likely to take a short trip, on 27 per cent.

Source: www.travelbite.com 14th March 2005

Think of three different ways you could check the information given in this article.

Find out what the current top short break destinations are. Cross reference your findings with other sources.

✱ REMEMBER!

Keep details of your sources as you do your research.

Carrying out primary research

✱ REMEMBER!

Refer to Unit 10 for the basic information on research methodologies.

Your research project should not entirely rely on secondary data. You should carry out some original research of your own. You will decide what type of primary research you want to do at the planning stage and incorporate it into your plan.

The most appropriate research methodologies for your project will be:

✱ interviews

✱ focus groups

✱ questionnaires.

Interviews

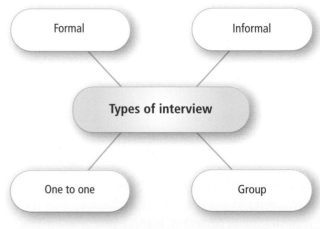

FIGURE 8.7 *The different types of interview*

A formal interview is very structured with a list of pre-prepared questions to be asked. It is similar to carrying out a questionnaire on a one to one basis or with a small group.

An informal interview allows more scope for the interviewee to develop the flow of the interview. You still need to prepare a list of topics that you want to cover in the interview but you can be flexible about what order they are covered in and if the interviewee suggests an issue that they consider particularly relevant you can include it in your discussion. Where this is done with a group it develops into a focus group.

In terms of your research project you are likely to find that an informal interview is more appropriate if you are speaking to an 'expert' such as a manager of a visitor attraction or a tour operator. The expert will bring points to the discussion that you may not have previously considered. This is most likely to be on a one to one basis.

On the other hand if you are interviewing ordinary consumers you may want to use a formal approach, if it is one-to-one, as the interviewees will depend on you to direct the interview. If you still prefer an informal structure consider carrying out a focus group.

Focus Group

A focus group is very useful if you want to find out consumer attitudes or perceptions about a company or service. For example, you might hold a focus group to find out attitudes towards booking holidays with travel agents.

It is also a technique that you can practise and develop during the course of your project. This research method is used extensively in consumer marketing.

A focus group is formed by the following methods:

✳ **Decide what kind of people should be invited** – for example, if your project is about attitudes to flying on low cost airlines, you must invite people with experience of travelling on these airlines.

✳ **Invite a group of people** – between 6 and 12 – to a pre-arranged venue.

✳ **Focus group participants are often paid.** You are unlikely to pay them but you might offer refreshment as an incentive to attend.

✳ **Prepare a list of discussion points but be prepared to be flexible** – the discussion should flow from the interviewees but if it goes completely off track you have to pull it back. This is where experience helps.

✳ **In a focus group an extrovert personality can easily dominate discussion.** Try to bring in quieter members.

✳ **Record the discussion** – you can't take notes and lead the session. You need a tape recorder or a scribe. Ask a friend or colleague to help you. You can reciprocate for them.

There are some useful techniques that an interviewer can use in running a focus group. These are:

✳ **Playing devil's advocate** – this means that the discussion leader deliberately takes an opposing point of view to a participant in order to stimulate a strong defence and further discussion

* **Sophisticated naiveté** - the leader pretends not to understand a participant's point in order to get them to expand on it

* **Closed book technique** – participants in a focus group are aware they are taking part in research and may not choose to reveal too much of their real opinions. The closed book technique is used to formally bring the focus group to an end. The leader thanks the participants and puts their papers away or turns off the tape recorder. The leader should be listening intently at this point as the participants will relax and may reveal some interesting attitudes to the leader or as asides to each other when they think they are no longer being recorded.

Questionnaires

Questionnaires are useful means of getting information from a large number of people. Remember you can use them in an informal interview if you choose. Refer to Unit 10 for guidelines on designing a questionnaire.

Presentation of project

You should start thinking about how to present your research project at the planning stage. Your tutor may have a preferred method of presentation such as a written report but most are flexible and if you have an innovative idea for presentation discuss it with your tutor. The two methods we will focus on here are written reports and oral presentation.

How to write a report

The following elements should be included in the structure of a report:

* Title page

* Contents page

* Introduction (Terms of reference in a formal report)

* Findings

* Conclusions

* Recommendations

* Appendices (if used)

* References/bibliography.

Reports can be informal or formal. An informal report is arranged under headings without numbering. A formal report has a system of numbering headings and then subheadings. The introduction is numbered '1'. The findings are numbered '2' and each sub section 2.1, 2.2, etc. The conclusions are numbered '3'. Recommendations are not always required but if so they are numbered '4'.

Contents page

You will do this at the end or as you go along. Ensure page numbers are given for each section. There is a system in Word to do it for you if you choose.

Introduction

This section explains the research issue and the aims of the report. You should also give an overview of the research methodology used. Remember that in a formal report this is headed terms of reference and will give more detail on the what, why and how.

Findings

This is the main part of the report and is where you report on all the research findings from both your secondary and primary research. This is where you present the main results from your research and analyse all the data that you collected. You may include description, facts, charts, graphs and quotes as long as they are referenced.

Conclusions

Having presented all your findings you should draw some conclusions. This will be a series of important points resulting from your research.

Recommendations

These are not always required but if so should be presented as a series of points for action resulting from the conclusions.

Use of appendices

You can attach information, statistical data and pages from the Internet in appendices. This means they are labelled Appendix 1, 2, etc. and attached to the back of your work. They must be referred to in your work. For example, in your report you might state something like "statistics show that Paris is the most popular short break destination - see Appendix 1". Sometimes the reader needs to see the statistics or graphs and charts as they read the report as they are important to understanding a point. In this case include them in the main body of the report and quote the source.

References and bibliography

The references are a list of sources from which you have made direct quotes or extracted data in the report itself. The bibliography is a list of all sources that you have used to carry out your research and produce the report. The Harvard referencing system is the one that is conventionally used. Ensure you include titles, authors, publishers and dates. There are many study skills books and web sites which explain how this should be done. You must include newspapers, journals and websites as well as books. Remember that direct quotes should be acknowledged within the text.

Plagiarism

Everything you write must be in your own words. It is unacceptable to copy from another source unless it is a direct quote. This must be acknowledged with details of the source and the date. If you do copy directly from a source without acknowledgement, this is called plagiarism and is very serious.

Third person

Reports are usually written in the third person. This means you do not use 'I found that…', for example. You say 'It was found that… '

> **✳ REMEMBER!**
>
> When carrying out research:
>
> ✳ plan well – don't just browse at random
>
> ✳ check the validity of your sources
>
> ✳ never plagiarise
>
> ✳ present your work in a logical way with appropriate headings
>
> ✳ use appendices and always refer to them in the main body of your report
>
> ✳ add a bibliography.

Oral presentation

You may decide to present your work orally. You will still have to do a lot of written work to keep track of your research, analyse findings and draw conclusions. However, you will not have to produce a full written report. Instead you can use your research findings to plan a presentation. From your notes you will plan a presentation which includes the following elements:

✳ **Introduction** – description of the research issue, the aims and the methodology chosen. You will also tell your audience what is going to be covered in the presentation.

✳ **Findings** – divide this into sections and make sure that the different sections are flagged up to the audience by using bullet points on an overhead, PowerPoint or by introducing each section verbally. You should use cue cards to remind you of the key points you want to make in each section. Practise your presentation so that you are not totally dependent on the cue cards and you are not tempted to read from them.

✳ **Visual aids** – your presentation will be of greater interest if you support it with visual aids. You may choose to produce a PowerPoint which can include charts and pictures; you may use a series of overheads or handouts. If you use handouts give them out at the beginning or the end but not when you want your audience to listen to you. They will get distracted by the handout and you will lose their attention.

✳ **Conclusions** – draw attention to the main conclusions from your findings.

✳ **Recommendations** – if these are appropriate, discuss these last.

✳ **Questions** – unlike a written report there is an opportunity with an oral presentation to invite your audience to seek clarification or expansion of points. You can limit the time for questions if you wish. If you get a question that you can't answer, throw it open to your audience as in 'Thank you for that question, who would like to comment on that?'

✳ **Thank your audience** at the end.

Evaluation of the project

You should consider different ways of evaluating your work and reflecting on what you have achieved and how you achieved it so that you learn from the experience for future research projects.

Here are some aspects of the project that you can include in an evaluation:

✳ Did my plan help me? How?

✳ Did I stick to my planned deadlines?

✳ Did I choose suitable research methodologies? Why were they suitable or not?

✳ Did my sources of information produce sufficient, relevant information?

✳ What other sources could I have used?

✳ Were my findings presented in a logical way supported by relevant data?

✳ Was my referencing correct?

✳ Were my conclusions valid?

✳ Did I produce viable recommendations?

✳ To what extent did I work independently?

✳ What would I do differently next time?

This assessment provides evidence for Unit 8. It covers assessment objectives:

2. Application of knowledge and understanding of the specified content and of related skills in vocationally-related contexts.

3. Use of appropriate research techniques to obtain information to analyse vocationally-related issues and problems.

4. Evaluation of information to make reasoned judgements, draw conclusions and make recommendations about vocationally-related issues and problems.

On completion of this assessment, you will be awarded a number of marks. These will contribute towards the marks for this unit. The quality of your work will determine the marks awarded. Your work will be assessed against the following criteria:

2. Application of knowledge and understanding of the specified content and of related skills in vocationally-related contexts.

1–7 marks
The project has been completed with guidance from others. It meets most aims and timescales set including final completion by the deadline stated. The plan was not updated with changes. Changes were within the control of the learner.

8–12 marks
The project has been completed with some guidance from others but mainly independently. There is evidence that the proposed plan has been followed and indicated aims and timescales have been met. Changes to the plan have been documented and were mainly as a result of factors beyond the control of the learner.

13–15 marks
The project has been completed independently. The plan has been followed and all aims clearly met and timescales adhered to. The plan is regularly updated throughout the process with an indication of how aims and timescales were met and the changes that were required. Contingencies were in place for deviations from the plan.

3. Use of appropriate research techniques to obtain information to analyse vocationally-related issues and problems.

1–9 marks
Research has been undertaken that uses a limited range of resources that have mainly been directed. There is some use of research methodology identified in the plan for the project. There is some analysis of the issue and its effect on the travel and tourism industry or a specific sector but this is mainly descriptive.

10–14 marks
Research has been undertaken that uses a range of sources, many of them identified and used independently. Sources are clearly referenced throughout. The sources used areas identified in the plan. There is clear analysis of the issue and its effect on the travel and tourism industry or on a specific sector.

15–18 marks
A range of research techniques is used to obtain data and sources of information have been obtained independently. Sources are fully and clearly referenced throughout. Sources used exceed those identified in the plan for the project and the need for these additional resources is explained. There is a clear and comprehensive analysis of the issue and its effect on the travel and tourism industry or on a specific sector.

4. Evaluation of information to make reasoned judgements, draw conclusions and make recommendations about vocationally-related issues and problems.

1–7 marks
There is an evaluation of the project but it is mainly superficial and subjective. There is an evaluation of the research methodology with some awareness of the limitations of sources of information available to support the project or some acknowledgement of the learner's own limitations in terms of the range and depth of research undertaken. Recommendations are made but these are not limited in detail and are not always feasible or appropriate.

8–12 marks

There is an evaluation that evaluates the project with some objectivity and some depth drawing valid conclusions that are mainly reasoned. There is an evaluation of the research methodology that acknowledges the limitations of the research where appropriate and the effect of these limitations on the outcomes of the project. Recommendations for improvement are made, some of them justified. Most have some detail and are appropriate.

13–15 marks

There is a comprehensive evaluation that is objective and in depth with valid and accurate conclusions that are clearly reasoned. Research methodology and data obtained are evaluated and where there are limitations these are clearly explained in terms of the effect on the outcomes of the project. Valid recommendations for improvement are made that are justified and presented in detail.

Assessment practice

Carry out the research for the current issue that you have chosen following the plan you prepared.

Update the plan as you proceed giving reasons for any changes. Indicate where you have worked independently.

Produce a written report of between 2000–4000 words on your research topic, analysing the issue and its impact on the travel and tourism industry or on a specific sector of the industry.

Produce an evaluation of the project and the research methodology with recommendations for approaches to be adopted for future projects.

Knowledge check

1. What is a PEST analysis?
2. Describe two drawbacks of a PEST analysis.
3. Give two sources of travel and tourism statistics.
4. How can you track your research?
5. What is globalisation?
6. What should be included in a research proposal?
7. Why do you need a research plan?
8. Give two examples of research methodologies.
9. When would you use a focus group?
10. Why do you need to assess the validity of an information source?
11. Think of two ways to present your work other than a written report or oral presentation.
12. What is the referencing system commonly used called?
13. What is plagiarism?
14. Why do you need to do an evaluation when you have completed your project?

Working in travel and tourism

This unit covers the following sections:

9.1 The range, nature and skills required for employment opportunities within travel and tourism

9.2 Teamwork

9.3 Personal skills and career development

In this unit you will be introduced to the wide range of employment opportunities in the travel and tourism industry. You may already be aware of many types of jobs through any experience of your own in travel and tourism. You are likely to have been a customer of a travel agent or have travelled by air. You may have visited many visitor attractions. In Unit 1, *The Travel and Tourism Industry*, you studied the structure of the industry and gained an awareness of the breadth of opportunity. Besides looking at such customer facing roles you will discover many behind the scenes opportunites discussed in this unit. You will also find out about the nature of employment in travel and tourism, that is, whether jobs are full time, part time, well paid or not, and learn about the skills required to succeed in the industry.

Good teamwork is essential in this industry so part of this unit is devoted to understanding what such skills are and developing them. You will evaluate your own skills by completing a personal skills audit and create your own personal development plan for employment in travel and tourism.

How you will be assessed

This unit is internally assessed by your tutor and externally moderated by Edexcel. A variety of activities and case studies is provided in this unit to help you understand all aspects of working in travel and tourism and to help you prepare for the assessment.

Your assessment evidence must show that you have:

* participated in a team, working towards completion of a significant travel and tourism related task

* analysed the range of employment opportunities and the skills and qualities required for a successful career in the travel and tourism industry

* prepared a detailed career development plan based upon a personal skills audit produced using information from a range of sources.

9.1 The range, nature and skills required for employment opportunities within travel and tourism

Introduction to employment in travel and tourism

In this section you will be introduced to the range of jobs in different sectors of the industry. Within each sector we will examine the types of jobs available at different levels, the nature of the employment and the skills and qualities required for that kind of employment. You will be encouraged to carry out your own research from a number of different sources so that you are able to produce a detailed analysis of the range of employment on offer in travel and tourism.

Scale of employment

You may remember from your previous studies that the travel and tourism industry is very

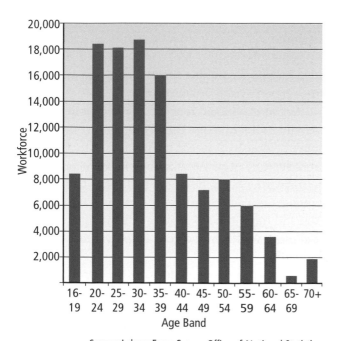

Source: Labour Force Survey, Office of National Statistics

FIGURE 9.1 *Age profile of the UK travel and tourist services workforce*

important as an employer in the UK. According to the government report 'Tomorrow's Tourism' the industry employs over two million people which amounts to about 8% of the UK workforce. One in six of all jobs created in the last ten years has been in travel and tourism.

Although the industry is dominated by large organisations such as First Choice and Thomson, most travel and tourism businesses are very small with 85% employing fewer than 25 staff so most people working in the industry work for small companies. It is a young industry, 17% of the workforce is under 20 compared with 5% of the national workforce.

Note that the bar chart relates to the travel and tourist services sector, e.g. travel agents and tour guides, not to the whole industry.

Nature of employment in travel and tourism

If you are hoping to work in travel and tourism you will need to research different sectors to find out the range of employment available and how the terms and nature of employment differ in different sectors. For example, travel agents are likely to work regular hours and be office based in one location. A tour representative works long, unsociable hours with little time off and is often expected to live and work abroad. You will need to decide what type of employment conditions suit you and find appropriate jobs. In this section we will look at the terms and conditions of travel and tourism work.

Types of contracts and seasonality

Much travel and tourism work is seasonal and much is part time. Obviously demand for staff fluctuates with the tourist season, particularly in the hospitality sector. Full time positions are more likely to be found with travel agents, tour operators and in event management than in hotels or in visitor attractions. If the work is seasonal you will be offered a temporary contract rather than a permanent contract. This is sometimes known as a 'fixed term' contract as it runs from the start of the tourist season to the end. Seasonality of tourism work can affect whole communities. For example, many people travel to resorts like Newquay to pick up summer jobs but find themselves unemployed in the winter. If you are working for a company you will have 'employed' status and will have tax and insurance deducted from your pay. If you work for yourself you will be 'self-employed' and will have to ensure you pay your tax and national insurance.

Pay

Pay varies considerably depending on the sector, the amount of experience you have and the promotions you have achieved. You will find some examples of rates of pay in the job examples given in this unit.

Working hours

When you consider what kind of travel and tourism job you would like, think about whether you are prepared to work long hours when everyone else is enjoying themselves or whether you prefer a 9 to 5 job. There are 9 to 5 jobs – they are most likely to be found in the public sector in tourism offices or in the private sector with travel agents. If you opt to work in hotel management or as a rep you will work long, unsociable hours so it is essential that you enjoy your work. Many waiters and chefs in hotels and restaurants work split shifts. This means they are there to serve breakfast, take a few hours break and then return to serve dinner.

Job location

If you hope to work in your home town you may find yourself restricted in your choice of travel and tourism jobs available. All towns have travel agents and hotels. Few have a tour operation head office, call centre or airport. These are centrally located, for example the Thomas Cook head office in the UK is located in Peterborough and Thomson is located in London. You need to find out what is available in your area. It is likely that you have already studied the scope of the local travel and tourism industry in Unit 1, *The Travel and Tourism Industry*.

Many exciting jobs in the industry require travel, for example, resort representatives, hotel contractors and airline personnel. Some jobs are only available in certain locations. For example, you may choose to work in an airport or at a ferry terminal. In these cases you will be expected to live within travelling distance of your place of work.

Skills and qualiites

The skills most often cited as important in travel and tourism posts are:

* computer literacy

* communication skills

* customer handling skills

* management skills

* team working skills.

Many types of employment in travel and tourism involve dealing with customers and therefore good communication and social skills are demanded by employers. The ability to work in a team is also essential. Of course, there are other skills which are also important. You should expect to present at least basic numeracy skills although in some roles advanced numeracy is desirable.

Some jobs require languages so it is a good idea for you to study a second language alongside your travel and tourism course.

As the travel and tourism industry relies more heavily on technology then IT skills become more desirable. A recent survey found that the introduction of new technology in travel and tourism was being hindered by lack of IT skills amongst workers, particularly in small companies. You still have time to acquire advanced IT skills and these will increase your employability in the industry.

When employers are looking for staff they place the basic requirements of the post in an advertisement.

This example illustrates the kind of job you could do whilst studying. It is enjoyable work, pays well and gives you experience in your chosen industry.

Development Directorate
Winchester Tourist Information Centre
SATURDAY ASSISTANT
Salary £6.05 – £7.46 per hour

Hours

Summer season (May to September)	*Week 1* 8.30am to 3.30pm
	Week 2 11.30am to 6pm
Winter season (October to April)	*Week 1* 9am to 3pm
	Week 2 12noon to 5.30pm

(Extra hours are available to cover annual leave, travel and sickness)

Are you reliable, enthusiastic and interested in Tourism? The Tourist Information Centre is seeking a Saturday Assistant to support its busy and friendly team throughout the year. This is a varied role which involves helping visitors with a wide range of enquiries, making accommodation bookings and selling souvenirs. You will have a good knowledge of Winchester and the surrounding area; be educated to GCSE level or equivalent and possess a working knowledge of Microsoft Office applications.

We operate a non-smoking policy. Committed to Equal Opportunities.

Source: Winchester City Council

You can see from the advertisement that the hours change according to the season, although overtime is available. The location is fixed and the requirements are knowledge of the local area, GCSEs and IT skills.

However, the employer has a very firm idea of the work that needs to be done and the kind of person they are looking for to do it and this information is produced in two separate documents, a job description and a person specification. Once you register interest in applying for the post these documents are sent to you to help you complete your application. The job description and the person specification for the Saturday Assistant post are shown here.

Job Title: Saturday Assistant

Department: Development Directorate

Post Number: LST 247

Grade: Scale 2

Accountable to: TouristInformation Centre Manager

Post Objective: To provide accurate and comprehensive information to customers in order to:

- enable visitors to make the most of their time
- support the effective management of tourism
- encourage repeat visits and referrals

Specific Tasks:

1. Provision of Information
   - Toprovide accurate and useful information to TIC customers, in person or by phone or email;
   - Toassist with updating information both manually and using information technology;
   - Tohelp maintain adequate supplies of free literature and keep display areas stocked

2. Accommodation bookings
   - Tomake accommodation bookings using the 'Visit' computerised booking system
   - To promote actively to customers the accommodation booking service

3. Sales
   - To sell souvenirs, publications, event tickets and guided tour tickets using correct till procedures;
   - To observe correct audit procedures for all sales;
   - To be pro-active in promoting sales opportunities to customers.

4. Other duties
   - To support the implementation of the TIC Business Plan and Community Services Business Plan;
   - To consider at all times ways of improving the services offered by the TIC, and relay these to the TIC manager, in accordance with the principles of Best Value;
   - To carry out any other duties as requested by the Tourist Information Centre Manager of Head of Cultural Services

Hours of Work:
   - 5–6 hours on Saturdays throughout the year
   - Additional hours available to cover staff leave and training
   - No weekend enhancements payable.

Requirements

Requirements		Weighting	Assessment Method
Skills	• Verbal ability in a foreign language • Computer literate with Microsoft Office • Team working • Good telephone manner • Good interpersonal skills	1 2 3 3 3	A/I A/I A/I I
Experience	• Knowledge of Winchester • Working with the public in a customer service environment • Retail and/or cash handling	2 3 2	T A/I A/I
Personal Qualities	• Good personal presentation • Articulate • Reliable • Enthusiastic • Flexible • Organised • Ability to fit in with team • Initiative	3 3 3 3 3 3 3 3	I I I I I I I I
Specific Job Requrements	• Weekend and Bank Holiday working	3	I
Qualifications	• GCSE level grade C or above in English and Maths.	3	A

Weighting   3 – Essential for the successful performance of the job
　　　　　　　2 – Desirable, but can be achieved through on the job training or experience
　　　　　　　1 – Useful but not essential for successful performance of the job

Assessment
Application Form	A	Interview	I	Tests		T	
References	R	Presentation	P	Evidence of Qualifications		Q	

Source: Winchester City Council

You will note that weightings are put against the person requirements. A weighting of 3 means that requirement is essential, a rating of 1 means it would be useful but is not essential. Note too that there are three methods of assessing candidates, the application form, interview and a test!

Throughout this unit you will have the opportunity to examine the specific skills required for different positions, either by using the examples presented here or by doing your own research.

Employment in different sectors of travel and tourism

Travel agents

If you choose to work in a travel agents you can work in leisure or business travel. Many travel agents deal mainly with leisure travel which usually means holidays and travel for pleasure. Business travel agents organise transport and accommodation for business clients. There are many similarities in the work but also some important differences. Business clients are usually more concerned about reliability and convenience than cost.

Leisure clients may be booking a long time ahead whereas business clients may be booking a few days ahead. Business travel agents may hold accounts for large companies and cater for all the company's travel needs. Some are even departments within a large company.

It is possible to work in a travel agency after A-level. You would expect to join as a trainee but could get promoted with experience to management. If you were to work for a large chain of travel agents like Thomson there would be more opportunity for promotion. The irony of working as a travel agent is that you don't get to travel yourself very much although you may be offered 'educationals'. These are trips provided by tour operators for agents to help them develop knowledge about the products they sell. Some specialist travel agents such as Trailfinders employ agents who have travelled extensively round the world so that they are able to give detailed advice to their clients who are often students or people taking sabbaticals from work. Travel agency hours are reasonable – often 9 to 5 and you would expect to get a full time permanent position with a travel agent.

Kwik Travel
Experienced Travel Advisors

1. Do you have excellent general product knowledge or expertise in a particular market?
2. Do you have at least two years' ABTA travel experience, accumulated during the last five years?
3. Are you PC literate, with proven sales ability?

If you can answer 'Yes' to each of these questions, read on.

By joining Kwik Travel as a self-employed, home-based travel advisor and selling holidays under our trusted and powerful brand name, the opportunity to develop your own successful business is well within reach.

Being ATOL bonded, you will even be able to create and sell unique, tailor-made packages directly to the public.

True success will only come from working together and in return for providing the following infrastructure we require that you are completely committed to making a success of your career.

Technology and Kit
You will be provided with all the tools necessary to run your own travel business from home, including:
- PC with CD Rom drive and 15 inch monitor
- BT cordless digital telephone and fax/phone/answer machine
- Two telephone lines, plus ADSL Broadband data connection (ISDN if ADSL is not available in your area)
- Colour printer and ink cartridges
- Internet and email facility
- Software to include 'TARSC' (back office system), 'Magic Desk Top' (booking system) and 'Travel Scan' (on line brochure library)
- Kwik Travel Intranet, your internal online help and news desk
- Global Travel Group 'Dynamic Packaging Solution' for tailor made packaging
- Global Rooms and Global airfares online for the best rates on accommodation and worldwide flights.
- Automated credit card authorisation
- Comprehensive office stationery pack
- All branded stationery, such as letterheads, business cards, compliment slips, luggage labels and ticket wallets
- A supply of first and second-class stamps

Please note that all telephone installation charges, line rentals and business call costs will be paid for you by Kwik Travel.

Administrative and Customer Services Support
Our highly experienced Central Office team will provide you with comprehensive support in all areas.

Our Customer Services team will deal with the vast majority of administrative queries, including customer confirmations and invoices, the dispatch of travel documents and the collection of balance payments.

Direct access to senior and middle management is also available for any queries that you may have, such as potential marketing initiatives and technical assistance.

Earning, Time Commitment and Commission Levels
In your first year working full time, we would expect your earnings to be between £12,000 and £15,000. As your bank of customers grows and your confidence develops, your earnings will increase year on year. What remains clear is that sales and profit are directly related to the time and effort expended.

We would expect you to be available for calls for at least 30 to 35 hours each week and if you form part of a team, you will be required to commit to a rota. You will however be able to work additional hours on top of your rota hours.

You will receive between 30% and 33% of the commission earned on your bookings. Higher commission structures up to 60% are available to established homeworkers or career travel agents who have established a customer database.

In your first year with Kwik Travel you can earn an additional 10% on nominated friends and family bookings.

A one off commitment fee of £295 + VAT is required on joining Kwik Travel and a monthly fee of £63 will be deducted from your commission each month.

The commitment fee will contribute to your setting up costs and the monthly fee will go towards your monthly running costs (i.e telephone, stationery, marketing, IT etc.)

Source: Kwik Travel Ltd

1. Carry out some research on the Internet and write a paragraph about each of the following:

   ✳ ABTA

   ✳ ATOL bonding

   ✳ Kwik Travel

   ✳ Dynamic packaging.

2. Rachel is 23, she has worked in a travel agent since she left school. She is considering leaving her High Street agency to work for Kwik Travel from her home. Draw up a chart weighing up the advantages and disadvantages of this way of working for Rachel.

3. Draw up a person specification for someone suitable for working at Kwik Travel.

Extension task: Find another example of a company recruiting travel homeworkers. Compare the conditions of work and the employment benefits with Kwik Travel.

Research tip: Travel Weekly and Travel Trade Gazette often carry advertisements for homeworkers.

Tour operations

Tour operation is one of the most exciting sectors in which to work as it offers a wide range of opportunities. If you want to work in tour operations in a head office role you will have to move to the head office location. Unlike travel agencies, tour operators are not represented in every town. Tour operator jobs are either at head office or in a resort, often overseas. There is a career structure in each.

If you look at the different departments of a tour operator you can see the wide range of jobs needed, many in specialist areas.

FIGURE 9.2 *Career options in a major tour operator*

Theory into practice

Choose one of the types of jobs mentioned above. Find an advertisement for this type of job in the trade press or on a travel jobs website. Give a detailed description of the job including:

✳ responsibilities

✳ work pattern, for example, seasonal, permanent, full time, shifts

✳ pay and conditions

✳ qualifications required

✳ skills required

✳ personal attributes required

✳ entry levels, for example, school leaver/BTEC National/A-level/graduate

✳ progression

✳ research tip.

Try the websites of the 'big four' tour operators to find jobs.

✳ www.firstchoice4jobs.co.uk

✳ www.shgjobs.co.uk

✳ www.travelrecruit.co.uk

✳ www.mytravelcareers.co.uk

✳ The Federation of Tour Operators website offers lots of information about the different roles within tour operating. www.fto.co.uk

Tour operators offer lots of overseas jobs too. The job you are likely to be aware of is resort representative.

Many students state resort representative as their chosen career and this is not surprising as it gives an opportunity to meet new people of a similar age and to live in a resort. Bear in mind that some companies look for over 21s so check the age requirement. Many ski companies offer jobs to over 18s as chalet assistants. Some resort representatives are employed all year round but there are many more positions available in the summer high season. This means there are jobs for students in their holidays. If you do get a permanent job you should expect to move resorts between winter and summer season.

The work is often low paid but accommodation is included and it is possible to earn commission and tips. This is how Thomson describes the duties of a holiday representative.

'You will be involved in a variety of activities including:

* Holding What's on Welcomes – these will be held soon after your customers arrive in the resort. This will be your opportunity to promote the accommodation facilities, to tell them all about the great things to do in the resort and to promote the range of excursion activities on offer.

* As well as establishing good rapport with your customers, you will also need to have excellent working relationships with your hoteliers, hotel staff and other suppliers.

* Another occasion where you will be together with your customers is when you are guiding. This is where you accompany an excursion. It is, of course, important that you are visible and attentive to the needs of your customers so that the trip meets, if not exceeds, their expectations.

* You may also be involved in escorting your customers from the airport to their accommodation and vice versa.'

Source: www.thomson.co.uk

Theory into practice

Draw up a list of the skills, qualities and qualifications you think are needed to fulfill the requirements of a holiday representative position with Thomson.

There are other types of resort representatives. You might work as a children's rep, a ski chalet host, a rep on a campsite or a transfer rep, escorting customers to and from the airport. There is also a career structure within a resort with promotions to management likely for those who work hard. The following example describes a position at Cosmos as an Operations Assistant in a resort. Note how the possibility of career progression is emphasised.

As an Operations Assistant you will be involved in all aspects of running a busy resort office, including handling hotel reservations, producing transfer lists, handling incoming calls to the resort office and dealing pro-actively with all issues. You will be computer literate and ideally familiar with Word and Excel. You will also have a strong attention to detail and be prepared to work flexible hours. All applicants must have a UK national insurance number.

As with our Overseas Consultant positions, you will need to be aged 21 or over, confident with an outgoing personality, show commitment and most importantly have common sense. Employment is initially for the Summer Season in a resort within our range of Eastern and Western Mediterranean resorts. However, many of our Overseas Consultants go on to work Winter Seasons and continue to work with us for several years. We are a forward thinking company with a strong commitment to staff development - we are particularly proud that so many of our Area Managers began work with us as Overseas Consultants and have progressed through the company.

Because of the wide range of destinations we offer, a knowledge of a foreign language is preferable, in particular, Spanish, Portuguese, Italian or Greek. Please note, we are only able to offer positions to those holding a permanent UK national insurance number. Additionally, holding a full UK driving licence is a great advantage.

We expect you to have the following personal attributes:

- Commitment to customer care
- Strong communication skills
- Confident, friendly personality
- An abundance of stamina!
- Flexibility
- Ability to meet targets and deadlines
- Sales skills
- Initiative.

Source: www.cosmos-holidays.co.uk

Think it over...

Have you got what it takes to be a resort representative? Think about the personal attributes given in the Cosmos list. Do you have them? Do you have evidence of them? What kind of resort representative do you think you could be?

Airlines and airports

Airlines employ a variety of personnel such as air crew/flight crew and maintenance crew. Some airlines contract out the maintenance and engineering to specialist companies. Most airlines also contract out services like baggage handling and check-in – ground handling companies based in airports handle these services.

An example of a ground handling agency is Servisair/Globeground. They offer many support services to airlines and therefore a variety of jobs. These include:

* check-in – working at the check-in desk ensuring passengers are checked in according to the airline's procedures

* customer service – deals with any specific problems that occur, looks after VIP departures and arrivals

* baggage handling – very physical work, loading and unloading baggage onto and from aircraft

* security screening – checking passenger baggage on x-ray and randomly searching bags or people.

* special services – looking after passengers with special needs on behalf of the airline and guiding them through the airport.

Many airports in the UK are expanding and that means there are more jobs available at airports. If you live near an airport you can visit and investigate the jobs on offer. The type of job available varies a great deal. There are many unskilled and relatively poorly paid jobs such as baggage handlers and catering staff preparing the aircraft in flight catering and bar carts. However these jobs do not have to be a dead end – famously, the head of British Midland Airlines, Michael Bishop, started out as a baggage handler at an airport and worked his way up to chairman of BMI! There are also highly skilled jobs at airports such as air traffic control (based in air traffic control centres like Swanwick) and operations management. Some jobs require very few qualifications if any and others are only open to graduates. At Manchester Airport 19,000 people are employed across 250 companies so you can see that the type of work is very varied. Remember that public services like immigration, customs, police and fire services are all provided at airports and each of these has its own career structure.

Many students are interested in air cabin crew positions with airlines – although the job itself is not very exciting, the prospect of European travel is very attractive and many young people take the job to visit several different countries whilst being paid.

Kerry is an inflight beauty therapist for Virgin airlines. She is easily distinguished from other members of the crew as she has a pristine white uniform whilst the others wear red. She works in the upper class cabin only and offers a variety of treatments on board. These are free for the upper class customers and usually include a neck and shoulder or hand massage. Kerry's duties begin after take off when she distributes the vanity kits offered to passengers. She then introduces herself to each passenger in turn, explains the treatments and finds out if they wish to have one. When she is giving a treatment to a passenger she works in a small curtained off space. She takes breaks during the flight and is accommodated in hotels on stopovers along with the rest of the crew.

Air cabin crew may be promoted to supervisor and then to flight manager. Some may choose to go into training positions. An example of a flight supervisor's position is given in the case study taken from www.aviationjobsearch.com

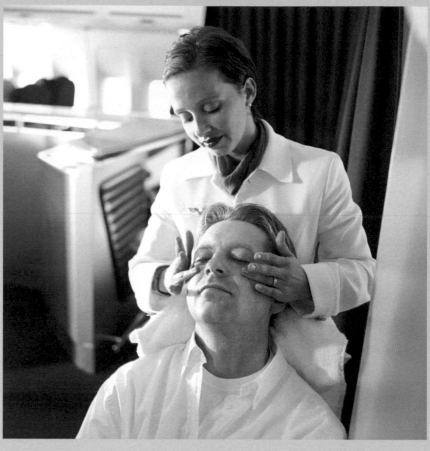

1. Visit www.virgin-atlantic.com Find the job profile of the inflight beauty therapist and find out what skills and qualities are required for the job.
2. Choose another job at Virgin which interests you and write notes on why it interests you and why you think you would be suited to that job.

Cruising

Not all jobs associated with the cruise industry are on board ship. There are many opportunities at corporate headquarters and at terminals. However, it is likely that if you are attracted to this sector then you are thinking about travelling the world as you work!

There are lots of different kinds of jobs on ships, some of which require specialist skills like engineering or catering. Others are open to those with general qualifications. Here are some examples of the types of jobs on board ship:

* Retail
* Entertainment
* Engineering
* Bars and restaurants
* Fitness
* Shore excursions
* Reception

FLIGHT SUPERVISOR – HEATHROW UK
Flight supervisor- bmi mainline FAST TRACK Programme

The role of the flight supervisor will put you at the heart of our business – managing and providing our on board product.

This challenging role provides the opportunity to work as the senior cabin attendant, in conjunction with the support of an experienced cabin services team, to deliver the bmi shorthaul product and in-flight service. The flight supervisor is also responsible for the welfare, discipline and motivation of cabin crew, whether operating onboard the aircraft or whilst nightstopping away from base.

This position requires an ability to demonstrate supervisory expertise, excellent organisational and problem solving skills, an adaptable approach to our operational and business environment and the ability to take ownership of all situations.

In addition to the cabin crew criteria you must be able to meet the following:

- Have at least 12 months continuous service as a senior cabin attendant or 24 months continuous service as cabin crew.

There should be a gap of no more than 18 months since last operational as cabin crew.

- Deliver excellent customer service and motivate others to achieve this.
- Be able to demonstrate strong leadership skills.

The fast track programme includes the following:

- Full initial training course
- Flying as crew for approx 3 months
- Flight supervisor promotion course
- Check flight

Further to our expansion plans to operate flights to Riyadh, Arabic speakers are encouraged to register their interest.

Please state which languages you can speak.

Source: www.flybmi.com

---

1. **Find out more about BMI – what type of company is it? How big is it? How many planes does it have? Where is it based?**
2. **Make some notes on the nature of employment as a flight supervisor at BMI. Include location, type of contract likely to be offered, working hours and benefits.**
3. **Summarise the entry requirements for a flight supervisor post.**

Extension task: Discuss the possible career progression for a flight supervisor, either within BMI or with another company.

Use the job advertisement to help you answer the questions and visit www.bmibaby.com or www.flybmi.com to do further research.

✱ Beauty and hairdressing
✱ Decks
✱ Housekeeping
✱ Tours
✱ Medical.
✱ Casino

What is it like working on a ship?
You will work long hours – it isn't a nine to five type of job. You might have to work seven days a week as well. You don't really get to be off duty because when you are not working you are still on the ship and you have to be pleasant to the passengers. You can't escape from the work

environment or your colleagues and that can be a cause of stress.

Accommodation may be pretty basic and you might have to share. However, the more senior your position the better your accommodation.

Your contract will be for a few months and you won't be paid in the off contract time. If you leave during the contract you will have to pay your fare home.

It will be your responsibility to make sure that passport, visas and vaccinations are up to date, although you will be told what is required.

So why do it? You will have the chance to see the world! There are opportunities to visit ports of call and the ship will revisit the same places regularly so you will get to know them quite well.

As you work so closely with colleagues, you will hopefully make friends that you will keep for many years. The staff will be multi-national and you can learn about different cultures and improve your language skills.

There is no journey to work, no commuting and even if you don't get paid much you will have food and accommodation provided. You will be able to save most of your earnings.

When a ship gets into a port most of the passengers go ashore so many of the crew are allowed time off to go ashore themselves. If you have a long term contract on a ship you will visit the same ports several times so you will have a chance to get to know them well. You will need to keep a base in the UK either with friends and family, or bought or rented, for the periods when you are not working.

If you want to apply for a cruise ship job:

* apply directly to individual cruise lines
* research the products and services offered by the line
* be specific about the jobs you are interested in
* describe your training, experience, talents, and skills.

Be careful when looking for a cruise ship job. There are many companies and websites who will try and sell you books on how to apply or CV services. It is best for you to apply directly to the cruise ship companies; this won't cost you anything.

Theory into practice

Do some research into the types of positions available on cruise ships at www.cruisejobfinder.com.

Hospitality

The hospitality sector includes hotels, bars and restaurants so it is very likely that some of you are already working in it as the sector provides many part time jobs.

In a hotel, you may start as a receptionist but can quickly move into reservations, managing housekeeping or managing events or business activities. For those people prepared to travel, the opportunities are even greater as many hotels are part of international chains.

Much of hospitality work is part time, 42% in hotels and 50% in restaurants. This compares with only 25% part time work across all industries. This might be a good thing in terms of flexibility for employees but the work is also low paid and often seasonal, in spite of strong criticism from trade unions. Employers are allowed to top up wages with tips. The employers argue that food and accommodation are often provided for workers and that this should be taken into account when setting wages. These factors can cause recruitment difficulties and jobs are often taken by those who find difficulty finding work in other sectors, such as refugees and people with few basic skills or those for whom English is a second language. Having workers who have problems communicating in English or lack other basic skills impacts on customer service and hotels and restaurants often have to keep people lacking such skills away from customer facing activities, for example in kitchen work. Even there a lack of English may cause other problems as instructions on catering and kitchen products can't easily be read. A market assessment carried out by People 1st the sector skills council for hospitality and tourism, found that there was generally a lack of training in management skills, in information technology, in basic skills, customer service skills and specifically in areas like food handling.

From this we can conclude that more training is needed across the sector. The kind of training most often undertaken is that which enables organisations to meet their legislative requirements such as food safety training, health and safety and first aid training.

The best quality training is usually available in the large companies, such as hotel groups where investment has been made in training and in policies to retain staff, so if you hope to work in the hotel business you should look at what the major hotel groups can offer you.

People 1st

People 1st is the Sector Skills Council (SSC) for Hospitality, Leisure, Travel and Tourism. It aims to represent the industry on skills matters, to optimise skills funding for the industry and to identify and endorse suitable training provision.

It is easy to research careers in hotels on the Internet as most large companies advertise their vacancies on their corporate websites.

On pages 92 and 93 are two examples. One involves working for Iberostar hotels as an entertainer. There are different types of entertainment team jobs on offer. Many of them require few, if any qualifications but may be seasonal in nature. If you want to work abroad, possibly for a gap year then these are interesting jobs to apply for. If you are looking for a career you can join a trainee scheme after A-levels or after a degree. The example from Accor hotels illustrates a product manager position ideal for someone with a tourism marketing degree.

Conferences and events

This is an exciting and growing sector of travel and tourism. There are many jobs in this sector and even many degree courses specialising in conference and event management. Jobs may be in the public or private sector. The main function is to plan, develop and promote special events. You need excellent communication skills to do this job as you will have to liaise with lots of different people including clients and suppliers. You need to be very motivated, be creative and have lots of initiative because there is little routine with this kind of work. You will have to be a multi-tasker, that is, able to manage lots of tasks at once. Conference and events management jobs can be found in hotels, visitor attractions, tourist offices and in specialist companies.

Theory into practice

Visit some hotel group websites and find information about jobs. Look only for trainee schemes either at A-level or graduate entry. Consider what it would mean for you to join one of these schemes.

* Where would you be located?

* What would you learn?

* What are the rates of pay?

* What other benefits are there?

* What would you need to do to be accepted onto the scheme?

* What career progression could you expect?

Compare at least two schemes and present your conclusions to your group.

When will you join us?

IBEROSTAR
HOTELS & RESORTS

| HOME | ABOUT US | JOBS | APPLICATION | F.A.Q. | WATCH US |

FUN

CASTING 2006

APPLICATION

CONTACT US

LINKS

Sports entertainment

As a sports entertainer you preferably have already got some experience as a sports monitor, aerobic teacher, tennis teacher, fitness monitor or similar. If not, that is no problem as long as you have a wide interest in sports and recreation games. Are you an active volleyball player, tennis player, swimmer, hockey player, etc? Perfect, the rest will be taught at the training course. You will get to know the rules of the different sports activities, you will be taught how to handle an air rifle, bow and arrow and how to organise and Olympic day or other tournament.

Once you start working with the guests at your hotel, remember that in the first place you are an entertainer and not an organiser. The aspect "sports" in the hotel means first of all fun for your guests. If you have a good relationship with your guests, you will easily find people to join in your activities.

Webdesign by OKP

Example of jobs in tourism (taken from the Internet)

Customer manager

Sales / Sales Administration

▷ Missions   ▷ Responsibilities   ▷ Profile   ▷ Skills
▷ Abilities   ▷ Where is this profession practised?   ▷ Links

Hotel industry
training
Conference and
banquet manager
Customer manager
Travel consultant
Table manager
On-board attendant
Barman

⊞ **Universities degrees**

⊞ **Other training**

**Internships –
Apprenticeships**

Testimonies

▶ Check our job
vacancies

Book on-line

Missions

The customer manager is the point of contact between the customer and the sales force, and is therefore responsible for transforming prospective corporate customers into actual customers. In the role of technical advisor, he or she supports the sales force in its customer development and loyalty objectives.

Responsibilities

- To ensure that the customer commitment is respected
- To deliver high quality service

Profile

- A-Levels/2 years' further education to BTS (vocational training certificate) standard or similar in sales
- Previous experience (business to business) in after sales service / customer service would be an advantage.

Skills

- Good IT skills
- Good language and writing skills
- Good relational skills: the ability to listen and be diplomatic
- Sales ability and a good telephone technique
- Sensitivity to customer needs
- Team working

Abilities

- Thoroughness: in administrative supervision
- Dynamism: he or she is an ambassador for the brand.
- Reactivity: caring about the quality of the services sold
- Self-sufficiency: managing his or her own portfolio

Where is this profession practised?

Accor Services

Links

From where...
- Hotels, Tour Operator: reservation agent
- Accor Services: office-based sales representative, call centre agent or sales asistant

...To where?
- Hotels: internal sales executive
- Accor Services: customer supervisor
- Operations or logistics management

Source: www.accor.com

Example of jobs in tourism (taken from the Internet)

Rashid works in hotel near Edinburgh. His job title is Conference and Banqueting Assistant and he reports to the Events Services Manager. This is Rashid's first job after completing his Event Management degree. He is enjoying it immensely but also finds it very tiring. He spent his first couple of weeks receiving training but of course he is learning more all the time. He has to know the hotel facilities and rates inside out. It took some time to develop this knowledge. It is his job to set up conference rooms, including the necessary audio and visual equipment. He has to meet the group leader when they arrive. He introduces himself and checks that the facilities are satisfactory to the client. He checks any breakout rooms, coffee and lunch times and arrangements and then he ensures that the group leader knows how to contact him at any time during the conference. This aspect of customer service is very important. Rashid also likes to see the group leader at the end of the conference to get some informal feedback on how things have gone. After this he asks the group leader to complete a feedback form which is passed to the Event Services Manager.

Draw up a job description and person specification for the role of Conference and Banqueting Assistant.

Use the examples on pages 81 and 82 to help you with the format.

If you are sure this area of work is for you then consider studying for a degree in Events Management. An example is given on page 95.

Visitor attractions

As in every other sector, visitor attractions require staff to provide all the usual business functions such as marketing, human resources and accountancy. Other jobs available vary according to the type of attraction. For example, at theme parks, engineers design and build the rides. At stately homes, guides are needed with a detailed knowledge of the history of the house and grounds. You will also find restorers working on ancient tapestries and paintings. Historic properties require managers and this is a likely career for you if you are interested in heritage or conservation and think you can mange a team of people. Visitor attractions have positions available at different entry levels. Here is an example of a basic position at Alton Towers.

Think it over...

Note that applicants for this job must live locally to Alton Towers or find their own accommodation. The position is seasonal as Alton Towers closes in the winter. No qualifications are required. What kind of people would find this job appealing?

RIDE HOST

Job role

You will help to operate the Park Rides and Attractions, helping guests onto and off the rides and attractions safely, checking that all safety and height restrictions are met. You will help our guests to enjoy a fun and friendly atmosphere whilst maintaining strict safety guidelines. Cleaning duties are also involved. Applicants should be available 5 days out of 7 until 30th October, excluding agreed leave/holidays.

Benefits

We can offer an excellent development opportunity as well as a comprehensive package of benefits including full training, subsidised transport, company pension scheme, various discounts including our spa, as well as free tickets for Tussauds attractions worth up to £1000. Please note that we are currently not able to help applicants from outside the local area find accommodation. Alton Towers is situated in Staffordshire, between Stoke-on-Trent and Derby.

Source: Hotonline

HND/BA (HONS) EVENTS MANAGEMENT

Julie Noble completed her placement year with events agency, Euro RSCG Skybridge.

"I was an Account Executive based at their London offices and my job was a mixture of the ordinary and the exotic. In the office I did the admin, researched venues, contacted suppliers and sent out invoices. I also travelled a lot and delivered events in Rio de Janeiro, Malta, Lisbon and Dusseldorf. I gained a lot of valuable experience and I sometimes forgot that I was still a student."

Talk to anyone involved in the industry and they will tell you that nothing compares to the buzz of delivering a successful event. The feeling comes from a combination of seeing your ideas work in practice, watching your client and their guests enjoy the occasion and appreciating the first class service your team has delivered.

Through this course you have the opportunity to acquire the essential knowledge and skills needed to be an effective events professional. Elective modules and assignments provide the scope to specialise in those areas of the industry that interest you most and your fellow classmates will not only be your friends but will also become an invaluable 'little black book' of key contacts in the events industry.

Level 1 compulsory core modules	Level 1 elective modules – choose one
The Events Industry	Themed Events
Events Marketing Activities	Sports Events
Event Planning Process	Conference and Meetings Planning
Event Support Services	Web Design and Development
Applied Technology and Finance	Language (usually French, German or Spanish)
Understanding Service Organisations	Work Based Learning (available to non-placement students only)
Personal and Vocational Skills Development	

Work placement

Students who do not have extensive experience in the events industry are advised to go on a 48 week work placement after completing level 1. Most placement opportunities are salaried and you can choose to work in the UK, Europe or overseas.

Source: Leeds Metropolitan University

There are many opportunities for further education in travel and tourism.

Visitor attractions often try to diversify their business and extend the season by entering the conference and events market and this means a range of interesting jobs are available. Alton Towers employ sales executives whose role is to sell the conference and events facilities at Alton Towers hotels and in the park. They follow up initial enquiries, show customers round the facilities and prepare quotes for the customer's event. They have sales targets to meet and must have an excellent knowledge of the facilities on offer as well as the ability to sell.

People applying for this kind of job would be expected to have A-levels or equivalent and some experience of conferences and events. IT skills are also important for this role. The benefits would be the same as the ride host although the pay would be better.

Public Sector

Most local government offices now have a tourism department to promote tourism in their area. In addition there are posts with tourist boards and tourist information centres.

Here is an example of a typical structure and the job roles likely to be in place in a medium sized town.

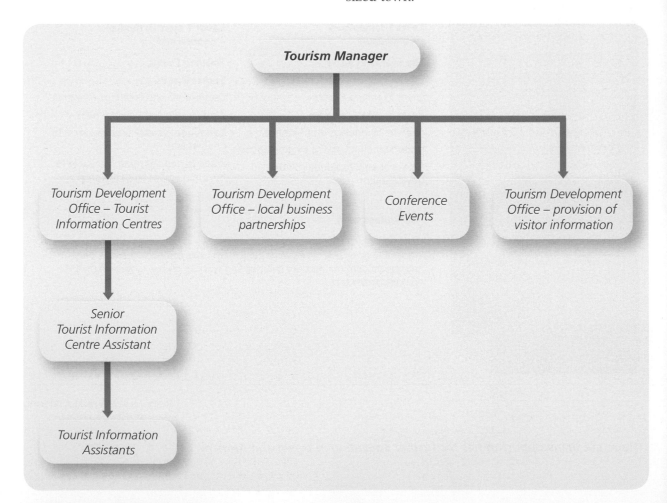

FIGURE 9.3 *An organisation chart for a tourism department*

Tourism Development Officers are often graduates so you would need to study for a degree before applying. Tourism Management would be a good choice.

Here is an example from West Oxfordshire District Council.

Tourism Development Officer

£17,922 – £21,654 pa plus Essential car user allowance

This is an opportunity for an ambitious graduate to join our Tourism Development Team, working to establish the area as a key UK tourism destination.

The role will make the most of the experience you have already gained undertaking research and project work, preferably in a tourism-related organisation. However if you are really going to succeed you will also need a good understanding of rural tourism issues such as countryside access and the implications of AONB designation.

As you will be working to promote the area, it is also essential that you have the communication skills needed to liaise with the general public, the media and a broad range of external organisations and partners. Moreover it is important that you are confident with IT and familiar with Microsoft Word/Access/Excel. A basic grasp of website publishing would be a definite advantage too.

Benefits include a minimum 24 days' holiday; flexi-time; generous contributory final salary pension scheme; discounted membership of the Council's leisure facilities and private medical insurance (dependent on grade).

Source: West Oxfordshire District Counci

Think it over...

What do you think are the advantages and disadvantages of working in the public sector rather than in another area of tourism?

Look in your local newspapers' job section or on the websites of tourist boards for examples of jobs in this sector.

Assessment guidance

This assessment provides evidence for Unit 9.1. It covers assessment objectives:

1. Demonstration of knowledge, understanding and skills.

3. Research and analysis.

To succeed in this assessment you must produce an analysis of the range of employment opportunities and the skills and qualities required for a successful career in the travel and tourism industry.

On completion of this assignment, you will be awarded a number of marks. These will contribute towards the marks for this unit. The quality of your work will determine the marks awarded. Your work will be assessed against the following criteria:

1–8 marks
Some research has been undertaken and is evidenced mainly through a bibliography. Sources used are those directed by others. There is some basic analysis of the nature and range of employment opportunities and the skills and qualities required for a successful career in the industry. The analysis is mainly descriptive.

9–14 marks
Research has been undertaken using different sources, some of which were obtained independently. Some evidence of research is referenced throughout the text, as well as in a bibliography. There is an analysis of the nature and range of employment opportunities and the skills and qualities required for a successful career in the industry. A range of employment opportunities has been included in the analysis, which is mainly clear.

15–18 marks
Research has been undertaken using a range of different sources that have been obtained independently. Much of the evidence of research is referenced throughout the text, as well as in the bibliography.

There is clear analysis of the nature and range of employment opportunities and the skills and qualities required for a successful career in the industry. A wide range of employment opportunities has been included in the analysis.

Jobs for the Boys (and Girls)

The careers department at a sixth form college is producing a series of informative brochures about vocational careers. They are currently working on health and social care, sport and recreation and travel and tourism.

The brochures are directed at students who have little experience of these industries and who are studying in more general areas. The brochures are intended to give up to date, factual and interesting information about employment opportunities in these industries.

One careers officer had the good idea of involving the travel and tourism students in the production of the travel and tourism brochure. Their tutor agreed that this would be a very useful project for all concerned.

Each travel and tourism student will individually produce a brochure. The one which is the most informative will be reproduced for distribution to other students. You are to:

✱ decide on the format of your brochure

✱ decide on a title for your brochure

✱ draw up a plan for researching employment opportunities in travel and tourism

✱ discuss your plan with your tutor

✱ carry out research into the range of employment opportunities in travel and tourism, ensuring you give examples across different sectors and at different levels

✱ discuss, in general terms, the skills and qualities required for a successful career in travel and tourism.

Choose a range of job roles in travel and tourism. They should be jobs which are of interest to you personally. Some should be jobs that you could take up immediately after your current course. Some should be jobs that you could progress to with experience or further qualifications.

Describe these jobs and make a detailed analysis of the skills and qualities required to make a success of them and to gain career progression.

9.2 Teamwork

You will have noticed in your research for employment opportunities that one of the most important skills required in travel and tourism is the ability to work well in a team. In fact teamwork skills are essential in most workplaces. You must be able to work with other people in a team even if you don't like them. Personal differences should be set aside. In travel and tourism teams may not always be physically located in one place. Even when you are not physically with the other members of your team, you can work together by contributing to a sequence of activities with a common aim. People who work as resort representatives abroad work closely with colleagues in the tour operator's head office in the UK.

In this part of the unit we will examine the different types of teams and what makes a team effective. You will find out about some theories relating to team work and learn about the role of the individual in the team.

Key terms

A team is a group of people who are working together to achieve common objectives.

Types of teams

Formal teams

Formal teams relate to the structure of an organisation and are planned in order to meet that organisation's objectives. The team will follow rules and regulations in its procedures and may meet to a pre-arranged schedule and complete administrative procedures. Examples in travel and tourism include sales teams and marketing teams. Characteristics of formal teams are:

* planning to meet the objectives of an organisation

* meeting regularly

* keeping records such as agendas and minutes

* including individuals chosen as they are able to contribute to the team's objective.

Informal Teams

Informal teams work within or outside formal teams. They are based on personal relationships between members rather than on work roles. They provide for members' emotional, social and psychological needs. Sometimes informal teams can work counter to a company's objectives as people may group together to share worries and concerns about their work. Characteristics of informal teams are:

* groups of people joining together from personal choice

* an ability to give a sense of belonging and develop self esteem

* lack of a formal, appointed leader – in fact leader may change according to the current needs of the group

* the group sets 'norms' of behaviour by which the group abide – may be unspoken and unconscious

* they often fill a gap not covered by formal teams in an organisation.

When you complete group work for assignments, you often choose with whom you wish to work. You choose to work with people whom you like and whom you know will be as committed as you are to the work. This is an informal team.

Short term and long term teams

Teams may be put together for a particular project and once the objectives of the project have been achieved and the project is completed the team can be disbanded. An example is the team working to put together the Olympic bid for London which was successful in 2005.

Ad hoc teams are put together for a specific purpose and are also short term teams. For example if a disaster occurs in a resort and a tour operator has to send a response team, they will put their contingency plan into play and put together an ad hoc team to deal with the problem. Ad hoc teams tend to be made up of people who are immediately available rather than ideal for the job to be done.

> *** REMEMBER!**
> Make sure you can define these different types of teams:
> * Formal
> * Informal
> * Short term
> * Long term
> * Ad hoc.

London completes its top team

Oct 29: London 2012 has made three more senior appointments, completing the management team bidding to bring the Olympics to Britain.

Debbie Jevans, a former junior Wimbledon champion and General Secretary of the International Tennis Federation (ITF), is to be Director of Sport.

Charles Wijeratna is to be Commercial Director and Neil Wood has been seconded from accountancy firm Deloitte to be Financial Director.

London 2012 Chairman Barbara Cassani said: 'The appointment of Debbie, Neil and Charles completes our management line-up. We have a highly talented, knowledgeable and dedicated team to lead our bid.

'Now that our senior management is fully in place, we can turn all our attention to our first submission to the International Olympic Committee in January.'

As Director of Sport, Debbie Jevans will be responsible for ensuring London's proposed venues meet all technical requirements and also for liaising with sports governing bodies.

In her role with the ITF, she has been responsible for tennis at the Olympics and will act as an adviser for next year's tournament in Athens.

She said: 'In the UK we have a strong sporting heritage. We have the skills and ability to host a fantastic Olympic Games.'

Neil Wood, a partner at Deloitte, added: 'I'm delighted to be joining London 2012. We've already made excellent progress and I look forward to being part of the team that brings the Olympic Games to London.'

And Charles Wijeratna, who was part of the initial team which set up London 2012, said: 'This is a once-in-a-lifetime project and I'm thrilled to be part of it.'

Source: 29th October 2003 www.london2012.org

The press release describes the completion of the Olympics bid team.

1. Is this team formal/informal?
2. Is it short term/long term?
3. What are the team objectives?
4. Why do you think these three people were invited to join the team?

5. Who was chairman of the team by the time of the bid? Why did this change in team members occur? What are the implications for the working of the team?

Extension task: Find out what has happened to the team now. Visit www.london2012.org for more information.

Think it over...

Can you think of examples in travel and tourism of these different kinds of teams? Discuss your examples with your colleagues.

The role of the individual in a team

Not everyone in a team is the same. Each person has their own strengths and weaknesses. If each person had the same weaknesses the team would not work. There needs to be a balance. A method of recognising the individual's strengths and weaknesses is needed. Here we will consider two approaches. Belbin roles and MTR-I team dynamics.

Belbin's roles

Dr. Belbin's nine team roles are:

1. Chairperson/co-ordinator – the group leader, likely to be relaxed and extrovert, also likely to be a good communicator. Will use the

Belbin's roles acquire a different level of importance according to the objectives of the team and the stage in the team's life.

strengths of team members and give them encouragement.

2. Plant – the ideas person in the team, a person who is creative in looking for solutions to problems, but not always good at details, and so may make careless mistakes.

3. Shaper – the task leader who unites ideas and effort. Needs to be dominant and extrovert in order to make things happen.

4. Monitor/evaluator – the team analyst, who is not so good at ideas but pays attention to detail, thus keeping the team directed towards its target.

5. Implementer – the organiser of the team, who is able to take the ideas of the plant and shaper and turn them into manageable and realistic tasks. A practical, stable and disciplined person.

6. Resource investigator – the person who always has a solution to problems, who is sociable and enthusiastic and good under pressure.

7. Team worker – a very people-oriented person, sensitive to others' needs. This person has good communication skills and will be good at motivating others. A natural mediator, who will deal with conflict within the team. Very good to have around in a crisis.

8. Finisher – a person who sticks to deadlines and likes to get on with things. Will probably be irritated by the more casual members of the team.

9. Specialist – this person is single minded and self starting, providing knowledge and skills in rare supply.

MTR-I model

Another team roles model is the MTR-I model. It describes individuals in a team in the following terms:

* **Coaches** produce agreement and *harmony* across the team, trying to create a positive team atmosphere and reach a consensus.

* **Campaigners** produce a sense of priority, stressing those issues that have most *importance* so that discussions are focused on the most valuable topics

* **Explorers** uncover new potential in situations and people and *explore* new areas and the possibilities that they present

* **Innovators** produce a sense of *imagination* and contribute new and alternative perspectives and ideas

* **Sculptors** bring things to *fruition*, producing action to address the most urgent matters, and using tools or techniques that they know (from experience) will work

Thomson Graduate Development scheme

New Media

The New Media department is the newest element with the Planning and Trading Division.

New Media is all about managing the TUI UK websites to maximize sales and contribution. The department is responsible for many websites, but principally Thomson.co.uk, Portland-direct.co.uk, Thomsonflights.com and ThomsonFly.co.uk. Our objective is to sell as many package holidays and flights as possible whilst developing the company's capabilities in the new but rapidly growing sectors of accommodation only sales and dynamic packaging.

The department is spilt into three equal sections:

1. Sales and Operations

The Sales and Ops section is responsible for both forecasting and reporting sales to highlight both new opportunities to exploit and expose issues with our sites that require resolution.

The Sales and Ops team interfaces with Planning and Trading to ensure we are promoting the best offers on the site to both clear distressed company stock but also maximise sales through the web channel. They also work with P&T to ensure we have the right level of online discount at any given time.

Finally this section is responsible for ensuring we have the right accurate, up to date content on the websites to persuade visitors to buy.

2. Development

The new development section manages all functional improvements to our existing site and all new web projects from business case through to delivery.

Development liaises with the rest of the business to understand opportunities to grow our web sales. Then it works with both external design agencies and with our IT Department to turn New Media requirements into functional specifications. Thereafter it manages the development process through to ensure the end result delivers against original objectives.

On a day to day basis Development fixes faults with our existing sites and proposes any implement improvements which will improve site usability.

3. Online marketing

The marketing team is responsible for online customer contact via email and online CRM. It works with external agencies and our central marketing team to formulate campaigns.

New Media Marketing is also responsible for multi-million pound on-line budgets which they use to drive traffic into our sites from search engines, banners and affiliated partnerships.

Source: TUI UK www.tui-graduates.co.uk

Summarise the objectives of each of these teams. Imagine you have graduated from university and you are applying to the graduate development scheme at Tui. Decide which of the new media teams you would like to join. Write an account of what you think the characteristics of a good team member in that team would be.

Extension task: Explain why you as an individual would be a good team member and how you would work in the New Media team.

* **Curators** produce a *clarification* of ideas and information, producing a better knowledge and clearer picture of any situation

* **Conductors** produce structure and introduce a logical *organisation* into the way things are done

* **Scientists** produce *explanation* of what is happening and the cause of problems, and generate models to demonstrate how things work.

Source: teamtechnology.co.uk

Theory into practice

Which of these roles do you fulfill in a team? Discuss your thoughts with your colleagues and see if they agree. Remember that you might fulfill more than one role.

Visit the website www.teamtechnology.com to find out more about MTR-I team dynamics and find out the positive and negative aspects of performance.

What are the benefits of being in a team?

* A sense of achievement in working together for the same goals.

* The team provides a sense of belonging and a sense of status.

* The team provides you with a support network.

* How can you be a good team member?

  * Respect and listen to other team members.

  * Admit your own shortfalls.

  * Share decision making.

  * Be tolerant of different views and personalities.

  * Be open to new ideas.

  * Help to resolve conflict.

  * Commit to the goals of the team.

The team role models that we have looked at demonstrate that there are many valuable roles in a team. Not everyone can be a leader and nor is it desirable – nothing would be achieved! There are other ways of contributing to the team.

Conflict in teams

Conflict occurs in a team when there is disagreement among team members which affects their interaction. The disagreement may be about leadership, team roles, the aims of the team or the means of achieving those aims. A high performing team will air disagreements and make an effort to resolve conflict. Conflict is usually viewed as a problem. However conflict can sometimes be positive. It can lead to a new approach to problems and more creative ideas. There are some common sources of conflict in teams.

Personality conflict

This affects the relationships among team members and distracts them from their objectives. It may manifest itself as hostility to one or more team members and the breaking of the team into cliques. Some team members may be reluctant to contribute through shyness. Others may be dominant and overbearing. This type of conflict can be resolved by allowing individuals to air their grievances openly and engage in free discussion. Quieter participants should be encouraged to express their opinion.

Task conflict

Team members disagree on how to achieve their objectives, for example on how to increase sales. It may promote a healthy competition amongst team members as they strive to prove their idea is most workable or it may unsettle the team and make them insecure. In a situation where individuals are able to get on with their own tasks within the team the effect will not be so marked. The management can help by setting clear policies and guidelines for the team. However, too much bureaucracy can be counter productive.

Disney teams to integrate next month

Integration of the UK teams of Disney's French and US theme parks is to start next month under the helm of former Disneyland Resort Paris managing director for UK, Ireland and Nordic regions Jo Rzymowska.

Rzymowska will oversee the first phase of the integration of the UK sales and marketing and back-office teams that work for Disneyland Resort Paris and Walt Disney Parks and Resorts.

Both UK teams already operate out of the same offices in Hammersmith, London, but will be merged to work as one to sell and market Disneyland Resort Paris, Walt Disney World Florida, Disneyland California and Disney Cruise Line.

Rzymowska could not rule out job cuts but said the aim of the merger had never been a head-count reduction.

'This is to offer a better service to our guests and travel partners. We are in the process of going through the merger but the aim has never been to reduce staff,' said Rzymowska.

She said the merger was planned because the UK is the number-one foreign market for the US and French theme parks.

Also research shows the brands are complementary with Disney theme parks seen as both main holiday and short-break destinations.

'Having analysed the market and looked at what customers and travel partners want, it makes sense to push the teams together. The resorts are complementary,' said Rzymowska.

Source: *Travel Weekly* 21st June 2002

1. **Identify the potential sources of conflict within the merging teams.**
2. **Suggest measures for resolving the conflict.**

Extension task: Find examples of good practice elsewhere in merging teams and make recommendations to Disney.

Developing an effective team

Understand the stages of team development

Understanding the theory of team structure and development will help you to understand the effectiveness of teams. Tuckman (1965) identified four main stages of team development.

1. Forming – at this stage, team members form their first impressions of each other and establish identities. They are sounding each other out and finding out what is expected of them.
2. Storming – the team has, by now, become more used to each other. Team members are prepared to put forward their ideas forcibly and openly. They are also prepared to disagree and so there may be some conflict and hostility.
3. Norming – the team now begins to establish co-operation. Conflict is controlled. Views are exchanged and new standards introduced.
4. Performing – the team is now working together, they begin to arrive at solutions and achieve their objectives.

There can also be a fifth stage 'mourning' where the team has disbanded and the members miss being part of the team.

Tips for effective teams

✱ Make sure teams are not too large – they must be small enough to come to decisions to be effective.

* Enlist team members who have a diversity of skills and personalities so that they complement each other.

* Make sure the team has a specific purpose and is not floundering.

* Hold team building events and activities.

* Get the team to produce its own mission statement and objectives as soon as it is formed.

Team building events are usually arranged as staff development exercises to bond teams and get them to work more effectively. When we think about these, outward bound, physically demanding courses come to mind. These are fun but not suitable for everyone. Other types of team building activities are available and there are companies which specialise in running them.

Theory into practice

You could organise a team building event for your group. You can find out about activities in your local area. What about devising your own team building course and running it for another group of students?

Characteristics of effective teams

* Good teams achieve synergy, that is, together you can achieve more than you can individually. You generate more ideas, energy and resources as a group than you do individually.

* A good team has a sense of shared responsibility – no-one wants to let down other team members.

* The team holds responsibility for planning and managing its activities.

* Team members have mutual respect and support each other.

* There is effective communication – ideas can be freely expressed in an open environment.

* Everyone listens to each other.

* People are willing to take risks.

* Well motivated team members.

Motivation

The motivation and commitment of employees is key to the success of a team and therefore to the company.

Think it over...

What factors motivate you to go to your job or your course? Think about one of your friends or family who has a good job. What motivates them? Is their motivation different to yours?

There are many ways of motivating staff. Here are some examples:

* **Shares** – some companies allow employees to hold shares. If the company is doing well they will be paid a dividend thus the employees have an interest in a successful company. British Airways operates such a scheme.

* **Performance related pay** – the better you perform or the more sales you make the more money you get.

* **Flexible working** – if employees get the hours they want they are better motivated.

* **Competitions** – staff are invited to enter competitions based on high sales or customer satisfaction.

Appraisal

A good appraisal scheme can be a motivating factor for employees if they feel involved in the process and are given constructive feedback.

Evaluation of team performance

It can be difficult to evaluate team performance. Management want to know whether a team has met its objectives but it is also important to measure the contribution of individuals in a team.

Here are some ways of measuring team performance. You should be able to use these yourself when you do your assessment:

* Match the team's results to its original objectives –

  • Which objectives have been achieved?

  • Have the objectives been achieved in the planned time frame?

* Carry out a SWOT on the team's performance.

* Keep ongoing records measuring a team's performance.

* Hold regular appraisals of individuals in the team.

* Assess the performance of the team leader.

* Ensure each individual is aware of performance standards.

✴ REMEMBER!

SWOT analysis means strengths, weaknesses, opportunities and threats.

Assessment guidance

This assessment provides evidence for Unit 9.2. It covers assessment objectives:

1. Demonstration of knowledge, understanding and skills.

2. Application of knowledge, understanding and skills.

   To succeed in this assessment you must participate in a team, working towards completion of a significant travel and tourism task.

   On completion of this assignment, you will be awarded a number of marks. These will contribute towards the marks for this unit. The quality of your work will determine the marks awarded. Your work will be assessed against the following criteria:

1–9 marks
A role will be taken within a team. The role may not be significant but has been agreed by other team members. Participation in the team has been effective although contribution may not be significant to completing the task. The contribution of others within the team is recognised.

10–17 marks
A significant role has been taken within a team. Participation in the team has been effective with a valid contribution made to completing the task. The contribution of others within the team is recognised and conflicts that arise are dealt with effectively. Evidence of involvement is drawn from a range of sources.

18–21 marks
A significant role has been taken within a team. Participation in the team has been consistently effective, with a significant contribution made to the completion of the task. Potential difficulties in meeting objectives are identified and alternative approaches suggested and adopted. The contribution of others within the team is clearly acknowledged and support provided to others as required. Potential conflicts are identified and solutions proposed and implemented. Evidence of involvement is drawn from a wide range of sources.

Travel and Tourism Careers Day

You and your colleagues have gathered a lot of information about employment opportunites in travel and tourism. You will remember that this information was intended to be distributed to other students in brochures.

Now, you have decided to hold a careers day in your school or college to give other students an even better opportunity to find out about employment in travel and tourism.

1. Start by discussing in your group where you will hold the careers day and what features it will have. You might consider:

   * displaying all the information you have already gathered

   * leaflets and application forms from employers

   * computer screens displaying travel and tourism job websites

   * talks from local travel and tourism employers.

   Make a note of your aims and objectives.

2. Decide on the roles of individuals in the team. Make sure everyone is in agreement about the assigned roles. Note who is responsible for what. Possible roles include:

   * marketing the exhibition

   * recruiting employers

   * finance

   * venue management

   * display planning

   * administration.

3. Keep a log recording the team's organisation of the event. The log should include:

   * regular recording of the team's achievement

   * regular recording of your own contribution

   * conflict occurring

   * how conflicts have been resolved

   * other problems

   * how problems have been resolved.

   An example of a log is given below.

LOG FOR TRAVEL AND TOURISM CAREERS DAY

DATE	GROUP TASK	INDIVIDUAL CONTRIBUTION	CONFLICT/ PROBLEMS	HOW RESOLVED	COMMENTS
1/12	Decide on list of employers to be invited to contribute to the exhibition	Contact college work experience co-ordinator for access to database – get list of work placement employers			
2/12	Send out letter to employers	Write draft letter	John has also drafted a letter	Discussed our two letters together and came up with a final draft	I wish I had asked if anyone else was doing a draft but it was the first item I had worked on with John and we worked well together. Will work on the letter again tomorrow

LOG FOR TRAVEL AND TOURISM CAREERS DAY					
DATE	GROUP TASK	INDIVIDUAL CONTRIBUTION	CONFLICT/ PROBLEMS	HOW RESOLVED	COMMENTS
3/12		Finished the letter – got it checked by the tutor	John didn't show up to class	Suggested that the group leader gets everyone's mobile numbers so we can check on absentees	Really annoyed!

4. Produce evidence of your involvement in the careers day.

Your log is one source of evidence but in order to gain more marks you need to show evidence from a range of sources. Make sure you collect some or all of the following:

✳ Witness statement from your tutor

✳ Appraisal from another member of the team

✳ Witness statement from an employer who was at the event.

✳ Group SWOT analysis of the event

✳ Feedback from visitors to the event

✳ Self evaluation.

9.3 Personal skills and career development

In this section of the unit you will learn how to evaluate your own potential and assess potential career opportunities in travel and tourism. You will discover how to carry out a personal skills audit and evaluate your own personal skills, attitudes, qualities, knowledge and experience. You will learn to develop a personal career plan based on your personal skills audit.

Skills for employment

Personal skills and attributes

These are the types of personal skills and attributes you will need to develop to gain successful employment in the travel and tourism industry.

✳ **Social/personal** – when you go to work you need to leave your personal problems at home and develop a professional attitude showing respect and consideration for customers and colleagues alike.

✳ **Analytical/critical/problem solving** – these are skills that you will have developed during your A-level programme – at work you will have to use your initiative to deal with any problems or incidents that occur. Learn to bear in mind your limitations and pass issues on to relevant personnel if appropriate.

✳ **Prioritising tasks** – again you have practised these skills in your current programme. At work you will be given various tasks to do, sometimes from different members of staff – learn how to decide which tasks are more important or urgent and do those first. If in doubt, ask.

✳ **Time keeping** – Punctuality shows your commitment to your work – you will be expected to return punctually from breaks as well as arriving on time for the start of work. It is unacceptable to be late for work. Plan to arrive at least ten minutes before your start time.

* **Self motivation** – this is about showing initiative and asking for things to do if you have no work, rather than waiting to be told.

* **Action planning/research techniques** – you are developing your planning and research skills on this programme – this will stand you in good stead when it comes to finding a job or moving on to another course.

Attitudes

* **Response to authority** – you will have to accept that someone – a line manager – is going to tell you what to do. If he or she is a good manager they will show you respect.

* **Honesty and reliability** – lapses in honesty will result in immediately losing a job. Good employees are reliable and keep to deadlines.

* **Respect for others** – treat everyone in the workplace with respect and friendliness no matter what their position.

* **Discrimination** – you will be aware of the laws regarding discrimination but you need to also examine your own moral code and make sure that you do not act in a discriminatory manner for any reason, be it gender, race, sexual orientation or disability. If you see discrimination be prepared to challenge it in a mature, adult manner.

* **Confidentiality** – in most jobs you will have access to customer details and other confidential information such as sales figures. You must be aware of the Data Protection Act and also conform to your company's confidentiality policy.

* **Knowledge and Experience**

  * **Travel and tourism** – you have a great advantage when applying for a job as your course has given you an extensive knowledge of the travel and tourism industry.

  * **Customer care** – experience of dealing with members of the public, suppliers and colleagues and the customer care skills you develop will be of use in travel and tourism – you may be developing these skills already through a part time job.

  * **Technical/practical** – some types of employment in travel and tourism entail the use of specialist equipment and resources, for example, reservation systems. We noted earlier in this unit that the industry lacks people with advanced IT skills so think about how you can gain these now.

Business skills

Business skills will be essential in the travel and tourism industry. These include:

* writing a business letter

* writing a memo

* using a fax machine

* communicating by email

* telephone skills

* making a presentation.

Writing a business letter

A business letter is a formal letter. It is often on headed paper, and it is always word processed. The most common format of a business letter is fully blocked format. This means that everything is aligned to the left. You should:

* include the name of the recipient if you can, otherwise write to Dear Sir/Madam. Never assume a particular gender

* use an ordinary font such as Times New Roman, size 12

* begin a new paragraph for each new point

* if you are responding to a job advertisement, include a reference to the advertisement

* end with 'Yours faithfully' if you started with 'Dear Sir/Madam'

* end with 'Yours sincerely' if you started with 'Dear (name)'

* print on good white paper

✱ check everything and then ask someone else to check it again.

An example for you to follow can be found below.

Your address   Fern Cottage
St John's Road
Cardiff
CH 6 4WA

Ms S Jones   *recipient's name and address*
First in Travel
Bond St
London
W12 1DH

3rd September 2007

Dear Ms Jones

RE: Vacancy for Contracting trainee   *reference to advertisement*

I am writing with reference to the above vacancy which was advertised in *The Independent* on 27th August 2007.

I finished my A-levels at Cardiff Sixth Form College in June this year and I gained an 'A' in Travel and Tourism and 'B's in French and Spanish. I would like the opportunity to work in tour operation and think that I would be suited to your company.

I have undertaken two periods of work experience. One was in a local travel agents and the other was in the reservations centre of Dreamworld (tour operator). I have excellent references from both placements.

At Dreamworld I was working with the reservations staff but was introduced to all departments and I was very interested in the contracting department.

I also have a part time job at Sainsburys and was recently promoted to supervisor. This job has given me a lot of customer service experience and team skills.

Note new point in each paragraph

I am sure I have the necessary skills and experience to succeed in the advertised post. I have pleasure in enclosing my CV and look forward to hearing from you.

Reference to enclosed CV

Yours sincerely

Jennifer Marshall

Writing a memo

Memos are not used very often these days as they have been largely replaced by email. However, you should know the format in case you need to write one. Sometimes memos are sent by email.

A memo is an internal document sent to a group or an individual to give them some information. The word 'memo' is short for memorandum. It is an informal document and there is no need to sign it.

An example for you to follow is below.

MEMO

From: Sanjit
To: Mary
Date: 30.4.2005
Subject: Meeting

The meeting scheduled for next Friday (6/5) has been cancelled.

Note the content is very brief.

Using fax

You will be expected to use a fax machine in the workplace. First complete a fax header form. This has the details of the sender and a space for you to enter the details of the recipient. Each machine differs slightly but the basic operation is simple. If you are using a manual fax machine, insert your papers as directed by the manufacturer's instructions, tap in the recipient's fax number and press send. If you are using a computer system you will have to attach documents held on file or scan your document to file and then attach. The computer will generate a header form to go with the fax.

Emails

Emails are less formal than letters but still important as there is always a record of what you wrote. This means it isn't a good idea to write them on the spur of the moment! If you are writing to an employer be professional although you do not need to use a formal business layout. Don't apply for a job by email unless expressly invited to do so. Record sent mail into your sent box. Learn how to send an attachment in case you need to attach your CV.

Telephone skills

You might have to make telephone calls to a prospective employer – you might even be interviewed by telephone. A telephone call can be very important. You create an impression even though you cannot be seen. You should prepare for your telephone call just as you would for a face-to-face meeting.

Before you call, think about its purpose. Is a telephone call the best means of achieving that purpose?

For example, if you telephone a company and say 'Hello, I am calling to ask if you have any vacancies', it's very unlikely that the answer will be 'Oh yes, we do, you just called at the right moment, can you come in tomorrow?' It would be better to send a letter.

Who do you want to speak to? What are you going to say if they are not in? You could leave your name and number or you could phone back having found out when he or she will be available.

Make a few notes about what you want to say or ask – but don't write a script or you will sound very unnatural. During the call:

* stand up – good body language will affect your voice

* smile, so that you sound friendly

* use an appropriate greeting

* introduce yourself - for example, 'Good Morning, this is Jennifer Marshall from Cardiff Sixth Form College. Is Ms Hendry available please?'

What if you don't know who to speak to? Ask the switchboard operator or whoever answers the phone for the name of the relevant person. For example, 'Hello, could you tell me the name of your human resources manager please?' 'Yes, that's Ms Hendry'. 'Thank you, is she available, please?' Write the name down so you remember it for next time.

Don't launch into your full speech to the wrong person - the switchboard operator probably won't be interested! When you are speaking:

* use your voice to make a good impression, vary the pitch, be clear and not too quiet or too loud

* don't ramble, but make your point briefly

* end the call properly - say thank you, make sure your name has been noted and say goodbye.

Making a presentation

There are two important aspects to an effective presentation, what you say (the content) and how you say it (the presentation).

To ensure the content is correct, make sure you have understood the brief. If you have been asked to talk about Barbados, don't talk about all Caribbean islands. Carry out your research thoroughly so that you know your subject inside out and are able to answer questions. Select relevant information from your research to fit the length of the talk. What is relevant? Decide what the audience needs to know, the essential facts and the most interesting information. You probably won't have time to include everything you found out if you did your research properly.

Prepare the structure of your talk into logical sections. Describe these sections to your audience by showing a contents page if you are using an overhead projector or PowerPoint, or tell them clearly what you are going to cover. Once you have introduced your subject in this way, present the information to the audience and, at the end, recap it again in summary.

The best presentation structure is to:

* tell the audience what you are going to say (outline)

* tell them the information

* tell them what you have told them (summary).

Keep to these basic presentation rules:

* Talk clearly and more slowly than usual.

* Use your voice – don't speak in a monotone.

* Flag up the different sections by telling the audience or using a PowerPoint slide or overhead transparency.

* If you have to include figures, give them in written form – on a screen or a handout.

* Don't use slang.

* Use cue cards.

* Never read out information – know your subject and use cue cards as prompts.

* Establish eye contact with the audience – practise scanning the audience, not fixing on one person.

* Practise giving presentations – you will improve!

Think about your body language too. You will probably stand; in fact it is better to stand even if you are allowed to sit – you will immediately feel more confident and in control. Stand up straight and don't shift from one foot to the other. If you have a tendency to play with pens, jewellery or tap your fingers then put everything down and fold your hands together. This will also stop you waving your hands about in excitement.

You should be smartly dressed – even if you are not in an interview situation.

Prepare for a presentation. The subject is you. Your tutor has asked for volunteers to act as greeters and receive the visitors at a careers event to be held in the main hall. Only two people can be greeters. Their task will be to welcome the visitors, charm them and make sure they are directed to areas of interest to them. Employers must be shown to the rooms where they will be giving talks. As you can imagine everyone in your group wants to be chosen to be a greeter. You have to sell yourself and persuade your tutor that you have the necessary skills, charisma and knowledge to be chosen.

Job application skills

Sources of jobs

You need to know where to look for jobs that might interest you. Here are some examples of sources of employment opportunities. Of course, you may want to apply for higher education so later we will look at how you might do that:

An example of a newspaper jobs page

* **Careers advisors** – they may be based in your college or school or in another centre, for example, Connexions. You will be able to secure an interview to discuss the kind of career you are looking for.

* **Newspapers** – Look at job advertisements in the local newspaper to find local employment opportunities.

* **Resource centres/websites** – if you are looking for employment in a specialist sector such as the airport sector, you will find that there is often a job centre or website for recruitment. Examples include Manchester and Stansted airports. These centres will have a range of jobs, at different entry levels, on offer.

* **Networking** – perhaps you have a family member or friend who works in travel and tourism. Use these contacts to find out what opportunities are available.

Once you have found a job that interests you, see if you can get further details in the form of the job description and person specification. These will allow you to assess your suitability for the job before you apply and to consider the career progression that the job will give you.

Here are some points you might consider to assess the potential:

* **Physical make-up** – does the job require any special physical characteristics such as strength, good eyesight or height?

* **Attainments** – what type and level of education is needed? What special occupational experience or training is required? Do you need to have a degree?

* **Special aptitudes** – is a skill in writing or drawing needed? Does the applicant need to be a car driver or speak a second language?

* **Disposition** – what type of personality is desirable? Are you expected to deal with the public or work in an office?

* **Circumstances** – does the applicant need to be mobile? Would you have to travel away from home?

* **What training** will be given?

* Will you be able to further your qualifications in that position?

* What are the opportunities for promotion?

* Will experience in this position help you to move onwards and upwards elsewhere?

Preparing a Curriculum Vitae (CV)

Curriculum Vitae literally means an account of your life. It is a summary of your work experience, education and skills. The purpose of your CV is to bring you to the attention of an employer and get you to the interview stage. Your CV should be constantly updated and although you will keep a basic CV on file you should adapt it to fit the particular requirements of each job that you apply for.

The CV should include:

* personal information

* work history

* education

* skills

* references.

We will consider these in more detail.

Personal information

Give your name, address, telephone numbers and email address. There is no need to give your gender, marital status or number of children, if any. Age need not be mentioned either but if you are young, it is a good idea to put your date of birth as there may be jobs that you are not eligible for because of your age. Some resort representative jobs are only available to over 21s. You do not want to reach interview stage and then be disappointed.

Work history

This is where you list all your employment starting with your current or latest job. If you have never had a job, include any periods of work experience or voluntary work you have done. For each job give the job title, the name of the company and what it does, if it is not well known. Add a list of your responsibilities in that position. If you can think of particular achievements in that position, list them too.

Education

As with work history, start with your most recent qualification or course. Include schools from secondary onwards. Do not include GCSEs at less than 'C' grade. Write the name of the college/school and against it the qualifications you achieved there.

Skills

List any other skills you have. Examples include language, with an indication of level, driving licence, first aid certificate and lifeguard qualifications. You can include any key skill or IT qualifications here. For IT say which software packages you can use.

References

It is usual to include the names and addresses of two referees. One must be an employer or tutor. You can state that they are available on request. This gives you time to ask the referees for permission to use them.

Profile

Some people choose to start their CV with a brief personal profile. It sums up your skills and experience and gives the employer an instant idea of whether you are suitable for the post. It can easily be changed to fit a particular post.

CV writing tips

* Keep it brief – 2 sides of A4 maximum.

* Don't try to be funny.

* Don't include visuals, squiggles, etc.

* Do not add a passport photo unless specifically asked for.

* Tailor the CV to the job.

* Don't put in anything negative.

* Print it on good quality paper.

* Ask referees before mentioning them.

* Get someone to check the grammar and spelling.

* Keep a copy of your CV on disk.

Example of CV

Jennifer Marshall
Fern Cottage
St John's Road
Cardiff
CH6 4WA
886 2121
jmarshall12@hotmail.com

Enthusiastic college leaver with 'A' grades in Travel and Tourism A-Level offers substantial language skills and tourism knowledge to employer.

Work history

June 2003 – present	Saturday supervisor
Sainsburys	Responsibilities include organising the work of a team of six in stock rotation and shelf filling. Responsible for organising their work rotas and breaks.

Work Placements

First Choice (travel agents)	Work experience – shadowing sales staff
Dreamworld	Work experience in the reservations department

Education

Sept 2003 to June 2005
Cardiff Sixth Form College
GCE A levels

Travel and Tourism	AA
French	B
Spanish	B

Sept 1986 to June 2003
Boddington Community School, Cardiff
GCSEs

Maths	C
French	C
Eng Lit	A
Eng Lang	A
Spanish	B
Geography	C
IT	CC

Skills

Full, clean driving licence
First Aid Certificate
IT Key skill level 3

References

Available on request

Follow all the guidelines and example given and produce your own CV. At the moment you should produce a basic CV which can then be adapted to fit a particular job.

CASE STUDY
Job applications

DREAMWORLD TRAVEL

Dreamworld Travel is based in Cardiff and is well known throughout Wales for its excellent range of holiday products and supreme customer service.

Customer Relations Executive

We are looking for a well organised, customer focused person who will be responsible for logging incoming correspondence, acknowledging customer complaints and liaising with other departments to ensure the customer complaint is resolved. The post is suitable for a new entrant into the travel trade and training will be given. As much of the correspondence is written, applicants will need excellent letter writing skills and must be confident in verbal communication. Knowledge of tour operators and their regulatory practices would be beneficial.

Adapt your CV, drawing on your own experience and skills so that your CV is suitable for this position. If you prefer, choose another job advertisement that better fits your skills.

Tips:

* List all the units relevant to this post from your A-level course

* In the profile add 'well organised'

* Under Sainsbury responsibilities add 'dealing with customer complaints.

Letters of Application

You should never send your CV without a covering letter. Remember your CV is only two pages long, at most. The purpose of your letter is to focus on why you are suitable for the job. If the letter is poorly presented you will not get selected so make sure you have studied the section in this chapter on writing a business letter. Letters of application may be speculative – this means you don't know whether a job vacancy exists but you are writing anyway. If you are writing in response to a job advertisement make sure you give examples of the skills and qualities you have which match the job specification.

Write a letter of application for the job advertisement shown in the previous case study. Use the letter writing guidance given earlier in this unit to help you.

Job interviews

Personal presentation

In the travel and tourism industry, workers often have direct contact with the public. Dress code is therefore important. Employers have the right to control their business image especially when employees are in direct contact with customers. Most travel and tourism companies require their staff to wear a uniform and have strict dress codes. Most airlines do not allow visible tattoos or piercings except for simple earrings.

In a resort, employees sometimes wear shorts and tee shirts depending on their role. This would be suitable for campsite couriers, for example. They are still part of a uniform provided by the company.

If you are preparing for an interview you should err on the side of caution and dress in a conservative way. This means wear formal business dress unless you are specifically told otherwise.

MEN	WOMEN
Suit – if you don't have one wear a shirt and smart trousers	Suit or smart trousers/ skirt and top – no mini skirts
Shirt or polo shirt – no tee shirts	No low cut tops or thin straps
Polished dark shoes – no trainers	Polished dark shoes – no trainers, heels not too high Wear tights with skirts – no bare legs
Hair – freshly washed and tied back if long	Hair – freshly washed

Make sure every item you wear is clean and free from creases. Make sure you are clean and sweet smelling. If you smoke do not do so just before you enter an interview. It will not give a good impression. Remember to smile.

Timing
Make sure you arrive in good time, remembering you might have to find your way.

Demonstrating your skills
Prepare examples of situations where you have demonstrated particular skills. You should be able to guess what would be appropriate from the job description. For example, think of situations where you had to solve a problem, where you demonstrated leadership or good customer service.

Preparing questions
At all interviews an opportunity is given for the interviewee to ask questions. Make sure you have some ready. Don't ask about the pay and holidays. You can find out later if they haven't already told you. Ask about training and promotion prospects. If interviewers want to give you a hard time they will start by asking for your questions. Don't be fazed, take out your pad of prepared questions and fire away!

Giving a presentation
At some interviews candidates are required to give an individual presentation on a given subject. You would expect to be informed of this prior to the interview and given plenty of time for preparation. It is a great opportunity to show what you are capable of and demonstrate your knowledge and research skills; nevertheless it is a nerve-wracking experience. There is no point planning an 'off the cuff' performance, the only way to give a good presentation is to prepare thoroughly and practise, and practise again. Use the section earlier in this unit to make sure you have prepared the presentation properly.

Know the company
Make sure you have carried out research into the company and its products and services. You might be asked about your opinions of the company. If you don't know anything about it you will look foolish. For example, an interviewee was asked what she thought about the company's new programme to Asia. She replied that she didn't know they sold holidays to Asia!

Skills Audits

The first stage of your personal evaluation could be a SWOT analysis. Refer to page 106 to remind yourself of what this is. Evaluate the strengths and weaknesses you demonstrated at your work-based experience. Identify any opportunities that arise from the experience. It is unlikely that you will find any threats unless your experience was completely unsuccessful!

Theory into practice

Complete the following chart

Personal SWOT analysis

STRENGTHS	WEAKNESSES	OPPORTUNITIES	THREATS
	Not good at IT	Take a CLAIT course in addition to A-level	
'B's in units taken so far		Improve to 'A'	
			Not many travel and tourism employers in this area
Full attendance on college course			

Theory into practice

Complete the following skills audit. Do this with a partner and discuss how you can improve on your skills and qualifications.

Skills Audit

SKILL AREA	ASPECT	GOOD	NEEDS IMPROVEMENT	QUALIFICATION HELD
Communication	Taking notes Spelling Writing letters Writing reports Oral presentation Interviewing			
Number	Calculating Interpreting statistics Presenting graphs and tables			
IT	Word Access Excel Internet Email			
Working with others	Contributing to a team Assertion Listening			

SKILL AREA	ASPECT	GOOD	NEEDS IMPROVEMENT	QUALIFICATION HELD
Improving own learning and performance	Time management Action planning Organisational skills			
Vocational skills in travel and tourism				
Languages				

Develop an action plan

Here are two examples of planning methods you can use to help set, plan and achieve your targets.

1. Setting targets

TARGET	FIND AN INTERESTING AND CHALLENGING JOB
1.	Gain A-levels with good grades
2.	Complete all assessments by deadlines
3.	Update CV
4.	Contact tutor about possible jobs
5.	Prepare CV and covering letter
Joint actions with tutor	Interview practice, regular reviews of progress

2. Action Plan

TARGET	HOW?	WHEN?	RESOURCES NEEDED?
Spend June to November in US at Camp America placement	Already arranged		
Apply to university	Research courses	Summer holidays	UCAS website, prospectuses, friends at uni
	Prepare personal statement	By beginning of October	UCAS instructions
	Complete application online	By October	Tutor or careers people help
	Prepare for interviews	By December	
Pass course	Keep to deadlines, prepare timetable of work	By June	Tutors, parents! Library and Internet
Go to university and study tourism management		Sept 2006	

This target setting form is suitable for someone wanting to go on to HE after a gap year. If you want to go to university straight after your A-levels you need to apply in the first year of your course. The same target setting format can be used for personal career development in terms of a job route.

There are hundreds of travel and tourism courses available at universities. Of course, you do not have to study travel and tourism. You may choose to study a different subject. Suitable courses include business studies, marketing and event management. All the details of courses are available on university websites. It is worth spending a lot of time researching courses as one travel and tourism course differs from another. If you have not already done so, begin by looking at the UCAS website. This offers you various search options, by subject, university or geographic location. Once you have found courses that interest you, you can link to the specific university website for more information.

Theory into practice

Design a similar target setting form or action plan to the one on page 119 and complete it for yourself. You can keep it confidential if you prefer or you can discuss it with your tutor. Use the form to show your personal career development.

Think it over...

If you get the opportunity during your course, take up a work placement. This will help you decide on your career options as it will:

✳ give you new skills and knowledge

✳ get you used to the discipline of working

✳ identify possible career pathways

✳ give you an opportunity to gain a reference.

Assessment guidance ···

This assessment provides evidence for Unit 9.3. It covers assessment objectives:

1. Demonstration of knowledge, understanding and skills.

4. Evaluations.

To succeed in this assessment you must provide a detailed career development plan based upon a personal skills audit produced using information from a range of sources.

On completion of this assignment, you will be awarded a number of marks. These will contribute towards the marks for this unit. The quality of your work will determine the marks awarded. Your work will be assessed against the following criteria:

1–9 marks
The career development lacks detail in some parts and may have some omissions although these are not significant. The focus of the plan may be on the short term rather than the medium term future. The plan makes limited use of the personal skills audit. The personal skills audit lacks some detail and is mainly subjective.

10–17 marks
The career development plan has some detail and some justification. There may be some omissions but these are not significant. The focus of the plan is on the medium term future. Use has been made of the personal skills audit to develop the career development plan. The personal skills audit is detailed and reasoned with some parts substantiated. Evidence is drawn from a range of sources.

18–21 marks
The career development plan is comprehensive, well reasoned and fully

justified making clear and sustained use of the personal skills audit. The focus of the plan is on long term career goals. The personal skills audit is comprehensive and detailed, drawing on evidence from a wide range of sources to fully substantiate conclusions.

Career Development Plan

The aim of this assessment is to help prepare you for seeking employment and determine your career intention.

1. You are to produce a detailed personal skills audit. This could include evidence from different sources and be put together in a portfolio. Examples of sources include:

   * personal SWOT analysis – example on page 118

   * skills audit – example on page 118

   * certificates detailing qualifications

   * tutor reviews

   * employer reviews from work placements or part time jobs.

2. Produce a detailed career plan. You can devise your own format. The examples on page 119 and the examples given here will help you. You can also use the activities you completed in the early part of this unit. Remember to link the career plan to the skills audit. Your plan should cover at least the next five years. Give reasons why your skills and qualities support your chosen career plan.

   The example given here has a few example entries to start you off but the career development plan must be individual to you and must be very detailed. Do not expect to fit all the essential information into a simple table.

Personal Career Development Plan

Career Goal: e.g. Resort Manager (*you might add an appendix with a job description*)

Types of job involved in achieving your career goal.

Knowledge, skills and qualities for this role.

How you will develop the skills and qualities required.

| *List here* | Already have | To be developed |

(You might add an appendix of your personal skills audit)

How you will gain the knowledge and experience required.

How you will adapt your attitudes to be successful in the career identified.

The timescales involved.

The sources of support that will be needed.

Reasons why your personal skills and qualities support your career goal.

Make sure that the skills that need to be developed for the chosen job role feature in your plan.

Example 1

CURRENT YEAR	TARGET	KNOWLEDGE, SKILLS AND QUALITIES	COST	COMMENTS
Year?	Apply to university	Research skills, etc. *List all skills likely to be developed in applying*	Minimal	
	Gap year *State where and what is involved*	Industry knowledge *List all skills likely to be developed*	Get paid but pay for air fares	
	Attend university to do Tourism Management Get part time job in a bar	*List all skills likely to be developed*	Tuition fees	
	Get a job as an overseas rep		Could be £16,000 salary	
	Get promoted to overseas rep			

Example 2

Knowledge check

1. Which skills are most commonly demanded in travel and tourism?

2. Which skill most needs to be developed amongst travel and tourism employees?

3. Identify three duties of a holiday representative.

4. Give three examples of ground handling services.

5. What employment opportunities are available in the public sector?

6. Describe two different types of teams.

7. Define an ad hoc team.

8. Identify two characteristics of effective teams.

9. Give three ways of assessing team performance.

10. Why is flexible working a good way to motivate staff?

11. What is meant by self motivation in the workplace?

12. Why are customer care skills important in travel and tourism?

13. Why are IT skills important in travel and tourism?

14. What should a CV include?

Promotion and sales in travel and tourism

This unit covers the following sections:

10.1 The sales process and buyer behaviour

10.2 The role of promotion in the marketing process

10.3 The promotion mix

In this unit you will learn about the marketing process and the role that promotion plays in marketing. We will examine different techniques used by travel and tourism organisations to promote their products and services. You will evaluate the effectiveness of different promotional techniques and campaigns.

In addition you will learn about the sales process and learn how to develop your own selling skills.

How you will be assessed

This unit is externally assessed. You will undertake a test set and marked by Edexcel. The test will consist of a series of short and long answer questions.

A variety of activities and case studies is provided in this unit to help you understand all aspects of promotion and sales in travel and tourism and to help you prepare for the assessment.

Your assessment evidence must show that you are able to:

* demonstrate knowledge and understanding of promotion and sales in travel and tourism

* apply your knowledge, understanding and skills of promotion and sales in travel and tourism

* use appropriate research techniques to obtain information and analyse problems and issues related to promotion and sales in travel and tourism

* evaluate information to make reasoned judgements, draw conclusions and make recommendations about issues related to sales and promotion in travel and tourism.

10.1 The sales process and buyer behaviour

Approaches to selling in travel and tourism

Selling is a vital activity in travel and tourism as revenue and profits are dependent on sales. Selling takes place in face-to-face situations with customers, on the telephone and increasingly, electronically (online).

The fundamental skills and qualities needed to sell are similar whatever the situation but when sales are made electronically there is no personal contact so selling represents a different challenge, although the desired outcome is the same.

Here are some examples of different selling situations in travel and tourism.

Face-to-face examples

Face-to-face selling is used by travel agents to sell holidays and a wide range of other products from insurance to currency. Some travel agents are paid by commission so they must try and sell as many add-ons as possible to increase their commission.

Hotel receptionists have to be able to sell. Even when a customer has pre-booked they will be offered extras on arrival. These include room upgrades, meals, newspapers and business facilities.

Resort representatives have responsibility for selling excursions. They begin this process with a presentation at their welcome meeting on transfer from the airport.

> **Key term**
>
> *Add-ons* All the extra products and services that are added on to the initial purchase.

Telephone examples

> **Key term**
>
> *Telesales* is the selling of products and services over the telephone.

There are many call centres in travel and tourism. Call centre employees may be selling holidays on behalf of a tour operator, insurance, car hire or flights. Even though the telephone is used there is one-to-one personal contact with the customer. There are particular demands on a call centre salesperson, for example, strict sales targets to meet and, as you cannot see the customer, you cannot get clues to their response to you and your products from their body language. In addition, the salesperson is desk based and cannot easily interact with their colleagues.

Qualities and skills required for face-to-face and telephone selling are:

* **the ability to empathise with customers** – to establish rapport

* **listening skills** – to establish customer needs

* **questioning skills** – the ability to ask the correct open questions

* **product knowledge** – to provide the right product

* **presentation skills** – this includes personal presentation. This is obviously more important with face-to-face selling but if you look smart and professional you will sell better, even on the telephone. Presentation skills also refer to the clarity of presenting the product. This is more difficult on the phone as you have no visuals to help you.

* **tone of voice** – especially important on the telephone as you must impart interest and enthusiasm through your voice

* **body language** – speaks volumes about your attitude face-to-face and even on the phone it affects the way you come across to the customer. It is important to sit up/ stand up straight and project positive body language. When you are face-to-face, make eye contact with the customer.

Making a cold call

personal contact is a great challenge. The skills and qualities needed to do this are rather different as the emphasis is on the technical skills needed to produce an effective website rather than personal skills. However, empathy with the customer is still important as the website designer needs to understand how the customer negotiates the website. The best websites are simple, informative and easy to navigate.

Think it over...

What do you think helps a customer make a purchase on a website? What kind of thing would make you abandon the website? What about speed, choice of product and clarity of presentation? How does a buyer behave when they are trying to buy through a website?

Think it over...

Remember that not only must the website be a selling tool the customer must find it easily. This means registering the website with appropriate search engines and sponsoring links.

Key term

Cold Calling – calling potential customers without any previous contact and trying to sell a product or service. Numbers can be taken from telephone directories, electoral registers or bought on a list. This practice is seldom used in travel and tourism apart from unscrupulous companies who try to sell time share related products. The salespeople get the respondents' interest by telling them they have won a holiday and reminding them of a survey they completed some months ago (which they probably didn't!). If you get these calls be very sceptical and remember nothing is free. Other types of companies who use cold calling are financial services, double glazing and kitchen design companies and mobile phone operators.

Electronic selling

This type of selling depends on the ability of a website to attract customers and take them through the process of AIDA – attention, interest, desire and action.

Producing a website that does this and takes the customer through the stages of a sale without

Useful examples of electronic selling include:

* tour operator websites
* airline websites
* consolidators such as lastminute.com and Expedia.

The Stages of Selling

Establishing rapport

This is the first stage of the selling process. It is about building a positive relationship with the customer so that they are relaxed and not under pressure to buy. You use your body language, tone of voice and the content of what you say to establish rapport. Start by greeting the customer and smiling. Give them your full attention and do not be distracted by what is going on around you. In a face-to-face selling situation, the environment is also important. Your desk and shop environment should be clean and uncluttered.

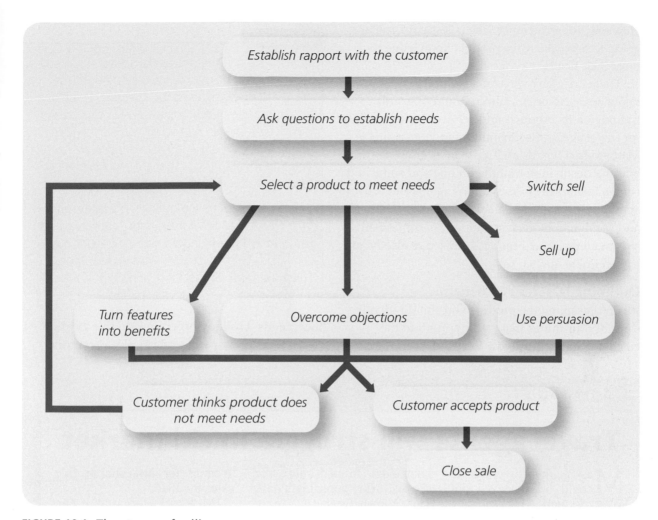

FIGURE 10.1 *The stages of selling*

Determining customer needs and expectations

Once rapport is established the next step is to find out what the customer needs. This is not as straightforward as it may seem as many customers do not know what they want or only have a vague idea. You will ask questions to establish the information. For example if you are selling holidays you will have a pro-forma to help you remember the questions to ask. You will be asking questions such as dates of travel, how many travelling, possible destinations and budget. You will ask open questions, meaning questions that begin with what, why, who, how, where and when. These types of questions will help you discover the underlying needs of the customer as well as the overt needs. You will also need to have good listening skills and practise 'active listening'.

> **Key term**
>
> *Active listening* – This is the process of demonstrating to a speaker, both verbally and non-verbally, that you are listening and that the information is being received. It is done by maintaining eye contact, nodding and expressing agreement in appropriate places. On the telephone it is more difficult. Here you can paraphrase what the customer says, for example, 'so you want to go somewhere hot' and encourage further information by 'tell me a little more about what you would like to do on holiday'.

Selecting the products to meet customer requirements

If you are lucky enough to have a customer who knows exactly what they want then this is easy.

However, for a customer who is less sure you are going to need extensive product knowledge to meet their needs.

There are many ways of acquiring product knowledge. An organisation should offer full training on its products and services to staff and, for travel agents, destination training is available. Many tourist boards and companies are now offering destination training on line and some of it is free. Examples of destinations agents can learn about on line include Canada, Thailand, Australia and Malta and more destinations are coming on stream all the time. Product knowledge also helps to 'sell up' or 'switch sell'.

Outlining features and benefits

When presenting the product you should identify three or four things that are important to the customer and explain how the product matches

their needs. Holiday brochures do this in print to sell their products. For example, a feature of

CASE STUDY

Travel agents will struggle in ski market

Mass-market travel agents could be squeezed out of the ski market because they lack specialist knowledge.

Crystal Holidays managing director Stuart McLeod said bad training often means customers know more about ski holidays than the average high-street agent. Speaking at Crystal's Ski Industry Report 2005, McLeod said: 'Agents do not have the product knowledge to add value for clients. Ski consumers are more knowledgeable and more sophisticated and they will be looking for agents who are too.'

He said specialist agencies such as Ski Solutions are better able to cope with consumer demands while more general agencies – which represent half of Crystal's ski sales – are falling behind and could account for just one in five sales by 2010.

McLeod denied the operator would actively court more direct business and urged agents keen to stay ahead to attend more ski educationals.

He also warned that mid-market operators which are not large ski or niche operators could struggle to survive in future.

Source: *Travel Weekly* 14th July 2005

This article shows the importance of product knowledge.

1. **Describe the following as used in the article:**
   * **Educational**
   * **Mid market operator**
   * **General agencies.**
2. **Suggest three ways that an agency could increase the ski market knowledge of its staff.**

3. **Why is specialist knowledge so important in this market?**

Extension task: Compare the type of knowledge needed to sell to ski customers with that of another specialist market, for example diving or trekking. Present your findings as a chart and discuss how this knowledge would be acquired.

For each product or service in the table turn the features into customer benefits.

PRODUCT OR SERVICE	FEATURE	BENEFIT
Item of luggage	Wheels and a key	
Aircraft seats	40" seat pitch	
Airport check-in	Self check-in	
Hotel room	South facing balcony	
Car hire	Insurance included in price	
Train	Buffet service	
Hotel room	Telephone and television in the bathroom at a hotel	

a swimming pool is the provision of a lifeguard. The benefit is that parents are reassured about the safety of their children. A feature of a flight is that meals and drinks are included throughout. The benefit is that the passenger does not have to take sandwiches or budget for buying food and drink.

Overcoming Objections

Customers may be reluctant to finalise a sale for many reasons. They may be anxious about spending their money or seeing something better or cheaper after they have bought it! You can help them make their purchase by overcoming objections. This is a skill and it improves with

CASE STUDY

Combat the hagglers with Seligo's list of defences

Accommodation only supplier Seligo has drawn up a list of defences for agents to use when customers try to haggle them down for a cheaper price.

Sales director Diane Mosson compiled the list of points to counter bartering attempts after watching the Tonight with Trevor McDonald report, entitled Holiday Haggles. She said: 'Agents face new threats to pricing – buyers increasingly think it is their right to haggle. But this list can be used by agents to highlight what advantages they can add.'

Mosson's tips include: Explain all the hidden costs that customers may not be able to immediately identify from an online price.

Tell the customer who the supplier is, and whether they are bonded health and safety checked, or if they offer overseas assistance.

Emphasise that you offer the customer someone to come back to should things go wrong. Agents invariably support a client's claim by dealing with the supplier on their customer's behalf.

Stress how using an agent's knowledge can save hours of online searching. Agents can show their worth by offering a range of other services including booking flights, airport transfers, hotels, car hire and extra activities.

Source: *Travel Trade Gazette* 11th February 2005

1. **Explain why customers try to haggle on price instead of accepting the price given.**

2. **Explain how the suggestions in the article will reassure customers when dealing with agents.**

practice in the same way that turning features into benefits improves. Objections may be about price – 'I didn't want to spend that much'. In this case you can explain what is included in the price and what good value it is.

Theory into practice

Carry out a role play. You are working in a call centre. You will need a brochure of city breaks which includes Prague. Take it in turns with colleagues to be the travel agent, the customers and observer.

'You have almost sold a city break to Prague to Mrs Fidler who wants to arrange a surprise for her husband's 40th birthday. She was very keen at first and happy with the flights and four star hotel you suggested. However, she is beginning to hesitate and you need that booking! She is raising objections. You have to overcome those objections and make the sale.'

The objections are:

* It's more expensive than I thought – I didn't know there would be a fuel charge.

* We'll have to get up very early to get to the airport for a 6am flight.

* We won't understand what anyone is saying in Prague.

* There might not be enough to do.

* I've heard the food isn't very good in Prague.

NB: When you are playing the customer add your own objections.

The observer should record the role play and feedback to the participants. The best way to do this is to divide a piece of A4 paper in half and make notes in two columns following the conversation. Quote exactly if a statement or phrase illustrates a particular point. Go through what was said with the participants at the end.

Extension task: The observer should assess the performance of the travel agent and make recommendations for improvement. Remember to give constructive criticism rather than negative feedback.

Closing the Sale

Once you have overcome objections you must look for signals that the customer is ready to buy. These may be things that are said (verbal signals) or visual signals. Examples include:

* customers nodding to their partner
* looking in their bag for their wallet
* asking you to reconfirm the price
* checking all the details again.

The customer should not be rushed but if you are sure they are ready, close the sale. Timing is very important as poor salespeople miss the signs, fail to close and lose the sale. There are ways of closing, for example, suggesting that the holiday will not be available for long or that an excursion is very popular and will be full. Offering a discount or something extra is also a close, as long as it is dependent on an immediate sale. You must be careful that your close is not counter productive. Some people are put off by a hard sell and will leave with you losing the sale. With experience you will come to gauge what kind of close and timing is appropriate in different situations.

After sales service

Informing customers about the after sales service can help you close a sale as it is reassuring to the customer to know that there is a point of contact in case of questions following purchase. The after sales service may be in the form of a guarantee – for example if you find the same product cheaper elsewhere the difference in price will be refunded.

Theory into practice

Choose a travel and tourism website. Study the website and describe how it takes the customer through the stages of selling. Comment on its effectiveness.

Call centre staff ditch the hard sell

Experts are worried customers are becoming annoyed by call centre operators trying to sell add-ons such as insurance and car hire when all they want is advice about their holidays. Some call centres are already adopting a different culture to avert a fall in sales. Robin Deller, managing director of ski specialist Fast Track, said: 'When we started three years ago, we used to do the hard sell but we found we never got any repeat custom, so we had to change how we did things. The sales take longer, maybe two or three calls "but we do now get a lot of repeat custom. Freedom Direct commercial and marketing director Nick Jackson admitted: 'Our sales techniques have changed. We do not use hard sell. You can hit people with too many things at the point of sale.' The director of the research company, Simon Gilman said: 'Customers can be put off if they feel agents are trying too hard to sell. Customer service expectations are getting higher. There is a loss of trust if the customer always feels they are under pressure to buy.'

Source: *Travel Trade Gazette*, May 28th 2004

1. **Think of two instances where you have had to deal with a call centre as a customer. If you have never spoken to a salesperson in a call centre interview a friend who has. Make notes on:**
   * **the greeting that was given**
   * **which stages of selling were apparent**
   * **what type of close was used**
   * **whether a purchase was made**
   * **overall opinion on the call including whether it was a hard or soft sell.**

Compare the two instances and write up your findings.

Theory into practice

Prepare a short report which outlines the skills and qualities needed to sell in the following situations. Make comparisons where possible:

* An airline reservation call centre
* A resort rep selling excursions at a welcome meeting.

10.2 The role of promotion in the marketing process

In this part of the unit you will be introduced to the marketing process and the key stages involved. At each stage we will examine the role that promotion plays.

Introduction to the marketing process

Before you try to understand the process of marketing and how it occurs in practice, you need to understand what is meant by the concept of marketing. If you ask people what they understand by marketing, they often mention advertising, promotion or selling. However these things are not marketing but only a part of it. Marketing embraces all business decisions to be made in order to get a product or service to the right customer, or consumer as they are called in marketing.

> *** REMEMBER!**
> Marketing and promotion are not the same thing – promotion is part of marketing.

A company which has adopted the philosophy or concept of marketing puts the customer at the heart of its business. Every product which is made has a customer who needs or wants that product, even if they don't quite know it yet. Every service that is offered is offered because the company has established that there are customers who would like to use that service. Of course, this doesn't always work out in practice. If it did then no companies would fail. Long term successful companies are those which are providing for the needs of their customers. Promotion is vital to the process because customers have to be informed about what products and services are available.

An organisation which practises marketing tries to have excellent customer knowledge and to anticipate customer needs. Most travel and tourism companies understand that putting the customer first is crucial to success in business.

Definitions

This is how the Chartered Institute of Marketing (CIM) defines marketing:

> 'The management process responsible for identifying, anticipating and satisfying customer requirements profitably'

There is an argument that 'profitable' is not essential to the definition. It is evident that not all organisations aim to make a profit. Charities give all the money they make to the cause they support. They have to market themselves to raise that support. Public organisations such as tourist boards provide services to consumers but don't usually make a profit. They still practise marketing to ensure that the services they provide are right for their customers. These organisations use promotional techniques extensively too.

Here is another definition provided by a famous marketer, Philip Kotler:

> 'Applying the marketing concept means that companies can achieve success by determining the needs and wants of target markets and fulfillling the needs and wants more effectively than their competitors.'

Adapted from Philip Kotler: Marketing Management: Analysis, Planning, Implementation and Control, 6th edition (Englewood Cliffs, N.J.:Prentice Hall, 1988)

Again the importance of the customer is emphasised but now there is also mention of the competition. Travel and tourism is a very competitive industry. Just consider how many holiday companies there are to choose from when you book a holiday. So we can see that to be successful the company has to not only provide what the customer wants but do it better than their competitors.

Theory into practice

Ask ten people what they understand by marketing. Write down what they say and bring your notes for discussion with your colleagues. How many people are close to the definitions given? How many people confuse marketing with just selling or just advertising?

The stages of marketing

Setting marketing objectives

Mission statements

Objectives can be summarised in a mission statement. This is a short statement, consisting of a few lines, which states what the company aims to do. Mission statements are usually published in company literature, on websites and in reception areas of company offices. The mission statement is useful to customers as it tells them something about what to expect in terms of product or service and so is itself a form of communication. It is also useful to employees as it focuses them on what the company wants to achieve. It would be surprising to find mission statements which say that the company wants to make lots of money, even if we think they do. It is likely that the emphasis will be on service.

Here are some examples of mission statements from travel and tourism organisations.

Kuoni Travel Group:

- 'We are committed to creating best value for our customers, employees, shareholders and business partners.
- We strive to be successful in our core business activities: Leisure Travel and Incoming.

- We motivate our staff by encouraging entrepreneurial spirit and innovation at all levels.
- We think and act internationally.
- We work to enhance shareholder value and support environmentally friendly solutions. '

Kuoni stands for reliability, cost-effective solutions, quality and fairness in business.

Source: www.kuoni.com

And here is the Thomsonfly mission statement:

'Our objective is to provide more choice, more flexibility and more opportunity by offering inspiring destinations, attractive schedules and, very importantly, low fares.'

Source: www.thomsonfly.com

Public sector bodies have mission statements too. Here is an example from Tourism Ireland.

'Tourism Ireland's mission is to market successfully the tourism attractions of the island of Ireland to achieve an increase in our number of overseas visitors. Within that remit, we have a special responsibility to support the Northern Ireland industry in reaching its potential.'

Source: www.tourismireland.com Tourism Ireland annual report 2003

Note that the mission statements do not mention promotion specifically but give an overview of their aims and objectives. In order to achieve their objectives, travel and tourism companies must make both consumers and trade customers aware of their products and services. The methods they use to do this are collectively known as promotion and form part of the marketing mix.

Some organisations write a vision statement as well. This summarises the goals that the company hopes to achieve in the long term, recognising that these goals are not likely to be achieved in the short term but they show the direction the company is working in.

Objectives

Objectives should reflect the mission statement but will be very specific. The objectives may be strategic (general) or operational (broken down to specific targets).

Examples of strategic objectives include:

* increasing sales
* increasing profits
* increasing market share
* reducing costs
* entering new markets
* improving corporate image.

The SMART approach is often used to help set objectives. This means that objectives will be:

* **S**pecific – it is evident what has to be achieved.
* **M**easurable – there will be evidence that the target has been achieved (or not).
* **A**chievable – it is possible that this can be done.
* **R**ealistic – it will move the company towards longer term goals.
* **T**ime constrained – there must be a time limit on when this is to be achieved.

Operational objectives are more specific and allow the organisation to achieve its strategic objectives. Promotion is more likely to be included in operational objectives than in strategic objectives as it is an essential tool to achieve the strategic objectives.

Here is an example from Tourism Ireland's 2005 marketing plan of promotional objectives designed to achieve growth in visitors from the Great Britain market.

'A redesigned 2005 destination campaign will be launched to maximise the promotion of the regions of Ireland in British regions that are connected with direct access services.

A year round advertising presence will be maintained in regional and national media.

British families will be targeted.

Business tourism promotion will be stepped up with increased investment.'

Source: Tourism Ireland Marketing Plan 2005

Market segmentation

Market segmentation is the process of dividing up the total market for a product or service into groups of consumers or customers who share similar characteristics.

Market segmentation and marketing research are closely linked as research helps a company establish the kind of person who is buying their products and services and determine new market segments to target. If all customers were the same then a company would only need to produce one product or service and one set of marketing activities to reach the customers. This is known as undifferentiated marketing or a total market approach. It is very unusual and you are unlikely to find examples of it in the travel and tourism industry.

It is more likely that the organisation has identified different groups of customers who share similar needs and characteristics. Having

CASE STUDY

Here are some examples of strategic objectives extracted from the easyJet annual report, November 2004.

Focus on our customers
We know what our customers value, and we design our core product and ancillary services accordingly. Every year, we aim to create better value for our customers, whilst decreasing our costs to maintain or improve competitiveness.

Own our markets
We will develop and aggressively defend our chosen markets against competitors. This means quickly establishing a strong base, offering numerous routes with multiple frequencies to existing and new points on the network, and establishing a strong brand in the market.

Reduce our costs
Management is focused on increasing the operating margin. We will continue to challenge industry norms and further reduce our cost base through being highly productive, innovative and taking advantage of our scale and local knowledge in procuring goods and services.

Source: www.easyjet.com easyJet annual report 2004

Remember that operational objectives are ways of achieving the strategic objectives. For example, one operational objective for Easyjet is to 'withdraw capacity from any existing markets that are poorly performing or airports which are over-priced and do not meet our strategy'.

Visit the Easyjet website and find the mission statement. You will find it in the 'information pack'. www.easyjet.com

1. Find two examples of operational objectives. You will find these in the section of the website entitled 'Investor Relations'. You will have to use your initiative. Objectives are not neatly labelled for you.
2. Comment on the relationship between mission statement, strategic objectives and operational objectives.
3. Explain how different approaches to promotion can help easyJet achieve its objectives.

Check your work with your tutor.

identified the market segments the company has to decide whether to cater for all the segments but have different products and marketing strategies for each one, cater for some of the segments again with different products and strategies, or cater for just one specific market segment. The latter is known as 'niche marketing' and is highly specialised.

The segments that the company chooses to target with its marketing are known as target markets. Market segmentation informs promotional activity as, having determined the market segments, a company must then determine the best promotional methods and appropriate media to reach its chosen target.

Market segmentation can be done in various ways. Most companies do not choose just one but use a combination of methods.

Demographic segmentation

Demographics are the study of the make up of the population. Demographic trends illustrate how the population is changing. Factors that affect the make up of the population are the birth rate and life expectancy. Currently, in the UK, we have an ageing population as people live longer and the proportion of people in older age groups increases. This is, of course, of interest to marketers who have termed this the 'grey market'. The birth rate is low at the moment but in the post war years many babies were born as people felt more secure and looked to the future. These babies are now in their fifties and due to the sheer numbers of them, they have been an influential and important market all their lives. They are known in marketing as the 'baby boomers'.

When demographic segmentation is used, consumers are grouped according to:

* age
* sex
* ethnic grouping
* family life cycle.

The family life cycle is a useful, if old fashioned, method of segmentation. The stages of the life cycle are as follows:

* Young singles
* Young marrieds
* Full nest 1 (youngest child under 6)
* Full nest 2 (youngest child 6 or over)
* Full nest 3 (older, but still dependent children)
* Empty nest 1 (children gone)
* Empty nest 2 (children gone, parents retired)
* Solitary survivor.

These life stages do not relate to age but to family development. The idea is that needs and wants change according to where we are in this cycle. Families with young children expect hotels to provide appropriate services and look for family holidays whereas an empty nest couple is looking for different services and may have a greater disposable income.

as they usually have access to their addresses on their database. The geographic area from which the customers are drawn is known as the 'catchment area'. The catchment area is very important for tourist attractions as they need to draw customers from as wide an area as possible. Organisations like VisitBritain need to know from which countries incoming tourists originate in order to target their marketing and promotional activities.

Socio-economic segmentation

The population is divided according to socio-economic grouping. These groupings are based on occupation not income. The classifications are used extensively by advertising media to describe their audience or readership.

Geographic segmentation

The marketing data company CACI produced 'A Classification of Residential Neighbourhoods (ACORN)' based on post codes. Every street in the UK is included and categorised into 54 typical neighbourhood categories. Streets of broadly similar people are categorised together. The classification is arrived at using information drawn from the Census and from market research data.

Theory into practice

Go to the website upmystreet.co.uk. Enter your postcode and then click on 'neighbourhood profile.' (These are based on ACORN profiles) Find out what your profile is. You can get a detailed profile of your neighbourhood if you wish.

Travel and tourism companies can easily find out the geographic location of their customers

Psychographic segmentation

With this type of segmentation, consumers are categorised according to personality types, lifestyle and motivation. When it is done well, it is very effective in determining targets but it is difficult to do accurately. It is very relevant to travel and tourism. For example, environmentally conscious people will be interested in sustainable tourism products.

Promotion can be used together with research into personality types. Thomson has done this in conjunction with a self discovery website called uk.tickle.com. Visitors to the website are invited to take a quiz which tells them what their travel personality is. The personalities are named Wilderness Warrior, Glocal (citizen of the world), Tender tourist, British Bulldog and Met-Setter. The clever part is that once someone has found their travel personality, Thomson then presents them with recommended holiday destinations and activities.

Theory into practice

Investigate at www.tickle.com and find out your holiday personality.

Over 50's leading holiday boom

More than half of those aged over 50 plan to take a holiday in the next six months, with 76% planning to travel within the next year, new research shows. The desire of 50 somethings to travel abroad is attributable to the relatively low cost of foreign travel – 61% of those aged over 50 said the cost of holidays abroad is the main reason for leaving the UK.

Similarly, 14% of the more senior tourists surveyed say a strong pound is a key factor in choosing a destination abroad, as Britons aim to make their money go further.

Source: report by Phil Davies 2/9/05 www.travelmole.com

1. **Why are the over 50's an important market?**
2. **Find three examples of how the travel and tourism industry promotes its products and services specifically to this market.**

Extension task: Suggest a travel and tourism product or service which would be suitable for this market and explain how it could be used to plan promotions.

Psychographic segmentation is the most interesting and challenging type of segmentation but can be fun too. Research firm Red Media carried out some research into premium travellers, meaning those who spend more than £800 a week, and came up with the following categories.

* Confident Culturalists – they are extreme travellers who want to travel for the experience and not for the relaxation. From trekking in the Himalayas to rafting on the Zambesi, these adventurers want to experience local customs and spend £1452 per week on average.

* Top Notch Tourers – these are the silver surfers of the travel world, looking for a mix of culture and luxury. They have said goodbye to their children and are looking to spend their substantial pension, enjoying more independent holidays at an average of £1540 a week.

* Discrete Elite – travellers who know what they like and don't care what other people think. Well-educated and – they believe – from the upper realms of society, they have incomes larger than their egos and spend an average of £1567 per person per week on holiday.

Assessment activity

Describe in detail two market segments for beach holidays. Choose two media that would be suitable for a promotional campaign to reach these segments and say why they are suitable.

Marketing research

Marketing research is imperative in the marketing process, especially in travel and tourism where not enough is known about why consumers behave as they do. Marketing research enables the organisation to find out about the market, the competition and what consumers want. Numerous different methods are used to carry out research depending on the purpose of the specific research project. Research may be done on behalf of a company by a specialist research agency or it may be carried out within the organisation.

Research may be related to any area of the marketing mix or to the market overall. The most complex area of marketing research relates to consumer behaviour. We will examine these areas of research in more detail before studying the methods of marketing research.

Market research

Market research is a category of marketing research that involves finding out about the market for a product or service. Remember that the market for a product is all the users or potential users for that product. Organisations want to find out who these people are. How many of them are there? What are they like? Where are they? They also want to know who else provides products or services in this market and how many sales (or market share) they have. Market share can also be measured in financial terms. If a competitor is performing better than they are, they need to find out why. They should find out what the sales are worth for the whole market and whether the sales trend is up or down.

Here is an example from the Marketing Intelligence department of Tourism Ireland.

August 2005 – Market Intelligence Update Great Britain

Total outbound trips from GB were up 4.2% from Jan – June, but with Western Europe only up +0.2%. Visitor numbers from GB to ROI were up +6.6 % in March 2005 over March 2004, and ytd figures for Jan – March 2005 were up +3% over the same period last year. Air carrier reports are positive, however, sea carriers and tour operator reports are significantly less positive.

North America
US
US travel to Britain was down as much as 7% before the July 7 bombings. The latest release from the CSO indicates that visitor numbers from North America to ROI were down -9.6% in March 2005 over March 2004, and ytd figures for Jan–March 2005 were down -10.6% over the same period last year. Carrier reports are positive, however this includes both inbound and outbound passengers. Tour operator reports are mixed, with a continued trend away from fly drive towards coach travel.

Source: Tourism Ireland www.tourismireland.com

Product research

For a physical product such as a new type of aircraft, a long period of research and development is needed, including testing the product to make sure it works and is safe. At the same time the developer must ascertain whether there is a market for the product. Is there someone who wants this aircraft? What features do they want incorporated?

Tour operators research destinations to add to their product portfolio. Again, they need to ascertain whether there is a need for the product. In this case, is anyone likely to go to that destination? These questions take the marketer from product research into market research.

CASE STUDY

London City Airport – Vienna Questionnaire

1) Do you travel between London and Vienna?
   ● Yes ○ No

2) Do you travel for business or leisure reasons?
   ● Business ○ Leisure

3) From which airport do you currently fly?
   ● Heathrow ○ Stansted

4) How many times do you fly between Vienna/London each month?
   ● 1–4 ○ 5–10 ○ 11–14

5a) How many people within your organisation do you think fly to/from Vienna?
   ● Up to 5 ○ 6–10 ○ 11–15 ○ 16–20
   ○ 21+

5b) How many times per month do they fly to/from Vienna (on average)?
   ● 1–4 ○ 5–10 ○ 11–14

6) Does your company have a travel policy?
   ● Yes ○ No

7) Does your company's travel policy dictate which airline you have to travel with?
   ● Yes ○ No

8) What company do you work for?
   [   ]

9) What would be your ideal number of flights per day from London City Airport to Vienna or Vienna to London City Airport?
   ● 2 ○ 3 ○ 4 ○ 5 ○ 6+

10) What time would you like to leave London?
   ● 0700–0800 ○ 0800–0900 ○ 0900–1000
   ○ 1000–1100 ○ 1100–1200 ○ 1200–1300

   ○ 1300–1400 ○ 1400–1500 ○ 1500–1600
   ○ 1600–1700 ○ 1700–1800 ○ 1800–1900
   ○ 1900–2000 ○ 2000–2100 ○ 2100–2200

11) What time would you like to arrive in Vienna?
   ● 1000–1100 ○ 1100–1200 ○ 1200–1300
   ○ 1300–1400 ○ 1400–1500 ○ 1500–1600
   ○ 1600–1700 ○ 1700–1800 ○ 1800–1900
   ○ 1900–2000 ○ 2000–2100 ○ 2100–2200

12) What time would you like to leave Vienna?
   ● 0700–0800 ○ 0800–0900 ○ 0900–1000
   ○ 1000–1100 ○ 1100–1200 ○ 1200–1300
   ○ 1300–1400 ○ 1400–1500 ○ 1500–1600
   ○ 1600–1700 ○ 1700–1800 ○ 1800–1900
   ○ 1900–2000

13) What time would you like to arrive in London?
   ● 0700–0800 ○ 0800–0900 ○ 0900–1000
   ○ 1000–1100 ○ 1100–1200 ○ 1200–1300
   ○ 1300–1400 ○ 1400–1500 ○ 1500–1600
   ○ 1600–1700 ○ 1700–1800 ○ 1800–1900
   ○ 1900–2000 ○ 2000–2100 ○ 2100–2200

14) What's more important to you?
   ● Fares ○ Flight Times

Any Comments/Questions
[   ]

Your Email Address
[   ]

Would you like to be kept up-to-date with London City Airport developments?
● Yes ○ No

Source: London City Airport

1. **Summarise the information that London City Airport will get from this research.**
2. **How does this information help London City Airport develop their product range?**
3. **Why is a contact email asked for?**
4. **What are the advantages and disadvantages of doing this research online for London City Airport? (The questionnaire is accessed via the London City Airport website.)**

Extension task: Suggest other methods of research which could support or extend this questionnaire. Give reasons for your suggestions.

Price research

The price charged for a product must represent good value to the consumer and to the seller. This does not mean the product has to be cheap. Research that concerns price might involve finding out what competitors charge for similar products or asking consumers what they would be prepared to pay.

Place research

This area of research means finding out whether the distribution methods being used are the most suitable to reach the consumer and finding new ways of reaching the customer.

Consumer research

Consumer behaviour research is very difficult to conduct as consumers themselves cannot often explain why they act as they do. Although challenging, this area of research is possibly the most useful as it can lead to an understanding of consumer needs, their attitudes to a product and help a company to determine what products or services will fulfil consumer needs.

Promotion research

This might include looking for new methods of promoting the product or the company, assessing a competitor's promotional activity or trying to evaluate the success of a promotional campaign. It is difficult to determine whether promotions work. Even if there is an increase in sales, it is never absolutely sure whether it is due to the promotion or some other factor, like the weather.

The tour operator, Kuoni carries out several types of in-house promotional research. They measure the effectiveness of a marketing campaign by consumer response, in terms of brochures requested, number of calls generated and the number of holidays booked.

Research methodology

Research methodology can use a variety of different types of data.

Qualitative and quantitative

Quantitative data consists of easily measured facts and figures, for example the number of people admitted to a museum in one day. Qualitative data is more difficult to collect and to analyse as it is about why people behave as they do and what they think. Sometimes consumers themselves have trouble knowing why they buy certain things.

Primary research

This is research that has been collected for the first time – it doesn't exist anywhere else. It is sometimes called field research. Researchers only do this type of research when they are sure that the information they require has not been collected elsewhere. Primary research often follows secondary research, that is research of the kind that you often do, on your course, looking at reports, data and statistics gathered on the Internet and information collected in previous surveys.

There are several methods used for collecting primary data.

Surveys

Surveys are carried out with consumers, and may be done by mail, telephone, personal interview or through an Internet site. They are usually based on a questionnaire rather than free discussion.

The table overleaf shows the advantages and disadvantages of the different survey methods.

Key terms

Questionnaire terminology

Respondent – the person who is answering the questions.

Closed question – one with a limited range of answers, sometimes just yes or no.

Open question – any answer can be given.

Filter question – allows the respondent to omit certain questions which may not be applicable to them – for example, 'If you answer no to question 5 go to question 11'.

Classification data – you write in the age, sex and occupation of the respondent – this is used later to group respondents into categories.

Quota – the number of people in different age or socio-economic groups you want to question.

SURVEY METHOD	ADVANTAGE	DISADVANTAGE
Personal interview	The interviewer can explain questions to the respondent	May introduce bias
	Response rate is good	Very expensive to administer because of interviewer's time
	Can use 'prompts' to aid recall	Difficult to recruit trained interviewers
Telephone interview	Easy to carry out	People find telephone calls intrusive
	Many calls can be carried out in a short time	No visual prompts
	Response rate fairly good	
	Personal contact with respondent	
Mail questionnaire	Cheap to administer	Very low response rate
	Few staff needed	Need an appropriate list to get addresses
Internet questionnaire	Easy to administer	Limited to respondents who access that website therefore biased
	Instant response	No explanation of questions to respondents

Advantages and disadvantages of survey methods

It has become common practice for tour operators to give their customers questionnaires to complete at the end of their holiday. The response rates are usually good for these types of surveys, particularly if the holidaymakers are travelling by plane. They are a captive audience and air crew can easily collect the completed questionnaires. The results of these surveys help with planning for the next season and show up faults in the package booked which the company can then investigate.

When designing a questionnaire, follow the guidelines given below:

* Before you write any questions make a list of what you want to find out.

* Go through the list and discard anything that is not absolutely essential.

* Go through the list again and try to order the information you require in a logical way.

* Write the questions asking general questions first and then more specific questions.

* Never ask more than one thing in a question.

* Avoid bias in a question.

* Try to use closed questions – the answers are easier to analyse.

* Use a limited number of open questions if you want to find out the respondent's opinion.

* Use a filter question if the respondent does not need to answer every question.

* Always put classification data at the end. It is not a good idea to start off by asking the respondent how old they are and what they do. The exception to this rule is when you need to establish whether the respondent fits your quota.

Theory into practice

Using the principles described above design a short questionnaire with not more than ten questions. The purpose of the questionnaire is to establish the respondents brand awareness of travel and tourism companies. For example, you might ask them to say which airlines they have heard of without prompting. Remember to include classification data.

Observation

Observation is a very simple and yet effective research method. There are several ways of doing this. In its simplest form observers can watch consumers, for example at airports, and report on how they behave. Cameras can be used instead of people and the tapes analysed at a later date. The observer will use a checklist or take notes to aid later recall.

Focus groups

This is also a type of primary research. A group of people is invited to participate in a group discussion in someone's home, hotel or office. They may be offered an incentive to attend such as a flight voucher. The objective of the discussion is to find out peoples' attitudes to a product or service. It could be used to test people's reactions to a promotional campaign. A group leader who is often a psychologist leads the discussion.

Secondary research

This refers to research that already exists and is available to the researcher. It sometimes has to be bought. It may be internal or external to the organisation. Secondary research is done 'first' as secondary means you are not collating the data – it is secondary to you. It may lead to primary research if you do not find everything you need to know.

This type of research is sometimes called desk research as it can be done at a desk, computer or in a library. Internal sources of secondary data include:

* Sales records
* Customer database
* Costs
* Profits
* Load factors (airlines)
* Productivity.

External sources of secondary data include:

* World Tourism Organisation (WTO) – statistics on worldwide tourism
* Tourist board web sites
* Visit Britain and Star UK web sites
* UK International Passenger survey – statistics on inbound and outbound tourism
* Social Trends and Cultural Trends (Her Majesty's Stationery Office (HMSO) publications)
* Keynotes and Mintel reports – regular reports on everything! Only available to subscribers but libraries often subscribe
* National Readership Survey readership figures for newspapers
* Department for Culture statistics
* Travel trade reports
* Newspapers surveys and reports
* BRAD – directory of media publications.

The Marketing Research Plan

Identifying the objectives of the research

There must be a reason for the research. What do we want to know? It could be we want to know:

* Has our advertising campaign been successful?
* Who is buying our product?
* Why are sales going up?
* Why are sales going down?
* What do people think of our image?
* What new destinations should we introduce?

The range of possibilities for research is endless but a particular piece of research should not try to cover too much ground.

Planning the research strategy

Once we know what we are trying to find out we can consider the methodology to find the information:

* Do we need to do secondary or primary research or both?
* Who do we want to ask?
* How will we sample?
* How will we reach them/what method of data collection should we use?
* Where will we do the research?
* Who will do the research?
* When will we do the research?

Sampling

We are assuming that we can't ask everyone to take part in our research. When we can, for example when every single holidaymaker is asked to fill in a questionnaire, this is called a census. A census covers the whole population, where the population is all the possible respondents for that survey.

It is more usual to interview a sample of customers as it is very expensive to carry out a census. The sample should represent the whole body of customers otherwise the results will be biased.

Random probability sampling

Every member of the population has an equal chance of being selected. The company could use their own database as the source of respondents and a percentage of these would be selected at random. When a national survey is undertaken, the electoral register can be used as the source of respondents.

Quota sampling

In this case not everyone has an equal chance of being selected. In fact the choice of respondents is up to the interviewer but they have a quota to fulfil based on factors such as age, gender and socio-economic group.

Stratified sampling

The population is divided into groups or strata according to common characteristics. Then, a random sample is taken from each group.

CASE STUDY

Thomson rethink the family holiday as British reach the third age of travelling

British families are entering the 3rd Age of travel, according to new research by Thomson Holidays. Thomson, the UK's largest travel company, has reported a growing trend for the 'third age holiday', as more and more families book holidays that allow all three ages of the modern family to travel together; the child/teen, parents and grandparents.

Thomson has reported that more than half a million families went on holiday with extra adults included in their booking, (either grandparents or other older family members as well as parents and children) in 2004 – a 33% increase from four years ago. But whilst many families are travelling in larger numbers, Thomson has also seen the number of holidays taken by single parent families more than double over the last four years – a further example of how the family market is diversifying. In order to remain relevant in this rapidly changing market the number of flexible deals and less restrictive family offers available by British holiday companies has increased on year by year basis.

As these new trends in the family market have emerged – and in order to support the move towards more flexible family holidays – for the first time Thomson has designed a brochure solely dedicated to this new family market.

Thomson Family will provide a guide to the best family accommodation across the entire holiday market, from budget apartments to prestigious hotels, all inclusive resorts and family-friendly villas for summer 2006, supported with more large family, single parent and free child offers than ever before, making it easier for families outside the '2.4 children' group to travel abroad.

Thomson responded to feedback from the hundreds of thousands of families who travelled abroad with the tour operator last year in order to tailor make a family brochure programme, which would be modern, flexible and relevant.

Thomson press release July 2005-09-07 www.thomson.co.uk

1. How do you think this research was carried out?
2. What was the aim of the research?
3. How has the research helped Thomson?

4. Suggest two other types of research Thomson could do to find out about their customers.

Collection of data

At this stage the research is carried out and the data captured. This may be on paper or electronically. Personal interviewers are usually issued with lap tops to make the whole process much easier.

Analysis of data

It is possible to analyse data by hand but time consuming and laborious. Computer analysis is the most common technique and ensures cross tabulation of data. It is more difficult to analyse qualitative data electronically due to the diversity of responses.

Evaluation

Once the data has been produced it must be interpreted and conclusions drawn from it. Recommendations will be made so that the findings can be acted on. The data, the conclusions and the recommendations should be presented in a report.

Analysing the key factors of the business environment likely to affect promotional activities

PEST

Travel and tourism companies must be aware of the external political, economic, social and technological factors which affect the operation of their business. An analysis of these factors is usually described as a PEST analysis. A PEST analysis should take place at regular intervals as part of a review of marketing activities. Management should be constantly aware of topical issues which may impact on business even when a formal analysis is not taking place.

We will consider some of the key factors which may affect travel and tourism companies and their promotional activities.

> **Key term**
>
> *A PEST analysis* means that an organisation takes stock of the external factors affecting its business, identifying political, economic, social and technological factors.

Political and legal factors

By legal factors we mean changes in legislation introduced by government. A recent example of legislation affecting travel is the 'Denied boarding, cancellation and delay' EU Regulation which became operational in 2005. This regulation gives passengers much greater compensation when flights are delayed or cancelled. Airlines had to inform travellers about the new regulations and so leaflets were produced (by each airline) indicating how they intended to interpret the regulations.

Some legislation directly affects advertising. For example, some airlines have been accused of 'unfair and misleading practices' in their advertising, contravening advertising regulations. This is because some airlines advertise free flights which are not exactly free as many extra charges are levied including airport charges and taxes. It is the responsibility of the Advertising Standards Authority to respond to such complaints. The Ryanair example here shows how the airline

Source: www.ryanair.com

Ryanair removed 'free' from their ads, replacing it with 'just pay taxes and charges'.

stopped putting 'free' on their advertisements and now states 'just pay taxes and charges'.

Tour operators have to be aware of the political situation in the destinations they use. Some places are very dangerous because of their political situation. This changes rapidly but tourists will avoid places where there have been serious incidences of unrest or terrorism. For example, the Bali bombings of 2002 deterred tourists for some time and at the time of writing, it is not advisable to visit many parts of the Middle East because of terrorist activity. Many such occurrences cause great problems to tour operators as they are unexpected and cannot be planned for. Tour operators may have to repatriate holidaymakers when an incident occurs and switch destinations for those who have booked to go. The foreign office website gives the current situation on safety in countries all over the world. Planned promotions and other marketing activities must be cancelled or postponed if a destination is no longer viable. This can result in a wasted marketing budget. It would also be insensitive to run advertisements about a destination that has suffered a disaster.

Economic factors

Profitability
When a company is profitable it can afford to extend its marketing budget and spend freely on promotion. When profits decline, cuts have to be made. Staff cuts are often made but also non essential costs will be cut and the marketing department would expect to have its budget cut.

Taxation
Changes in taxes affect tourism as they impact on costs. Passengers on airlines have got used to paying air passenger duty as we are also used to paying our road tax. When taxes are raised or newly introduced they become contentious. In the States you will find that a room tax is added to your hotel bill. In the Balearics an environmental tax was introduced in 2001 for tourists and caused so much controversy that it was later removed. Tourists have to be informed of such changes in taxes through the media.

Interest rates
Interest rates affect a company's borrowing. When interest rates are high the company is less likely to borrow to fund expansion or marketing. The consumer is also affected by interest rates. High interest rates affect mortgage repayments and result in less disposable income. Less income means fewer holidays.

Competition
It makes good business sense to constantly watch the competition. If a major tour operator advertises cut prices then others will follow. If a competitor takes a stand at an exhibition, for example the World Travel Market, then you can't afford not to be there too.

Social factors
This includes changes in society in terms of patterns of behaviour and people's interests. Earlier in this unit you read an article about the patterns of holiday taking amongst over 50s.

Environmental factors
Environmental factors are also important as in today's society people are more environmentally aware. Sustainable tourism is currently very topical as people are more aware of the impact of their lifestyle on the environment. Travel and tourism companies need to develop an environmental policy which they can then flag in promotional literature. The purpose is to reassure customers that the company is environmentally friendly and in some cases to promote their products to a particular target market.

Technological factors
This is probably the area of greatest change, with rapid developments in technology.

Changes in products and services resulting from new technology must be communicated to customers. For example self check-in is becoming more common at airports, including checking in your own baggage.

The Internet has revolutionised the way we book our holidays and travel. On line booking systems are common for all modes of transport and for many holidays. Hotel bookings can also be made on-line allowing a view of your room and facilities. Travel agents are under great threat from the Internet. Their commissions have been slashed as operators cut costs and encourage Internet bookings. Travel companies have embraced the 'New Media' and most have departments whose function is to develop websites that are appealing to consumers and promote their products and services.

Developing a marketing mix

We are going to study each of the 4 Ps in turn but remember that they are interdependent. For example, a holiday product cannot be sold unless the public is aware of it (promotion), they know how much it costs (price) and they know where to buy it (place).

Product

'A product is anything that can be offered for acquisition or use that satisfies a particular need or want in a market. It can be physical and tangible or it may be a service and intangible.'

Adapted from: *Principles of Marketing*, Kotler and Armstrong

The definition shows that a service is also considered to be a product, and in travel and tourism, businesses are predominantly concerned with the marketing of services. The marketing for services may be different from that of a physical product as it is highly dependent on the people delivering the service. A fifth 'P', people, is often added to the marketing mix for services.

Nature of the product

When you buy a product, it is usually *tangible*. Travel and tourism products are rarely tangible. Another challenge for marketers is that the service is inseparable from the person providing it. In a restaurant, the food may be of consistent quality by using good produce and standard recipes. However, the diner's experience will still be ruined if the waiter is having an off day. Hence, the reason for introducing the important fifth 'P', people.

Travel and tourism products and services are often *perishable* (like food going off in the supermarket). Once a flight has left the airport it is too late to sell its seats. They have perished.

Airlines have to make sure their flights are as full as possible to make a profit. Of course, the airline seat is tangible but it isn't usually the seat that is the important part of the purchase, although you might be interested in its seat pitch and comfort. You certainly can't take it home. What the customer is buying is the travel to get them to their destination. Not many people fly around on aircraft just for the sake of it!

Seats on planes are perishable items.

Theory into practice

Look at a holiday brochure. Choose a holiday. Write down everything that is included in the price. You can include items that are supplemented if you like. Try to decide which aspects are tangible products and which are services. Make a table of your findings and compare it with a colleague's.

Example: A free children's tee shirt is tangible. Services of the rep are intangible.

Another way of looking at products is to examine the product features and benefits as you did when you looked at the stages of selling. The product features represent the core value of the product. For example, the features or core of a package holiday are the accommodation and transport. There will be a whole range of added features depending on the holiday chosen. These might include food, sports facilities and entertainment. The benefits on offer may be relaxation, the opportunity to go sightseeing or to learn a new skill such as windsurfing.

Companies are always looking for new features to add to their products and services. They want to give further benefits to the customer and maintain competitive advantage.

Branding

The brand is the name that identifies the product, and it may suggest something about the product itself. The travel agent 'Going Places' is a good example. Some brand names such as 'Thomson' or 'Thomas Cook' do not suggest anything about the product but still work as they are well established brands and have built up a good reputation. The public has a high awareness of these traditional brands as they are used extensively in promotion. In fact it is almost impossible to have a promotion that does not include a brand name.

Think it over...

There are lots of holiday brands. How many can you think of? Do the brands suggest anything about the company?

Branding can cost a lot of money as companies carry out research trying to find exactly the right name. It is particularly important when the brand has to work in several countries. Marketers must always check that the name makes sense in the languages of the countries they are using. Finding a name often starts with a brainstorm activity where lots of people are asked for their ideas and they are listed. A short list is then made and more research carried out with consumers before a name is selected.

Branding is used as part of 'differentiation'. Differentiation is where an organisation tries to ensure that its product or service is different to that of the competition. It is promoted in terms of its differences, usually claiming to be of better quality.

Niche products

Much of the UK holiday market has been characterised by mass market tour operators throughout the nineties and at the beginning of the 21st century. There has, however, always been room for niche operators – those operators who are usually smaller and highly specialised. They may specialise in a particular type of product, for example diving holidays or a particular area – say – Madeira or market to a particular group of people – perhaps the over 50's like the organisation, Saga (niche marketing).

The Product Life Cycle

This concept is used to show how a product moves through different stages in its life until

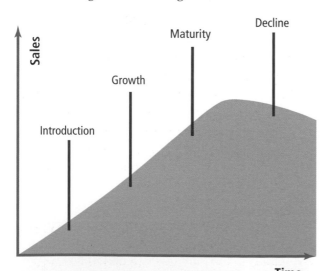

FIGURE 10.2 *The Product Life Cycle.*

it becomes obsolete. It is useful in marketing as the stage of the life cycle has an impact on how the product is marketed. It is also important that a company has products in each stage of the life cycle. If all the products were in the decline stage the company would soon be heading for bankruptcy.

1. Introduction

The launch of a new product is a very exciting, but tense, period. Consumers have never heard of the product so a lot of the marketing budget is assigned to promotional activity to let them know it exists. Developing the product will have cost both time and money. For reasons of high expense and few sales, little or no profits are expected in the introduction stage. If the product is accepted onto the market then some contribution to costs will be made. The people likely to buy the new product or try out a new service are known as 'innovators'. They are the kind of people who like to be the first to try something new. The price charged at this stage is often high – this appeals to innovators who do not mind paying for exclusivity – and it helps to recoup costs. Some products never get beyond this stage. Recently, an airline failed before it had even flown a single plane. It failed because its finance deal broke down.

2. Growth

Growth is the most profitable stage in the product's lifecycle and companies are eager to reap these profits while they can. Word of mouth promotion is important as consumers hear about the new product and want to try it. Competitors rapidly enter the market bringing out their own versions of the new idea. Due to this increased competition, it is important for companies to try and build up some brand loyalty. The promotional budget is usually devoted to stressing the product's benefits over competitive products (differentiation). Internet booking of hotels and holidays is still in the growth stage.

3. Maturity

Competition is at its most intense at this stage. Weaker competition is squeezed out of the market by aggressive marketing strategies. Marketing efforts focus on being competitive, often by promoting low prices. The low cost airlines are currently in maturity, having had years of unprecedented growth. In spite of this, newcomers are still entering the market. Entrants are not usually successful at this stage. Maturity is the longest stage of the life cycle.

4. Decline

Sales and profits start to fall at this point. Marketers must recognise when products are likely to move into this stage, as they must decide whether it is worth staying in the market. An organisation should be diversifying into other markets or products at the beginning of the decline stage (at the latest) to ensure survival. There are examples of companies who have managed to stay profitable staying as the only player in a market that everyone else has abandoned. In effect they become niche marketers.

5. Obsolescence

A product is obsolete when there is no longer any need for it.

Successful companies have products at each stage of the life cycle. It is difficult to predict how long each stage will last, as many external factors affect the product's life. In travel and tourism the product life cycle can be applied to products, services and destinations.

Price

The second element of the marketing mix is price. Travel and tourism organisations must use pricing as a means of achieving their objectives. If the company doesn't get the price right they will not make a profit. The simplest approach to pricing is the 'cost plus' method. The organisation calculates the cost of producing the product and then adds a percentage to give the return they want for profit. Although it is simple it is not the most effective approach to pricing. If sales targets are not met there won't be a profit. Also, this approach ignores the basic premise of marketing about identifying customer needs. Every approach to pricing should start with the principle of asking 'what is our customer prepared to pay? Are all the customers going to pay the same price?'

There are many different pricing strategies. The company will determine the strategy to be adopted by considering the stage in the product life cycle, competitive activity and prices of other products within the company.

Market skimming

This strategy normally applies to a new product, particularly anything that involves new technology. When the product is launched costs are high and the company needs to recoup the costs as quickly as possible. The new product appeals to innovators who can afford to pay a premium price for it. This introductory high price gives the product an air of exclusivity, but may be lowered as the product enters the growth stage of the life cycle, in order to attract new customers. This strategy would be used for deluxe products in travel and tourism, such as hiring your own jet.

Market penetration

Again, this is a common strategy for the introduction of new products. In this case, a very low price is set. The idea is that the low price attracts customers and builds market share quickly. The most common use for this type of pricing is with fast moving consumer goods (FMCG). These are household products and groceries. It is a useful short term strategy but problems may arise in trying to hold onto the customers when the price rises to a realistic level. Low cost airlines use this strategy to attract custom but it is not always successful and many low cost airlines have gone bust.

Competitive pricing

This is used in highly competitive markets where companies keenly watch the prices of their competitors and react quickly to low prices by reducing their own. It happens constantly in airline and tour operation businesses. It also relies on lack of brand loyalty amongst customers as they must be prepared to switch brands to get the best price. It can be a dangerous strategy as prices drop so low that weak companies fail and others lose money.

Odd pricing

This is a very simple approach to pricing and can be used in conjunction with any of the others. Customers are supposed to think that the price is cheaper than it is because it is £499 rather than

£500, for example. Although it is common practice no one knows if it works. What do you think?

Promotional pricing

This is where price is linked to a special promotion for a limited period of time. Sometimes the customer has to collect tokens to get the special price. It draws attention to the product and gets publicity so it especially useful for new products. Tourist attractions use this method of pricing a lot.

Differential pricing

Different prices are charged for different groups of people. For example in museums and cinemas, senior citizens and students can expect to pay reduced prices. On trains, the purchase of a rail card, (family or young person's) gives the holder access to discounted fares. These special deals are often promoted through leaflets.

Hotels have set rates but they are entirely flexible. If you are looking for a hotel room and you book on the day you want it, always ask for their 'best rate'. You are sure to get a discounted price as remember the hotel room is 'perishable'. If no one is in it, it hasn't made any money.

Seasonal pricing

This is particularly important in the tourism industry. The whole season is divided into three broad seasons. These are peak, shoulder and off peak. Peak season always coincides with school holidays and is when prices are at their highest. This causes problems for parents who have to pay the highest prices. Some parents take their children out of school to avoid peak season holidays but now that they can be fined £100 for doing so, it is likely to be a less popular option.

It is not just tour operators who charge higher prices at times of high demand. Airlines charge more on Friday afternoons and at the end of weekends and rail fares cost more during rush hours.

Place

This is the element of the marketing mix that considers how to get the product or service to the customer in the right place. The means of getting the product to the customer is known as the channel or chain of distribution. In the travel and tourism industry, the channel is complicated by the fact that there is often no tangible product to pass from one to another through the channel.

Types of distribution channel

The traditional channel of distribution in travel and tourism is:

![Get ready to travel. It's a Happy Monday. £20 off all flights for 24 hours. opodo.co.uk. Holidays - City Breaks - Hotels - Car Rental - Flights. Offer valid for bookings on Monday 5th September only. Use the flight e-voucher code "Monday" to receive £20 off flights to any destination. Terms and conditions apply. See Opodo.co.uk for full details]

Source: www.opodo.co.uk

This advert shows the company using promotional pricing to attract customers.

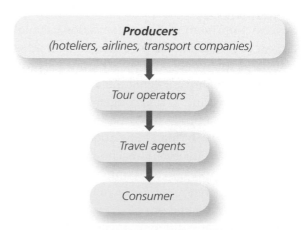

FIGURE 10.3 *Channel of distribution*

There are many variations on this channel today.

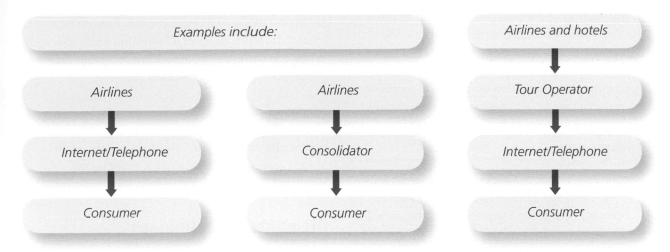

FIGURE 10.4 *Variations on channels of distribution*

The Internet has considerably reduced distribution costs to airlines. Some low cost airlines take more than 80% of bookings via the Internet. This is good news for the airlines and for consumers but it is not such good news for travel agents. Television channels also act as distribution channels for holidays. In fact, annual holiday sales through television channels have reached 400,000.

Tourist attractions have different considerations in terms of the place mix. The customers have got to travel to them in order to enjoy what they have to offer. This means the location of the attraction is important, as it must be accessible to customers. Purpose built attractions such as Disneyland Paris, are located near to major road networks. Hotels and ample parking are provided in the vicinity to ease access for visitors and to encourage them to stay longer.

Channels of distribution are still essential to allow visitors to buy tickets. Travel agents will sell tickets to attractions, as will tourist offices. The Internet is a source of direct booking and tickets can also be booked directly by telephone to most attractions.

Tourist attractions are very aware of the educational market and sell group tickets directly to school and colleges at a discount, combining price and place.

Theory into practice

Choose a travel and tourism organisation and carry out research into that organisation. Find its objectives – remember that a good source of this information is its marketing plan or its annual report. Describe each element of the marketing mix in turn, that is:

* the products and services that it offers

* the pricing strategies it uses

* the distribution channels it uses

* the promotions it undertakes.

Explain how these elements are mixed together to help the company achieve its objectives.

Prepare an oral presentation with visual aids, of your findings.

10.3 The promotion mix

In this section of the unit you are going to learn the key terms associated with promotion. We will examine different promotional techniques and evaluate where they are most effective and appropriate. You will also learn how to evaluate promotional materials and campaigns and how to put together a promotional plan.

Key terms

Promotion – Dibb, Simkin, Pride and Ferrell offer us this definition of promotion, 'The role of promotion in a company is to communicate with individuals, groups or organisations with the aim of directly or indirectly facilitating exchanges by informing and persuading one or more of the audiences to accept the firm's products.'

Source: *Marketing: Concepts and Strategies* 3rd edition 1997 Houghton Mifflin

Promotional campaign – all the promotional activities relating to a particular theme which help to achieve a marketing objective.

Marketing communications

We see that the role is 'communication' and this branch of marketing is often described as 'marketing communications'. The individuals, groups or organisations at whom the promotion is targeted are known as the 'target audience'.

The role of marketing communications is neatly summarised by Tourism Ireland:

> *'The function of the Marketing Communications Department is to manage the development, implementation and evaluation of the Tourism Brand Ireland communications programme to world class standards in order to promote the Island of Ireland as a tourist destination overseas.*
>
> *With a dedicated Head Office team located in Dublin, it manages brand communications. Brand Communications includes advertising, publicity, e-marketing, brand management/merchandising and photography.*
>
> *Collectively the department's role is to ensure that Tourism Brand Ireland is communicated in a consistent and compelling manner around the world.'*

Source: www.tourismireland.com

Communication Channels

The means of transmitting information from an organisation to its customers is known as a communication channel. Communication channels include the media but also other channels such as direct mail and press releases.

Media

The Media refers to anywhere that advertising can be placed. This includes print media such as newspapers and magazines, cinema and television.

Promotional techniques

These are all the methods used to communicate messages to the customer; they include advertising, brochures, displays, direct marketing, public relations, sponsorship, sales promotions and personal selling. We will examine each of these techniques in detail and consider some examples of their use in travel and tourism.

The aim of promotional activities is to take the consumer through four key stages that lead to the adoption of a product, service or even an idea.

The stages are known as AIDA:

* **Attention** – the promotion is such that it attracts the attention of the customer or recipient

* **Interest** – having spotted the promotion, the customer is sufficiently interested to want to know more

* **Desire** – I want it! The information about the product has stimulated the customer's desire for the product. They want to buy it or go there.

* **Action** – the final stage, the actual purchase.

Promotional materials

This term refers to the artwork, posters, mailshots and literature that are used as part of a promotion. Some examples are given in this section of the unit and you will have the opportunity to research your own examples.

Purpose of promotion

The definition given by Dibb et alia (page 152) suggests that the purpose of promotion is to inform or persuade. This is often the intention of a promotional campaign but remember that promotion is being used with the other elements of the mix to help the organisation achieve its marketing objectives.

The purpose may be:

* to inform the public about a new product or service
* to inform the public about a change to the product or company
* to increase sales
* to increase market share
* to give reassurance to existing customers
* to respond to competitors' promotions
* to remind consumers that the company is there
* to re-inforce corporate image.

There are a number of promotional techniques that can be used by a company.

Advertising

The Advertising Association describes advertising as 'messages paid for by those who send them, intended to inform or influence people who receive them'.

Advertising is paid for and is placed in the media. The media is the collective term for television, newspapers, radio, magazines, directories, outdoor sites and transport. It also includes the Internet although this still tends to be described as 'new media'. New media also includes new forms of advertising such as text messaging. Advertising expenditure in the United Kingdom rose by 5.6% to £18.4 billion in 2004 (before allowing for inflation). (Advertising Association figures)

Television

There are two organisations responsible for television broadcasting in the UK. One is the British Broadcasting Corporation (BBC) which does not carry advertising and is funded by payment of a licence fee. The second is Ofcom. Ofcom is the regulator for all UK communications industries not just television. It also covers

TABLE 10.1 *Total advertising expenditure by media sector at current prices.*

	1995	1996	1997	1998	1999	2000	2001	2002	2003	2004
National Newspapers	1433	1510	1650	1824	1991	2252	2062	1930	1902	1973
Regional Newspapers	1963	2061	2238	2390	2483	2762	2834	2878	2962	3132
Consumer Magazines	533	583	660	709	727	750	779	785	784	819
Business and Professionals	897	1018	1106	1209	1195	1270	1202	1088	1048	1082
Directories	639	692	737	780	831	868	959	990	1029	1075
Press Production Costs	514	550	577	620	650	702	669	643	634	660
TOTAL PRESS	5679	6413	6967	7531	7877	8604	8504	8314	8359	8741
Television	3136	3379	3704	4029	4321	4646	4147	4349	4499	4740
Direct Mail	1135	1404	1635	1666	1876	2049	2228	2378	2467	2469
Outdoor & Transport	411	466	545	613	649	810	788	816	914	986
Radio	296	344	393	460	516	595	541	547	584	604
Cinema	69	73	88	97	123	128	164	180	180	192
Internet	–	–	8	19	51	155	166	197	408	653
TOTAL	11026	12080	13340	14415	15412	16988	16537	16780	17411	18385

Source: The Advertising Association, World Advertising Research Center (www.warc.com)

radio, telecommunications and wireless communications.

Ofcom's mission statement is:

'Ofcom exists to further the interests of citizen-consumers through a regulatory regime which, where appropriate, encourages competition.'

Ofcom publishes codes about what is and is not allowed on television advertising. Here are a few examples:

✱ Only seven minutes per hour of advertising is allowed (on some channels 12 minutes are allowed)

✱ It must be evident what is a programme and what is an advertisement so there must be obvious breaks in between

✱ Some programmes must not be interrupted by advertising, for example religious programmes or Royal ceremonies.

Source: Ofcom

The codes are very detailed but you can find out more about them and the role of Ofcom by visiting the Ofcom website.

Advertisers wishing to choose television have dozens of commercial channels to choose from with the advent of cable and satellite services. Advertising is sold in 'spots'. One spot is usually 30 seconds. There is no fixed rate for a spot as the price varies according to time of day – peak time is 5.30-10.30pm when most people are watching. This is the most expensive time but premium rates will be charged if a particularly popular programme, such as an important football match, is being shown. Advertisers buy a package of spots. If you watch television for any length of time you will note that the same advertisements are repeated often. This is to ensure that the message reaches as many people as possible. The number of people viewing an advertisement is called the 'reach'. The final episode of Friends was broadcast in May 2004 in the US. It attracted over 50 million viewers and advertisers paid over £1 million for 30-second spots. All the spots were sold by January 2004.

The advantages of television advertising are:

✱ it reaches a mass audience

✱ it is possible to target a region

✱ it has movement, colour and sound

✱ it can demonstrate a product or a place (holidays).

It is, however, very expensive. Not only are spots expensive but there are also production costs to cover.

Think it over…

Find some examples of current travel and tourism television campaigns. They are most prolific just after Christmas. Why do you think this is?

Local and National press

This includes newspapers and magazines. National Readership Survey Ltd is a non-profit making body who provides estimates of the number and type of people who read Britain's newspapers and magazines. The survey covers about 250 publications. The reader profiles are broken down into age, sex, regionality, and other demographic and lifestyle characteristics. Publishers of press media use these profiles to sell advertising space and advertisers use them to target the correct audience through appropriate media.

National newspapers

The UK has 12 daily newspapers and 11 Sunday newspapers. The Sun has the biggest circulation of all the national dailies and the News of the World is the most popular Sunday newspaper. Between them they attracted advertising spend of £1973 million in 2004 (Source: Advertising Association).

Advertising is sold by the page, half page or column. Prices vary according to the position of the advert. The front and back pages are most expensive, as they are most prominent. The newspapers with the highest circulation command the highest rates; therefore The Sun is the most expensive. The advantages of national newspaper advertising are:

✱ most people in the UK read a newspaper

✱ very precise profiling possible

✱ very flexible as there is only a short time from placing the advert to publication

* can have colour

* can tie in with topical events.

Theory into practice

Find out the latest circulation figures for Britain's newspapers. You can do this by looking at a newspaper's website, looking at the National Readership Survey website or by studying a publication called BRAD in your library. Draw up a bar chart comparing the figures.

Regional newspapers

There are hundreds of regional newspapers, some of which are free. Some are very highly regarded such as the London Evening Standard and the Yorkshire Post. Circulations vary and some are very small but for a company that wants to advertise its services in a particular locality, they are useful and inexpensive. Regional newspapers attracted a spend of £3132 million in 2004, even greater than the national newspapers (Source: Advertising Association). Much of this spend goes on classified advertising which is more likely to be read in a regional paper than in a national.

Radio

As with television, it is the commercial sector that carries advertising. BBC radio stations are funded by the same licence fee as television. There are many, local commercial stations and you should note who they are in your locality. There are also some national radio stations, for example, Virgin Radio. You can find out about the radio stations by visiting the Radio Advertising Bureau website. This is an independent body that gives information on advertising issues to industry members but also to the public. Spots are sold on radio in the same way as on television, with peak times attracting greater revenue. In 2003/2004 commercial radio advertising revenue was £611.6 million in the UK, according to the RAB. Radio advertising is becoming more popular. One of the reasons is the advent of digital radio which allows greater targeting. Advertisers who wish to reach 15–24 year olds often use radio as they represent a large part of radio audiences, with RAB reporting a 20% growth in listening hours for this group since 1999.

The advantages of radio advertising are:

* it can be used in a national or regional campaign

* it is a cost effective medium

* it can be used alongside a television campaign to increase awareness

* radio audiences are growing

* digital radio allows better targeting

* production costs are less than television.

Audience research for radio – including the BBC – is carried out by Radio Joint Audience Research (Rajar). Ofcom is the regulatory body.

Cinema

As with any media, marketers look at the audience profile before deciding on a medium for a campaign. For cinema, Cinema and Video Audience Research (CAVIAR) provide this information. Advertisers aiming to reach 15–24 year olds may well choose cinema advertising as cinema going is the number one leisure activity for this group. Overall, 86% of the population say they go to the cinema. However, the current annual average is only three visits per person. There is also a seasonal pattern to cinema going. The busiest months are August, October and December, all school holiday periods. Total advertising spend on cinema in 2004 was £180 million, according to the Advertising Association, much less than any other form of media. The advantages of cinema advertising are:

* the audience is seated and highly receptive

* it can be targeted regionally

* it is good for reaching 15–24 year olds

* still advertisements are cheap to produce for small local businesses.

However, production costs of full advertisements are high and your advertisement will not have the same reach as television.

Magazines

There are different categories of magazines. These are:

* consumer magazines

* business and professional journals.

There are over 3000 titles of consumer magazines in the UK so the advertiser can be very precise about target audience. One of the biggest sellers is the Radio Times which has a circulation of over one million whereas some hobby magazines only sell a few thousand copies.

There are several travel magazines aimed at consumers and many aimed at buyers or owners of property abroad. These can be useful media for transport companies. Women's magazines are also an important category of consumer magazines.

Business and professional publications are aimed at people within particular industries. There are two important ones for travel and tourism with which you should be familiar. These are Travel Weekly and Travel and Tourism Gazette.

The advantages of magazine advertising are:

* precise targeting

* colourful, glossy adverts

* can use 'inserts' and target regionally.

A disadvantage of magazine advertising is that the copy must be ready to go to press quite a while before publication, so it is not as flexible as newspaper advertising. It is not suitable for last minute discounted offers, which are popular in the tourism market.

An advertorial is a promotion that is written in the style of a feature. It looks like editorial pages but is promoting a company or a product. Readers will probably assume that it is a feature unless they look closely at the small print which will state 'advertising feature'.

Internet Advertising

In 2004 advertising on the web overtook radio advertising for the first time. The value of website advertising rose to £653.3 million according to the Interactive advertising bureau. Figure 10.3 shows the types of advertising available on the Internet.

Display advertising could include paying for pop-ups on a website or banner advertising. Advertisers choose sites which they think their potential customers will visit. Paid-for search listings are those that pop up on the right when you 'google'.

The digital media mix

% share of revenues for
Jan to June 2005

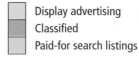
Display advertising
Classified
Paid-for search listings

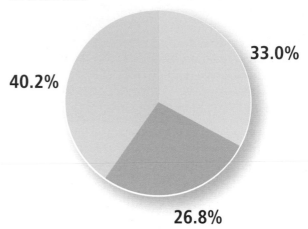

33.0%

40.2%

26.8%

Half year total - £490.8 Million

Source: The Internet Advertising Bureau

FIGURE 10.3 *The digital media mix.*

Theory into practice

Try googling for 'holidays in Ibiza'. You should get about two million hits. You will also see a list of 'sponsored links'. These are paid for and they are the reason you get to google for free.

Think it over...

What kind of travel and tourism companies are likely to use pop-ups and banner advertising on the Internet? Try surfing some well known travel booking sites like Expedia and lastminute.com and see what you find.

Billboards and posters

These are placed all over the country in strategic sites, usually on roadsides. Companies which specialise in outdoor advertising sell the space to advertisers. Advertisements can also be placed on taxis, buses, in the tube and at bus stops. Large colourful posters are excellent for the travel and tourism industry, reminding commuters that they can get away to sunnier places.

Point of sale

Point of sale refers to sales promotion literature or posters literally used at the point of sale. The most common use of this material in travel and tourism is in travel agents where you will find many poster, leaflets and special offers.

Holiday brochures

These are essential promotional tools for tour operators. They are costly to produce but provide a showcase for the company's products and services. Getting the brochure out on time is important as if it is not available when the booking of main holidays starts sales are lost. This means that the information in the brochure has to be collated and prices fixed a long time before the actual season. This can cause major headaches for tour operators and may lead to extensive discounting during the season.

Brochures are costly, each brochure will cost between 75p and £1.20 to produce, taking up a large chunk of the marketing budget. First Choice estimated that 25% of their marketing spend went on brochures. Many of the brochures never reach a customer. As second and third editions appear travel agents have to bin the old ones. One agent reported spending £500 on binning them. This amounted to more than three skips of brochures.

Travel agents also devote a lot of valuable storage to brochures.

E-brochures

The advantages of e-brochures are that they do not waste paper, money or space. They also can be more precisely targeted as a travel agent or other intermediary will download information that is of interest to a specific customer. However, holidaymakers like collecting piles of brochures and browsing through them at home and this is not possible with e-brochures.

Key term

E-brochure – an electronic version of tour operator information of the type that traditionally appears in print.

Displays

Point of sale material is used in displays. You will see displays in travel agents and also at exhibitions. Travel agents, windows are traditionally covered in posters and cards showing available deals. However, recent research has suggested that customers find such displays messy and unappealing.

CASE STUDY

Celebrity's first-class delivery

Cruise line employs butlers to deliver its new brochures. Robin Searle reports

Agents often gripe about bundles of brochures being dumped on their doorsteps before finding their way to a pile in a storeroom.

So one cruise company has decided to make sure its new programme doesn't suffer the same fate – by sending its ship's butlers to hand-deliver the information to its top 300 trade partners.

Celebrity Cruises' butlers will be accompanied by chefs and masseurs who will cook meals and provide treatments for agents as they talk them through the line's new programmes on August 1.

Source: www.ttglive.com July 15th 2005

1. **How effective do you think this promotion was? Consider it in terms of AIDA.**
2. **Is it a one off or could it be repeated?**

Extension task: Come up with an idea of your own for getting a travel agent's attention to a brochure. Explain and evaluate your idea in detail, including materials to be used and target audience.

Uncluttered Displays

This week Thomson announced an overhaul of its window displays to make them less cluttered. It wants potential customers to be able to see what is going on inside a shop, rather than be confronted by a wall of cards and bargain-basement promotional posters. Thomson research found that only 14% of passers-by looked in travel agency windows, and that those who did stop only spent three to 17 seconds considering the window information.

Thomson retail and commercial director Derek Jones said: "One comment that kept coming up in our research was: 'All travel agent windows are the same', which is fairly damning for a market that is highly competitive.

"Travel agents have lost sight of what shop windows should communicate. Windows are still a great way to create urgency and drive demand through tactics like

The old face of Thomas Cook

handwritten late deals, but travel agency windows look outdated on the modern high street."

Thomson shop windows will now have "linear designs, inspirational images and a more modern look".

The company wants "to create a clearer customer communication strategy, drive customer interest and footfall while also refreshing the public's perception of high street travel agents.

"These new designs will make us stand out from the crowd of other travel agents and spur customers to enter our shops, where the agents will then have an opportunity to influence them," added Jones.

"Staff spend a significant amount of time installing and creating window displays. We'd like to give them the opportunity to revert to doing what they do best – meeting customers and selling holidays."

Late deals will be grouped by category – such as sun, ski or cruise – so customers can easily find offers relevant to them. The range of products will be visually expressed to avoid mixed messages.

Source: www.ttglive.com 'Agencies show new high street fashion sense' 29th July 2005

1. Visit a branch of Thomson and analyse the effectiveness of the display. Consider:
   * AIDA
   * Whether the window expresses the 'clear communication strategy' outlined in the article

* Your own opinion.

Write a brief article for the Travel Trade Gazette reporting on the display.

Theory into practice

Design your own travel agency window and produce a poster of your design which can be displayed in your classroom.

Direct marketing

Direct mail

Direct mail is a form of direct marketing, where advertising comes directly, in the post, personally addressed. Advertisers call these 'mail shots'.

They are also referred to as junk mail – but by consumers not advertisers. This is because we receive a lot – 5438 million items in 2003 – and throw a lot of it away. The response rate is about 11% but it is still a popular promotional tool in travel and tourism. (Source of figs: Direct Mail Information Service)

Direct response

This form of direct marketing does not depend on the mail, it can be used in all the same media as advertising but a response is solicited. The reader might be invited to send for a brochure or send an email asking for information. The value of direct marketing is that it is easier to monitor than advertising. You are able to measure the response rate and with every response you gather more customer information.

Telemarketing

This is similar to direct mail except the telephone is used. Cold calling, that is making unsolicited calls, is very unpopular with consumers and is not often used in travel and tourism. However telemarketing is important in selling holidays and travel to callers who are responding to advertising or other forms of promotion and there are many call centres in travel and tourism businesses.

Public relations

This is a major part of the promotional mix and very important to those travel and tourism companies who have small marketing budgets. This is because public relations activities are much cheaper than other forms of promotion. Public relations may be carried out in-house or contracted out to a specialist PR agency.

The responsibilities of the public relations department may include the following:

* generating press releases
* media liaison
* organising events
* organising exhibitions
* publication of newsletters
* organising receptions
* community relations
* corporate communications.

Press releases

Press releases are used to plant favourable reports about a company in the media or to inform them about a new product. They are extremely cheap to produce and can result in lots of free publicity. A good press release should have the following features:

* It should be targeted at the right audience, via appropriate media.
* It should be presented in such a way that it can be inserted into a news page or feature with little alteration – this saves work for the receiving editor.
* There should be an attention grabbing headline.
* The press release should be dated and show the corporate logo and address.
* If an event is being publicised, the venue, date and time must be given.
* A photo can be included.
* Contact details for further information must be given.

Theory into practice

Your group is to hold a careers exhibition. Produce a press release giving the following information:

* It is to be held at your school or college.
* Make sure you include the date of the event.
* Many travel and tourism employers will be represented – you can name some if you like.
* The employers will be exhibiting careers information and giving talks.
* You will be the contact for further information.
* Give a quote from a student or employer to add interest to your press release.
* You can add a photo if you like.

Sponsorship

Advertisers are keen to be associated with events or celebrities who will help sell their products.

Advertisers may sponsor rock tours or sports events.

Television programmes can be sponsored. Sponsors pay to be associated with a programme and their logo and product shots appear at the beginning, end and at either side of a commercial break.

Sales promotion

Sales promotion includes all those activities which aim to bring about an early or extra purchase of a product, and they are found extensively in the travel and tourism industry. A sales promotion is very useful for boosting sales in the short term but will only run for a few weeks, otherwise the impact is lost.

Examples of sales promotion are:

* money off coupons
* competitions
* buy one, get one free
* discounts
* free gifts
* special offers
* loyalty schemes.

Most hotel chains offer incentives such as free nights to regular guests through loyalty schemes. Airlines also operate loyalty schemes, the most famous of which is the Airmiles scheme. This has even been extended to some shops.

Trade promotions are very common in travel and tourism where call centre and travel agents receive financial or other incentives on sales.

Personal selling methods, such as face-to-face, telesales and cold calling can all be used as part of a promotional drive.

Devising a promotional plan

A promotional plan forms part of a promotional campaign. It is the detailed schedule of promotional activities that are to be undertaken, where and when they are to be undertaken and the cost.

If this is carried out by an expert, for example by an advertising agency, then the expert is known as a media planner. A media planner has a detailed knowledge of all the different media and their costs and places the bookings to secure advertisements in the media. He or she is not responsible for actually creating the promotional materials.

A good promotional plan will give:

* **Coverage** – that is it will reach a good proportion of the target market.
* **Frequency** – this means there will be opportunities for the message to be repeated throughout the campaign.
* **Good value** for the given budget.

Budget

Promotional budgets can run into millions. It is easy to see why when you consider that a 30 second spot on national television can cost as much as £25,000. Companies can only spend what they can afford and it is possible to have a good campaign on a very tight budget by using regional media or by devoting the budget to cheaper public relations activities. A company will use past experience to set budgets for new campaigns and may set a budget as a percentage of estimated sales to be derived from the campaign.

Timing

The right time is when the purchaser is at the stage of deciding what to buy. Holiday companies traditionally start their major campaigns just after Christmas. Once the festivities are over, people start to think about their holidays.

Theatres send out programme guides at the beginning of each season so that people can book ahead and plan their theatre trips. Timing is not just about the right time of year, marketers must also consider what day and what time to place advertisements. These decisions will be constrained by their budget.

Target audience

The entire budget is wasted if the promotional campaign does not reach its intended audience. Usually the advertiser wishes to reach a particular group of people and will choose a medium where the profile of the audience matches the profile of their intended customer. All media publish profiles of their audience, that is, their gender, age group and socio-economic group. These profiles help advertisers to select appropriate media. There are several companies who carry out 'audience research' to produce these profiles. One example is the National Readership Survey which tells us who reads which

Evaluating promotional campaigns

Points to consider include:

* Does the campaign reach the target market?
* Has an appropriate media been used?

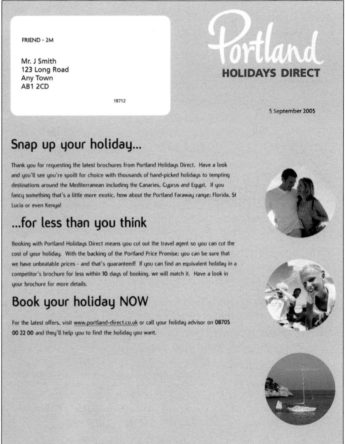

Portland mailshot

* Does the campaign meet the company objectives?
* What is the purpose of each individual promotional activity in the campaign?
* Are the promotional materials effective?
  * Use of colour.
  * Company logo and strapline included.
  * Contact details.
* Presentation.
* Clarity of message.

Theory into practice

Choose a current promotional campaign for a travel and tourism company. You can choose a trade or consumer campaign.

Collect materials from the campaign or make detailed notes on the campaign materials and media schedules.

Evaluate the campaign using the criteria given on pages 161/162.

Write a report on your findings suggesting recommendations for improvements.

CASE STUDY

Center Parcs

Center Parcs' target market is ABC1 families with young children, young professionals and empty nesters. The Center Parcs Marketing Department's main aim is to identify and satisfy guests' needs and demands for their short break holiday. Guest questionnaires are provided in each villa to provide valuable feedback on our total product offering. It allows us to assess the success of Village operations and consequently plan developments and marketing activities at each Village with an integrated approach to enhance the Center Parcs brand.

The Center Parcs experience is marketed via an annual brochure and primarily television advertising, with supporting information on teletext. The television campaign is timed to support the brochure mailing in September with a heavy emphasis in January, a key period for planning holidays. The company has its own in-house Reservations department which deals with both bookings and brochure requests. The computerised system can handle up to 5000 calls per day.

Direct Marketing is becoming increasingly important to Center Parcs as more and more of our guests are repeat visitors. Communication with our guests takes many forms, e.g. booking incentives during off-peak periods; informing guests of Village improvements; and encouraging repeat bookings.

The Company's database provides a foundation for all strategic mailing activities.

Source: Center Parcs Ltd

Produce a promotional plan for Center Parcs covering a six week period following Christmas. You are to include:

* television advertising
* newspaper advertising
* direct mail.

Include details of media to be used and costs. Give reasons for your choice of media and evidence that you have researched the costs.

CASE STUDY

The Kuoni UK brand has always been about offering inspirational travel experiences and personalised holidays whilst appealing to many different segments of customers. 'Dream holiday, think Kuoni', the instantly recognisable Kuoni globe and the strapline 'World of Difference', all represent the attributes that are associated with the brand's equity and attention to detail.

Kuoni uses a number of different media to market their products and marketing efforts are split into targeting both the consumer and trade. Typical marketing activities include newspapers, magazines, radio and direct mail (the latter using the company's specialised database).

The extract gives details of Kuoni's promotional activities to both the trade and the consumer.

CONSUMER	TRADE
* Kuoni Traveller – monthly email newsletter	* Advertising in the trade press, e.g. Travel Weekly, Travel Trade Gazette. Kuoni News – full page in Travel Weekly appears each week and updates agents on the latest product news from Kuoni
* Classified and display adverts in national newspapers	* Overseas agent educationals and seminars
* Direct Mail – customer loyalty magazine, 16 page newsletter, bespoke items	* UK regional training days
* Competitions/promotions	* Brochure Launch Roadshow
* Adverts in consumer magazines	* Travel agents' website
* Window displays in the two Kuoni retail shops	

Source: www.kuoni.co.uk (student pack)

Consumer promotions
1. Visit Kuoni's website – Who would you expect to be targeted by the email newsletter?
2. Which magazines would be appropriate for Kuoni advertisements and why?
3. Find an example of a classified or display advertisement for Kuoni in a national newspaper. Discuss the effectiveness of the advertisement including choice of media.
4. Suggest a competition that could be used to promote Kuoni.

Trade promotions
1. Who are regional training days and educationals aimed at?
2. What is the purpose of an educational?
3. Find an example of a trade advertisement for Kuoni. Comment on the effectiveness of the advertisement including choice of media. Contrast the advertisement with the consumer advertisement you found earlier.

Knowledge check

1. Give three examples of personal selling in travel and tourism.

2. What is meant by telemarketing?

3. Why do sales people need product knowledge?

4. What is meant by 'overcoming objections'?

5. Explain the difference between strategic and operational objectives.

6. What is market segmentation?

7. Give the advantages and disadvantages of conducting an interview by telephone.

8. What is meant by consumer research?

9. What is the difference between primary and secondary research?

10. What is the difference between quantitative and qualitative research?

11. What is the marketing mix?

12. What is an intangible product?

13. What happens to promotion at different stages of the product life cycle?

14. Explain promotional pricing.

15. What is meant by Marketing Communications?

16. Give three examples of the purpose of promotion.

17. What is an e-brochure?

18. Explain AIDA.

19. What are the features of a good press release?

20. What is a media schedule?

Special interest holidays

Unit 11

This unit covers the following sections:

11.1 The range, geographical distribution, features and providers of special interest holidays

11.2 Itineraries for special interest holidays

11.3 Appeal and popularity of special interest holidays

11.4 Factors that influence the popularity of special interest holidays

Introduction

In this unit you will learn about different types of special interest holidays and where they take place worldwide. You will look at the features of special interest holidays, the features of the destinations where they occur and also you will get to know about the tour operators who supply special interest holidays. You will assess the factors affecting the popularity of these types of holidays with tourists and recommend suitable special interest holidays for given tourists. You will also learn how to put together an itinerary.

How you will be assessed

This unit is internally assessed by your tutor and externally moderated by Edexcel. A variety of activities and case studies is provided in this unit to help you understand all aspects of special interest holidays and to help you prepare for the assessment.

Your assessment evidence must show that you have:

* completed maps showing the geographical distribution of different types of special interest holidays

* given a description and explanation of the geographical distribution and providers of a range of special interest holidays

* produced an itinerary for a special interest holiday based at one destination and an explanation of how the itinerary meets the needs of tourists as provided to you by your tutor in the form of a pen portrait

* produced a comparison of features, tourist types and popularity of two different types of special interest holidays; one involving a tour and one based at one destination

* produced an assessment of the factors influencing the popularity of two types of special interest holidays; one involving a tour and one based at one destination.

11.1 The range, geographical distribution, features and providers of special interest holidays

In this part of the unit we will examine the different types of special interest holiday. You will find out where these holidays take place geographically and their key features and providers. You will have the opportunity to practise some map work so that you are able to locate the destinations for special interest holidays.

What is a special interest holiday?

There is no one accepted definition of a special interest holiday in the travel and tourism industry but in general terms it is a holiday taken for the purpose of following a particular hobby or participating in a particular activity. These types of holidays differ greatly from the mass market package holidays of the 1980s and 1990s as they allow for individual tastes and choice and reflect the growing demand from people to have holidays tailor made for their needs rather than accepting a 'one size fits all' product. The range of special interest holidays is immense from cultural holidays to cookery to trekking through mountains. The trend is up for special interest holidays as people are now more confident about travelling abroad and looking for something other than sun and sand holidays. Also many people have the means to take more than one holiday and therefore may take a special interest break in addition to their traditional holiday. The market research organisation, Mintel, has carried out research into activity holidays and found that over 16 million activity holidays were taken in 2005. There are no figures available specifically for special interest as the term covers such a wide range of activities but the overall market is greater than just the activity sector.

In this unit we will examine the range of special interest holidays and study some specific examples. First we will look at holidays which take place in one specific destination.

> **Key term**
>
> *Special interest holiday* – A holiday that is undertaken with the purpose of participating in a specific hobby or activity.

Cultural holidays

Cultural and heritage holidays are often linked together as they appeal to similar groups of people. People who take a cultural holiday are likely to be visiting museums and galleries or going to music festivals or opera. For this reason city breaks are often taken with the purpose of discovering the culture of a particular city. Cultural holidays take place not just in cities throughout the world, but also in trips to follow the Inca trail in South America, to Egypt to visit the pyramids and similar trips. These could also be designated cultural holidays. Pop culture is important to many people and pop and rock festivals take place throughout the summer. There are many in the UK which can be accessed by road or by public transport.

In 1990 the European Commission designated cultural tourism as a key area of tourism development in Europe. In 2008 Liverpool will be the European Capital of Culture and will have an opportunity to attract tourists both domestically and internationally. It is expected that being designated capital of culture will bring millions of pounds in investment, new jobs and many tourists. The idea of European Capital of Culture started in 1985 with the purpose of bringing European citizens closer together. It was then known as European City of Culture. Many cities have had capital of culture status, including Dublin, Glasgow and Prague.

Find out the names of all the cities which have enjoyed European City or Capital of Culture status. Locate them all on a map of Europe and label them. Choose one city to research. Find out what particular cultural features attract tourists in that city. Evaluate how the city has benefited from being designated Capital of Culture.

Search tip: www.culture.gov

These pop concerts in the U.K are all accessible by road and rail.

T in the park - Scotland's 'Glastonbury', held at Balado near Kinross

V Festival - also in August headlines big name bands such as Oasis and The Scissor Sisters. Has two sites, Chelmsford and Western Park Staffordshire.

Green Man Festival Hay-on-Wye - held in August, has folk, indy, electronic and acoustic music.

Glastonbury - the biggest and the most famous of them all - started in 1970, it runs over 3 days in June

Reading and Leeds are run by the same company, Mean Fiddler, and headline the same bands who go from one concert to the other.

Live 8 Hyde park - a one off in 2005 to attract attention to AIDS issues in Africa.

Get loaded in the park - Clapham Common in London - August bank holiday in 2005 had the Happy Mondays, Fat Boy Slim, The Farm, Stereo MCs and DJ sets from Van Helden and Guilty Pleasures.

Bestival Isle of Wight - Newport winds up the festival season in September - more difficult to access as involves a sea crossing.

FIGURE 11.1 *Accessible UK pop concerts.*

CASE STUDY

The Leeds/Reading August Bank Holiday Music Festival is one of the best organised amongst the array of 'highly commercial now' UK music festivals. Bramham Park, the location for the Leeds Music Festival is part of the success. It's spacious, with campsites spread out so you don't feel like cattle herded into a cramped field! Last time I went they even had showers on the campsites, a festival luxury! Other facilities on this ideal site off the A64 eastbound include a choice of bars, cash points, first aid and paramedics, food and other stalls including funky and cheap clothing and herbs and natural high tents, general information tents, left luggage, a meeting point, market stalls, various merchandise, showers, and a Welfare Tent. Another bonus at the Leeds Music Festival is that under 13 (12 and under) are admitted free but they must be accompanied by a ticket holding adult. The Leeds Music Festival always has a good family feel about it, with plenty going on for kids!

Source: www.iknow-yorkshire.co.uk © 2005

Sam, Francesca and Parminder want to go to the Leeds festival at the next August bank Holiday. They are 18 years old and have just finished their A levels. Parminder is not allowed to camp so the girls are going to look for a bed and breakfast in the area of the festival. They live in Manchester and will take the train from Manchester to Leeds and then take the festival bus. You are going to help them plan their visit to the festival by:

* providing information about band line-up at the festival
* finding a suitable bed and breakfast
* giving them information on train times and on transport to the festival

When you have prepared all this information, evaluate what you have done and explain how it meets the needs of the group of girls.

Religious holidays

Religious holidays focus on visits to places of religious and historical significance, for example a 'Holy Land Tour' or a visit to Lourdes in the south of France. There are often opportunities for people to pray or reflect whilst on holiday so they are suitable for people who wish to have a quiet break and possibly reflect on their own particular cause. There are specialist companies which arrange such holidays. For example The Pilgrimage Trust, a registered charity which arranges Pilgrimage Holidays to Lourdes for children and adults with disabilities and Tours for Churches, a specialist tour operator.

Theory into practice

Do you know where the 'Holy Land' is located? Make sure you know where it is and can locate it on a map. Can you think of any problems in travelling to the Holy Land? Find out about other places that are visited for religious holidays and mark them on a world map. Make a few notes about each one explaining the main features.

Heritage

Heritage tourism includes tourism activities such as visits to sites of historical importance, scenic landscapes, natural areas and locations where historic events occurred. Tourists are interested in heritage so that they can learn about the culture and past of a country or region in an enjoyable way. Heritage includes the natural as well as the built environment, such as monuments and ruins.

The Ancient Monuments and Archaeological Areas Act of 1979 gives protection to nationally important archaeological sites as Scheduled Ancient Monuments. There are about 19,000 entries listed. The list includes sites such as prehistoric standing stones, Roman forts, medieval villages and wartime pill boxes.

Many of our heritage attractions are given special status to protect them from development or too many visitors. This could be the status of a national park, an area of outstanding

Beachy Head in Sussex

natural beauty or heritage coast. Thirty-two per cent of English coastline is designated heritage coast. This means the coast is protected to conserve its natural beauty. If possible, access for visitors is improved. One of the most famous coasts and the first to be designated is Beachy Head in Sussex.

Theory into practice

The map below shows the designated national parks in England, Wales and Scotland. Choose one of the national parks and carry out some research to find out the features of the national park which make it suitable for special interest holidays such as walking. Consider the following:

* climate

* landscape

* transport routes and accessibility

* accommodation

* local services

* activities and facilities.

Produce an information sheet with your findings.

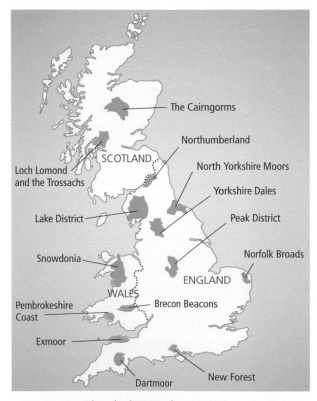

FIGURE 11.2 *The designated national parks in England, Wales and Scotland*

Sporting holidays

People may go on holiday to actively participate in their favourite sport or they may go on holiday to watch a sport. Examples of participation include diving and golfing; both of these are particularly popular. Spectator sports include cricket, rugby and football. Specialist operators have developed, offering packages for all of these.

Some companies arrange participative tours for all types of sports, for example:

> Burleigh Travel specialises in arranging group sports tours and producing tailor-made itineraries to suit the specific requirements of our clients. We offer tours to all the main sporting destinations for all the major team sports including Rugby, Hockey, Football, Netball and Cricket. Our team have in depth knowledge and experience of these sports from a participation and touring perspective and they are waiting to assist you in arranging a memorable tour for your school, university or club.
>
> Source: Burleigh Travel

Some tour operators specialise in arranging holidays for spectators to watch their favourite sports. You are able to book a package with the usual travel and accommodation but you will also get tickets to watch the sport. You might choose from one of the following:

* a rugby 6 nations weekend

* a cricket test match in Barbados

* a city break in Barcelona or Madrid including tickets to a football match

* a weekend in Monaco to watch the Grand Prix motor racing.

Specialist activity holidays

These are a growing market sector as tourists look for holidays where they can indulge in a hobby or learn a new skill. The range is varied with holidays available to learn languages, do painting or cooking or learn how to dance.

Most activity holidays are provided by small companies who specialise in particular activities, particularly in the UK market. However, many large tour operators have acquired specialist tour operators in order to gain representation in a growing market for activity holidays, particularly overseas holidays.

CASE STUDY
Scuba Diving

There are several specialist diving tour operators catering for the niche diving market. I love to dive operates holidays in Lanzarote but the best known operator in the UK is Regaldive (www.regal-diving. co.uk) owned by Holidaybreak.There are an increasing number of divers who will take at least two dive holidays per year. The main destination for UK divers is the Red Sea but market growth is in long-haul holidays, as divers are looking worldwide for more adventurous trips.

It is estimated that there are about 200,000 divers in the UK of whom about 80,000 take regular diving holidays. UK divers used to dive mainly in the Mediterranean but cheaper travel and wider availability of facilities means that they can travel further and experience warmer waters and a better climate even in winter. Popular locations include:

* Fiji
* The Great Barrier Reef
* Caymans
* Cancun
* Cozumel
* US Virgin Islands

* Bahamas
* Red Sea
* Hawaii
* Jamaica
* Thailand
* Maldives
* Dubai, where artificial reefs have been built.

Divers like to experience coral reefs, marine life, shipwrecks and caves on dives – to make life interesting.

1. Locate and label all the diving destinations mentioned on a world map.
2. Research one specialist dive tour operator and summarise the range of destinations they offer. Choose one holiday that would be suitable for a newly qualified diver and describe the features of the holiday. Explain why it is suitable for a novice.

Extension task: Interview someone who goes on diving holidays. Find out what features they are looking for in a destination, whether they book packages or go independently. Ask how often they take diving holidays and where. Produce a display or information sheet of your findings.

An activity holiday which is of particular interest to younger people is a clubbing holiday. Ibiza was the first destination to become famous for its clubbing scene and it still retains its reputation with clubs like Amnesia, Eden, Pacha and Privilege. In recent years the clubbing scene has also moved to other destinations like Ayia Napa, Falaraki, Malia and Magaluf. Research from Mintel reported that three per cent of over 18s go clubbing every night on holiday. Younger clubbers are particularly influenced by price so Greek resorts have become popular with clubbers as they are good value for money.

Use the Internet or brochures to find suitable holidays for the following people.

✳ Melanie James is determined to learn salsa dancing. She saw Ricky Martin in concert last year and thinks if she knows how to salsa she might get to know him. She wants to combine learning to dance with a holiday in the sun and she has a few hundred pounds in savings which she is prepared to spend. She is willing to travel alone as long as she is meeting up with a group of like minded people. She can take her holiday at any time of year.

✳ Jonah longs to paint. He is a frustrated artist. His wife and children have booked a weekend at Center Parcs without him and so he thinks he might look for a short break where he can paint in beautiful countryside. He hasn't got a lot of money to spare – a couple of hundred pounds at the most and he must be able to drive to his holiday from London.

✳ Martine is an excellent cook. She loves to cook! She wants to spend her holiday learning some advanced type of cooking but she is not sure what yet. Find her a suitable holiday in the UK for up to five days. She will go alone and can drive or go by train.

For each, describe the holiday you have chosen and explain its features and why they meet the customer's needs. Present the holiday to your customer (played by a colleague).

Health and fitness

Health and fitness holidays are those based around an activity such as yoga or tai chi or may be spent in a hotel which has many health and fitness amenities such as a spa hotel. This market has huge potential for growth as people become more and more health conscious.

According to research from Mintel about 20,000 spa holidays were sold in the UK during 2003-2004.

There are many new spa hotels opening all over the world. Some are extremely luxurious and very expensive. They offer beauty treatments and fitness classes or even a complete detox – which means you pay a lot of money to eat very little!

CASE STUDY

FIVE BEST MIND SPAS IN THE UK

Yohm Retreats – Swanky five star yoga, pilates, detox and fitness retreats in London and Wales. Kickstart a health regime, get back on the wagon and reward yourself for all your healthy living. Visit www.yohm.co.uk

Holy Island – Yoga, meditation, qigong and working holiday retreats on a magical island off the northeast coast of England that has been a retreat from modern life for centuries. Log on to www.holyisland.org

The Barn Rural Retreat Centre – This simple Buddhist centre in Devon focuses on meditation and organic gardening (you're growing food for future guests). See www.sharpham-trust.org/barn.htm

Agoy Holidays – Meditation and yoga weekend retreats with personal development therapists. See www.agoy.com

Taraloka Buddhist Retreat Centre – Women-only introductory meditation and Buddhist programmes in Shropshire; visit www.taraloka.org.uk

Source: *Grazia*, 29th August 2005

1. **Choose one of the spas mentioned in the article. Go to the relevant website. Describe the features of the holiday. Draw up a profile of the kind of person that this spa would appeal to and explain why. Present your information as an article for a magazine.**

Weddings and honeymoons

According to a Mintel survey one in ten couples gets married abroad. This amounts to 35,000 weddings a year, a large amount of potential business for tour operators. Since 1998, the number of people choosing to marry abroad has risen by more than 50%. There are many reasons for people choosing to have their wedding abroad, one of the main reasons is cost. The average cost of marrying abroad is £3000 – £4000 and of course that includes the honeymoon, whereas a UK wedding costs on average £15,000.

Think it over...

What are the other reasons for getting married abroad? Discuss the advantages and disadvantages with your colleagues.

When you think about a wedding abroad you are most likely to imagine a beautiful beach and hot sunny weather and it is true that this appeals to some couples. Couples must be aware of climate information if that's what they are looking for.

However, beach weddings are not the only option. Tour operators are coming up with new ideas for weddings abroad all the time to try and get a larger share of this lucrative market. All major long haul tour operators offer wedding packages. Here are some of their ideas:

* Virgin offer a wedding ceremony on the 86th floor of the Empire State building in New York.

* Las Vegas is a popular wedding destination – couples can get married in one of the wedding chapels on the Sunset Strip and the bride can even get Elvis (or a look-alike) to give her away.

* Kuoni offers the possibility of marrying in Sydney on a sunset harbour cruise or outside the famous opera house.

* Most of the beautiful Caribbean islands are geared up for weddings on perfect sandy beaches.

* A white wedding in Finland where the chapel is made of ice and the newlyweds can stay in an igloo.

Some tour operators have a wedding list service where family and friends can contribute to the

ESSENTIAL FACTS FOR WEDDINGS AND HONEYMOONS

How's the weather?

Bali: tropical climate with a dry season during our summer and a rainy season in our winter; year round showers. Average temperature 30°C.

Caribbean: sunny and warm all the time, but beware hurricane season from late September to early October. Temperatures between 25°C and 30°C.

Cyprus: very hot in the summer, mild the rest of the year; lots of sunshine. Temperatures between 15°C and 35°C.

Florida: sunny all year round, very hot and humid in the summer but can be chilly in mid-winter, particularly in Orlando. Temperatures 15°C and 40°C.

Greece: very hot in the summer, mild in winter, year-round sunshine. Temperatures between 5°C and 30°C.

Kenya: year-round warmth, with a dry season in our winter and a rainy season in our summer. Temperatures between 25°C and 30°C.

Las Vegas: sunny all year, extremely hot in the summer and cold in the winter. Temperatures between -5°C and 40°C.

Mauritius: year-round tropical warmth. Temperatures between 25°C and 30°C.

Maldives: warm all year, with a rainy season during our summer. Temperatures between 30°C and 35°C.

New York: very cold and snowy from November to March, steaming hot in mid-summer. Temperatures between -5°C and 35°C.

Sri Lanka: hot and humid all year round with two distinct monsoon seasons from May to July and December to January. Average temperature 30°C.

Sydney: seasons opposite to the UK so warm in our winter and cooler, though never really cold, in our summer; can rain in winter, but consistently sunny in summer. Temperatures between 12°C and 25°C.

Source: Trade Travel Gazette

cost of the wedding in lieu of a wedding gift or can buy add-ons to the holiday, for example, a yacht trip, a helicopter ride or a special dinner for two.

Theory into practice

Plan a wedding holiday for a special client – you! Imagine you are going to get married abroad. Think of all the features you would like your holiday to have and find a suitable wedding holiday to fit. Use the climate information on page 173. Check the location of all the destinations described on a map. Take a blank world map and label all the destinations mentioned on page 173 with notes about the features of each one. Make a poster of your wish list and the holiday you find.

Working holidays

Many working holidays are aimed at gap year students and you may be planning to take one of these yourself. A lot of information is available both on the Internet and in publications. A very interesting source of information is www.workingabroad.com. This extract from their website shows what they offer in terms of working holidays:

Short, medium and long term, unpaid: These positions can last from anything between a couple of weeks to nine months, and are suitable for many people, including students taking a year off, professionals taking sabbaticals to work on a specific project, individuals wishing to gain further 'hands-on' practical field experience and so on. Usually, they must pay for their transportation to and from the project. In most cases, volunteers pay a monthly fee which covers living costs, project materials, etc., which cannot be paid by the volunteer organisation. Costs depend upon country, but as a general indicator, volunteers may be asked to contribute between 100 to 400 GB pounds per month.

Short term expeditionary eco-conservation projects: There are also opportunities for people who are limited by time, and wish to take part in conservation and wildlife surveying projects as an alternative to a holiday. Such projects are usually located in tropical and remote areas and volunteers are expected to be self-funding and to pay for the costs of the expedition.

Source: Working Abroad www.workingabroad.com

The projects on offer are exciting and unusual and can be of appeal to the whole family. For example, one project involves tracking brown bears in Sweden and learning basic wilderness skills. Volunteers live in wooden huts in the forest and whilst working can expect to see lots of wildlife.

Of course, working holidays do not have to take place abroad. There are plenty of opportunities in the UK. The National Trust runs working holidays with volunteers participating in all sorts of activities, including painting properties or planting trees. Interested parties can go for a couple of days or for a week and the holidays are cheap and you get food and hostel accommodation.

Theory into practice

Plan your own working holiday. Decide how long it should be – from a weekend to a whole gap year. Be adventurous and team spirited.

You can get some information from these websites but look for your own sources of information as well:

* www.seasonworkers.com
* www.workingabroad.com
* www.worktravelcompany.com
* www.gapwork.com
* www.bunac.org
* www.nationaltrust.org.uk

Describe all the features of your chosen holiday and explain why it suits you. Summarise the costs and transport routes to your holiday. Write a short report on your findings.

Working holidays are offered by specialist companies like those mentioned here. Major tour operators do not offer working holidays.

Conservation holidays

We have just seen that many working holidays involve conservation and indeed all conservation holidays by their nature involve working! Conservation may apply to places, historical sites, the natural environment and to different animal species.

BTCV is a registered charity in the UK that specialises in conservation holidays. It runs over 500 such holidays a year, not only in the UK but throughout the world. Examples include learning how to build a dry stone dyke in a remote area of Scotland and spending a weekend felling trees in Nottingham forest.

> ### Think it over...
>
> What qualities do you think are needed to go on a conservation holiday? Have you got what it takes?

Special interest holidays with travel

All the special interest holidays we have looked at so far take place in a specific destination so now we will examine those holidays which involve tourists moving around during their stay.

Many of the holidays that involve moving around include an element of adventure and physical exercise as people choose to look for excitement and thrills on their holidays. A survey in the London Evening Standard reported on the top ten adventure holidays. The most popular options were various types of trek, kayaking in Canada, mountain biking in Mexico, looking for polar bears on the ice in the Arctic and even a gorilla safari in Uganda.

Trekking

Trekking is a popular special interest holiday as it offers adventure yet can be tailored to the ability and wishes of different groups of travellers. Families can trek together in destinations such as the Atlas Mountains in Morocco or the Pindos mountains in Greece. Experienced climbers

can visit steep and tricky mountains such as the Karakoram range in Pakistan or the sheer-sided Mount Roraima in Venezuela. Billed as the ultimate wildlife experience, a gorilla trek to the gorilla sanctuary in the Parc du Volcan rainforest in Rwanda offers excitement and helps ensure the survival of the gorillas.

Potential trekkers have to decide whether to arrange their trek independently or book with an operator. It is a good idea to book with a reputable operator if you are inexperienced as they will provide a local guide and will ensure that no risks are taken with health and safety. An example of a trekking operator is Exodus Travel which has over 30 years experience and organises travel to Europe, Africa, Asia, South America, North America, Australasia and the Antarctic. An independent trek might work out cheaper but could be difficult to organise, as a guide would have to be located and transport in remote areas might be difficult to find.

Cycling

Cycling holidays account for about five per cent of activity holidays taken. Serious cyclists can take their own cycles by air and carry their gear on their bike or on their back. All specialist cycling operators will provide bikes for those who want them and most offer a range of different cycling holidays ranging from extremely taxing mountain bike tours to gentle rides through the

CASE STUDY

Best For Families – High Atlas, Morocco

Why? Child-friendly culture, no problems with altitude, short flight time and little travelling on arrival; mules are available for tired little legs.

When? May to October.

The Big Ticks: Mount Toubkal, the highest peak in North Africa at 4165m; staying in a Kasbah; seeing snake charmers and acrobats in Marrakesh.

Short-haul Alternative: The Corfu Trail (11 days) is accessible by cheap flights and has *My Family and Other Animals*-inspired nature.

Best For Culture – The Inca Trail, Peru

Why? Machu Picchu isn't the only Inca ruin here: the whole four-day trail is lined with the Inca equivalents of motorway services – inns, rest houses and other, mysterious ruins. Local guides expertly bring these to life.

When? April to November.

The Big Ticks: Dead Woman's Pass (4198m); the first view of Machu Picchu from the Sun Gate; spending the day exploring Machu Picchu; time in Cuzco.

Short-haul Alternative: Northern Romania maintains a traditional life village life – try the Maramures region.

Best for Nature – Torres del Paine, Chile

Why? Condors, guanaco (a cousin of the llama), rheas (giant, flightless birds), armadillos and possibly the odd puma, all set among the most diverse and astonishing scenery on Earth with blue lakes, calving glaciers, huge forests and vertical peaks.

When? November to March.

The Big Ticks: The Paine Circuit (eight days) – a complete circling of the massif; the Torres walk to the base of the iconic rock spires (one day).

Short-haul Alternative: The Alpujarras, southern Spain, are carpeted with flowers in spring, and still have a healthy population of boar and snake.

Best for Softies – Annapurna Treks, Nepal

Why? Facilities in the Annapurna foothills are second to none. Stay in hotels the whole way and have your daypack carried by your own porter while trekking amid some of the most exciting scenery in the world.

When? March to May; October to December.

The Big Ticks: Views of Machhapuchhare (Fishtail) one of the most beautiful mountains in the world; sunrise over the Himalaya from Poon Hill (3210m, six days); the flowering forests of rhododendron in May.

Short-haul Alternative: Tuscany is a lovely base for gentle walking – spend a week in the hills around Siena.

Best for First-Timers – New Zealand

Why? If you're at all active, New Zealand delivers on every level; sublime scenery, great facilities and it's compact enough to do a couple of different treks in one trip.

When? December to March, but expect rain.

The Big Ticks: The Tongariro Crossing, possibly the best day-walk in the world; the Milford Track (four days), for big peaks, fjords and waterfalls (but be sure to book now for next year); the Abel Tasman Coast Track (five days) for fantastic, sunny coastal walking.

Short-haul alternative: The central section of the GR10 long-distance path in the French Pyrenees (five–twelve days) for good food and easy access.

Best for Photographers – Everest Base Camp, Nepal

Why? The biggest collection of neck-cricking peaks on the globe; Sherpa culture; yeti skulls in monasteries and beautiful, lively villages.

When? March to May; October to December.

The Big Ticks: Kala Pattar (5545m), a hill above base camp that delivers the classic view of Everest, Everest Base Camp (5300m, 14 days), only there in spring, the most famous campsite in the world.

Short-haul alternative: The Tour of Mont Blanc (11 days) for close-up views of an extraordinary mountain seen from three different countries.

Best for Altitude Junkies – Mount Kilimanjaro, Tanzania

Why? At 5896m it is the highest point in Africa. As it is a fairly easy-angled volcano, it is as big a mountain as you can climb without crampons.

When? June to February.

The Big Ticks: Standing atop one of the seven continental summits; seeing snow on the equator; nipping off for a quick safari afterwards.

Short-haul alternative: Corsica's GR20 long-distance path – there's nowhere steeper (but it's worth it).

Trekking holidays

Source: *Wanderlust* April/May 2005

1. **Locate all the trekking destinations mentioned on a world map.**
2. **Choose one of the treks and do some research to find out more about it. Describe the features of the destination and explain why those features make the destination suitable for this type of trek. Consider climate, landscape, transport routes and accessibility, accommodation, local services, attractions, local culture and facilities. Present your work in the form of a leaflet which includes all this information and can be used to promote the destination.**

Extension Task: Draw up a detailed profile of the type of customers your trek would appeal to. Add this to your leaflet.

countryside. Climate is an important consideration for customers taking a cycling holiday. If it is too hot then the cycling is uncomfortable and too taxing. Landscape must be carefully considered to fit the cycling ability of the group. Those taking cycling breaks in the UK can easily drive to their destination. Norfolk and Suffolk are popular cycling destinations in the UK and there are many easy routes for weekend biking in Kent. If a package holiday is booked then accommodation is included. It is usual for different accommodation en route to be taken although it is all pre-arranged. One or two nights will be spent in each hotel or guest house. Cycling is a fantastic way to see local attractions and feel part of local culture but if the weather is bad it can be a miserable experience.

Some cycling operators make the experience so easy for cyclists that they don't even have to carry their bags! Headwater is one such operator. Customers choose from various destinations in Europe for their tour. A week's tour will include bikes, a repair service if there is a problem with the bike, detailed routes and accommodation and meals in very good hotels. The customers' bags are collected for them from their hotel and moved to the next hotel en route. The cyclist just takes money and water for the journey by bike.

This extract from the Headwater website explains:

All cycling holidays are independent, with generally 2-8 people on each. Independent doesn't mean unsupported, though. Headwater staff meet you, fit you out with your bike, tell you all about the things to see and do, and move your bags from hotel to hotel. Otherwise they won't intrude on your independence, although they're at the end of the phone if you need them. You move on between hotels every two days: we transport your bags, so you don't need to carry a lot in your panniers. In-between days are an opportunity for exploring locally, with the help of Headwater's detailed maps and notes. Or you can lounge by the pool, go shopping, or whatever!

Source: www.headwater.com

At the other extreme some specialist operators offer tours for serious cyclists which take in classic cycle races such as the Tour de France. The cyclists travel by bike to watch various stages of the tour, staying in hotels along the route. This kind of trip allows cyclists to indulge in their hobby whilst also watching the professionals.

Cruising

UK consumers took more than 1.14 million ocean and river cruises in 2004. The UK market has shown year-on-year growth for the seventeenth year in succession and recorded the second-largest annual increase in UK cruising history of 11.9% between 2002 and 2003. Mintel's consumer research indicates that 13% of the UK population has been on a cruise holiday. Cruises from homeports are increasing in popularity with 306,000 choosing to cruise from UK ports in 2004 rather than flying to a foreign port to start their holiday. This represented a 13% increase on 2003.

The chart shows the increases in ocean cruising.

GROWTH OF UK CRUISING

	Annual % rise	Passengers
1992	19	229,000
1998	27	662,000
2004	6	1 million
2007 estimate	7	1.3 million
2010 estimate	7	1.5 million

Source: *Travel Trade Gazette Expert Cruises* 2005

FIGURE 11.3 *The growth of UK cruising*

To cater for this demand and to encourage growth in the market, the cruise lines are building new ships and providing a greater variety of types of cruises. Another factor leading to growth in the market is that for the last three years, prices of cruising have been heavily discounted as more competition enters the market. Lower prices have encouraged first time cruisers and changed the profile of the market.

All the major cruise lines offer fly cruises and that means that the prices quoted usually include the flight and all the arrangements are made for the passenger. Flights may be charter (specially booked for the travellers) where the ship is large enough to warrant charters arriving from various departure airports, or they may be scheduled. The more expensive cruises often use scheduled flights because of the extra flexibility and the perception of luxury. Also included in the prices are the accommodation, in cabins, all meals and usually room service, activities and entertainment on board. Fly cruises take the biggest market share for UK travellers with 72% of all cruises fly drive (Annual Cruise Review 2004).

World cruises appeal to lots of people but they can't usually afford the time or the money to do them! Prices start at around £11,000 per person and can be two or three times that depending on choice of accommodation. Also it obviously takes some time to sail around the world so work commitments might get in the way. The customer

profile tends to be older retired people – with plenty of money.

Mini-cruises have been developed as a means of bringing more business to passenger ferries. These ships have improved in the last few years and offer a good range of facilities to passengers, including cabins, restaurants, shops and cinemas. The cruise may be for one or two nights and is sometimes combined with a city stay in the middle. They depart from many UK ports including Hull, Harwich and Newcastle. Cruises to Amsterdam from Newcastle are very popular with students, especially as the cost can be as low as £34.50!

CASE STUDY

Destination breakdown

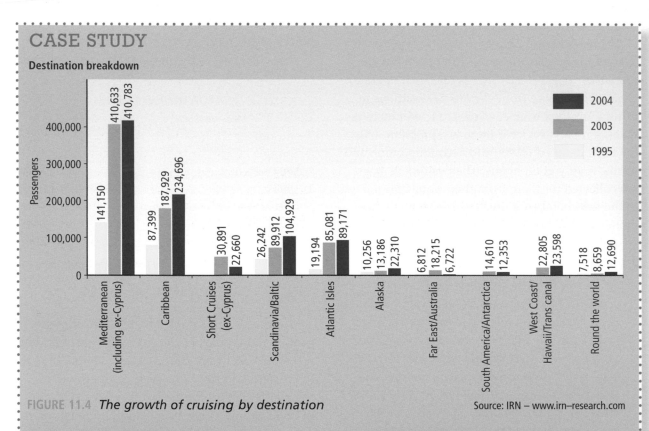

FIGURE 11.4 *The growth of cruising by destination*

Source: IRN – www.irn–research.com

Write down your answers to the following:

1. **Work out the increase in cruises in the Mediterranean from 2003 to 2004.**
2. **What do you think is the appeal of a Mediterranean cruise?**
3. **Why do you think there is such a big increase in world cruise bookings?**
4. **Why are many short cruises taken out of Cyprus?**

5. **What islands are included in 'Atlantic Isles'? (Consult a map.)**

Extension Task: Give a summary of the range of destinations used for cruise holidays. Explain why these destinations are suitable for cruising. Give examples of providers of cruises to these destinations. Present your work as a brief report.

River cruises, particularly on the Nile, are very popular. River cruising and ocean cruising are quite different experiences. On a river passengers are close to shore and can see sights very clearly. Often shore excursions are included in the price. This is important because passengers are unlikely to want to spend all their time on the ship as the facilities are not as varied as on an ocean going liner due to restrictions on space. A river vessel may carry 100 or 200 passengers rather than thousands.

Niche cruise operators offer a more unusual product, focusing on unusual destinations like Christmas shopping in Rio, offered by Discovery World cruises, or the Indian Ocean offered by African Safari Club. Ships used by niche operators are often smaller and can access ports which are inaccessible to larger ships. These specialist cruises are likely to be more expensive than mainstream cruises.

Many of these specialist cruises cater for a younger clientele who are looking for more activity on their cruise and a little bit of adventure. Some Alaskan cruises offer excursions like dog sledding, whale watching and rock climbing.

There are cruises which are planned around a particular theme, for example playing bridge, dance or health and fitness. Those who are not interested in the theme can still go on the cruise and carry on with the usual activities.

Cruises are usually sold through travel agents reflecting the high cost of the product and the level of risk in choosing the right cruise. Most customers (90%) prefer to take advice from a travel agent to choose their cruise. However, this is expected to change as it has in other sectors of the travel business as customers become more confident about booking online and as cruise operators improve their websites to encourage internet booking.

Theory into practice

On a blank world map label the major cruising destinations. Give some information on the particular features of each one such as climate, access and attractions.

Rail journeys

The reasons for taking rail holidays are that passengers are able to see spectacular sights from trains which they may not see by road. In addition trains themselves have appeal especially if they are luxurious and offering accommodation and dining experiences like those on the renowned Orient Express.

Less luxurious but also popular is the use of trains as an easy way of visiting Europe for backpackers. A Eurail pass allows anyone under 26 to visit 17 countries on one ticket which costs just under £300 for a month's travel.

Famous trains and journeys which you should note include the Blue Train, the Orient Express and the Trans Siberian Rail.

Blue Train

The Blue Train is a luxurious train which travels through South Africa. The train itself has luxurious suites with baths and double beds. All meals are included. There are various routes, mostly of one to two days duration. An example is Cape Town to Port Elizabeth and back, known as the Garden Route. The route goes through the Langeberg mountains and wine regions of Robertson and Swellendam. Passengers can enjoy spectacular views over the Indian Ocean. The train stops to allow passengers to go on excursions, for example to an ostrich farm (where rides can be taken on an ostrich!) or to underground caves. Once at Port Elizabeth, a historic town, passengers can visit the town or some nearby game reserves before returning to the train for their trip back to Cape Town.

Orient Express

Venice Simplon-Orient Express offers several rail journeys, all of which are in the luxury category. Domestic day trips are available in the UK on the British Pullman and Northern Belle; an example of a day trip on the Northern Belle is from Manchester to Edinburgh with a visit to the Royal Yacht Britannia in Edinburgh. For £235 passengers receive brunch with Bucks Fizz on their outward journey and a four course dinner with champagne on their return. Passengers may also have a week's Northern Belle holiday staying in hotels along the route. The train has six dining carriages, with a maximum capacity of 252 passengers.

The most famous Orient-Express rail journey is from Paris to Venice onboard the Venice Simplon-Orient Express train. The trip is perfect for celebrating a special occasion and may be combined with a stay at some of Venice's finest hotels. It costs £1,165 for one way, excluding hotels, or £1,690 for the return trip. This extract from the Orient Express brochure explains what to expect.

ITINERARY

Day 1 – Board the blue and gold carriages of the Continental Wagons-Lits in Paris. Throughout your journey you will be attended by your own personal steward. After you have settled into your comfortable private compartment it will soon be time to dress for dinner. Why not sip a pre-dinner cocktail before making your way to one of the magnificent restaurant cars. Here you will be served a delicious four-course dinner, prepared by our skilled French chefs. After dinner you may want to linger in the bar car, listening to the sound of the baby grand piano. When you are ready, retire to your compartment, which has now been transformed into a cosy bedroom.

Day 2 – You awake to the magnificent scenery of the Swiss Alps as breakfast is served in your compartment, at a time to suit you. Spend the morning in the bar car chatting to fellow travellers over coffee. Enjoy a leisurely three-course lunch served in another of the beautiful restaurant cars. While away the afternoon relaxing in your compartment admiring the spectacular scenery as the train travels through the Italian Dolomites. Later, afternoon tea is served in your compartment as you travel through the Brenner Pass. All too soon it is time to prepare to disembark as the train crosses the Venetian Lagoon and pulls into Santa Lucia station.

Source: www.orient-express.com

CASE STUDY

FIGURE 11.5 *The route of the Orient Express in Peru*

The map shows the rail network between Machu Picchu and Arequipa in Peru, a famous rail journey offered by Orient Express.

1. **Do some research into Macchu Picchu and explain why it appeals to tourists. Consider all the features that make it attractive to access by rail. Write up an information sheet with your findings.**

Extension Task: Find three examples of other famous rail journeys and compare their features and the features of the destinations they serve with the Macchu Picchu trip.

Trans Siberian railway

There are three main routes on the Trans Siberian railway. There is a seven day journey from Moscow to Vladivostok, a journey of over 9000 kilometres. The journey isn't as expensive as the Orient Express but nor is it as luxurious. It costs about £370 for a return trip for which you get a berth in a two berth cabin and access to a restaurant car. Those passengers heading for China can take the train from Moscow to Beijing. The route via Mongolia is very exciting. It takes six days and crosses Siberia, Mongolia and the Gobi desert into China and through the Great Wall. Two berth luxury cabins are available and the fare is only £246 return. The third major route is also to Beijing but via Manchuria.

Wine tasting

Wine tasting tours take place in wine growing regions. Wine buffs have the opportunity to tour the different chateaux and taste the wines. They usually buy those which are of interest. Such tours are offered by specialist tour operators. An example is Cellar Tours who have tours in the regions of La Rioja, Ribera del Duero, Penedes & Cava Country, Priorat, Mallorcan Wine Country, Somontano, Costers del Segre, Sherry Country, Rueda, Toro, Txacoli, and Rias Baixas in Spain. They also have tours in Portugal and Italy.

California is another important area for wine tours with many tours available in the Napa Valley.

Source: Vienna Tourist Board

A wine festival in Vienna aims to attract tourists for the duration of the event.

Not all holidays focused on wine are tours. There are often wine festivals in cities which serve to attract tourists for the duration of the event.

Overland adventure

Overland tours are a means of getting down to basics of survival and having an adventurous trip. These trips have their origins with young hippies travelling in groups in the seventies. Tourists, or rather travellers, travel in a truck and carry camping equipment with them. Each time the group stops everyone sets up camp together and takes it in turn to do cooking and pitching camp. The truck itself is maintained by the drivers who carry spare parts for repairs. This extract from www.oasisoverland.co.uk gives a flavour of what a trip is like.

On an Oasis Overland trip, a typical day 'on the road' is around eight hours and will go something like this: After breakfast of cereal and toast, tea and coffee and everyone has packed up their tents we 'hit the road' around 8.30am as our exciting overland truck expedition begins. We stop along the way for photos and snacks, etc. and usually have lunch around 12.30pm, whether it's in a town or on the side of the road. If the latter it usually consists of salad, sandwiches and fruit or if we are in a town or city you may have the opportunity to try the local food stalls. En route on our overland safaris we will stop for food and water in a local town or city so as to give the cooks for that evening's meal a chance to buy fresh produce! We camp up for the evening around 5.30pm. Our overland tours are about pitching in and working as a team: whether it be in a campsite or bush camp, everyone puts up their tents with their tent partner and then helps setting the tables and stools out, getting the fire going (whether it be gas or wood), getting water boiling for a hot cuppa, and helping the cooks prepare the fine fare for the evening meal (this is your chance to impress or flop!). Don't panic – your crew and other group members will have plenty of advice for you!

If we are at a campsite the majority do have a bar and showers! Usually our days on the road on our overland truck expeditions are between one and two days. However, there are times when we are on the road for two to three days, but this is rare and we will then be parked up somewhere for several days, e.g. Zanzibar 4 days, Victoria Falls 4 days, Olympus 3 days, Dahab 4 days, Cuzco 6 days and Iguazu Falls 3 days.

Source: www.oasisoverland.co.uk

Think it over...

What is the difference between a tourist and a traveller? Is it a state of mind?

Overland tours can take place just about anywhere where the terrain is suitable and there are sights to be seen. Tours take place in the Middle East to Egypt, Syria and Jordan or to South America exploring the Amazon jungle in Ecuador or following the Inca trail. Trips vary in length but are really targeted at those who want to spend a month or more travelling. Overland tours are offered by specialist operators. Examples include Oasis, Exodus and Kumuka, all of whom have websites. Some overland tours are also safaris.

Theory into practice

Complete this worksheet outlining the problems and benefits of overlanding as you see them. An example is given to start you off.

BENEFITS	PROBLEMS
Builds teams	Have to cook

Safaris

A safari is another type of overland tour. It is an expedition, often through land full of wildlife. People going on safari can be exploring or they could be on sightseeing trips. As such these can be luxurious or extremely basic depending on the choice of the customer. Most major tour operators offer safaris in packages mainly in Kenya and in Tanzania.

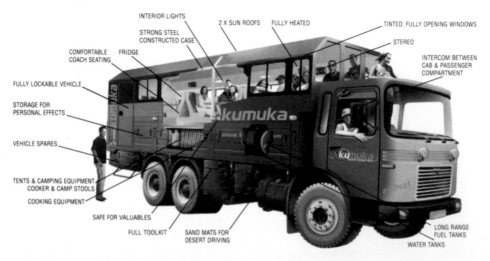

FIGURE 11.6 *The facilities offered by an overland tours truck*

Source: www.kumuka.com

Backpacking

Backpackers are usually younger people; the majority are 18–24 years old. Backpackers are usually taking an extended holiday either as a gap year before or after university or as a long summer holiday. Mintel estimates that the backpacking market within the UK and abroad is just under one million holidaymakers per annum. The research company also suggests that the market is growing and that more older people are taking career breaks to go backpacking or 'travelling'. Mintel describes 'yuppie' backpackers. These are people who travel with all mod cons including hair driers, Ipods, etc.

The point of backpacking is that it is independent travel so there are no tour operators specialising in this market. However, there are two well known companies who specialise in finding cheap round the world tickets and providing a product range suitable for young travellers. They are Trailfinders and STA Travel.

Theory into practice

Plan a three month backpacking trip for your best friend. She is going alone so give her some health and safety advice as well as choosing destinations that you know would interest her. Explain the features of the destinations that will appeal to her and label them on a map. Give examples of places to stay. Decide how she will travel and find out prices of tickets. Present your information to your friend and invite questions about the trip.

Providers of special interest holidays

Mass market and independent tour operators

You have met the four major tour operators in the UK market in previous units. Known as the big four they are:

* Tui UK
* Thomas Cook
* My Travel
* First Choice.

These operators are traditionally mass market operators, that is their product ranges do not differentiate greatly between different customer groups but assume that most people are satisfied with a similar package holiday. However, in the last few years these large tour operators have started to look at ways of satisfying increasingly sophisticated customers who want to have a holiday product that suits their personal needs. Some of the tour operators have acquired specialist holiday companies who offer special interest holidays, others have created their own divisions selling specialist products.

First Choice

First Choice now has an activity holidays division with several brands with it. These have been acquired over the last few years with The Adventure Company and Caradonna Caribbean Travels bought in 2004 for £6.2m. The chart shows the First Choice brands.

Sunsail	Yacht charter and watersports holidays all over the world
Platinum	Yacht charters with crews provided
Crown Blue Line	Holidays in hire boats on canals and rivers in Europe
Connoisseur	Also waterway cruises
Emerald Star	Boating holidays in Ireland
Exodus	Offers adventure active holidays across the world – examples include Kilimanjaro, Machu Picchu, the Ice Hotel and walking holidays in Tuscany
Adventure Company	More adventure holidays
Adventure Center	Offers walking and hiking vacations, cultural tours, African safaris, Antarctic expedition cruises

Trek America	Specialises in 'off the beaten path' adventure travel across the Americas
Waymark	Offers organised or independent holidays for walkers and cross-country skiers, specialising in Europe
Caradonna Dive Adventures	Offers scuba diving holidays throughout the Caribbean, Mexico, Central America and Florida and with customised dive packages for divers and new divers
Lets Trek	Trekking holidays in Australia and in New Zealand
Trips Worldwide	Specialist in travel to Latin America
Flexiski	Exclusive tailor made skiing holidays and weekend breaks

Activity holidays

First Choice has invested millions in the growing special interest market by acquiring specialist businesses and it is likely that further acquisitions will be made.

Tui UK

This is the largest travel group in the UK. It has had a specialist holiday division since 2000 as well as the Thomson Ski and Snowboarding brands.

> ### Key term
>
> *Horizontal integration* – one company buys out another at the same level in the chain of distribution – in our examples here tour operators have bought other tour operators.

Thomas Cook

Thomas Cook is the third largest tour operator in the UK. It owns Neilson, an activity specialist, which was acquired in the late 1990s. Neilson has a good reputation and was voted best mass market ski operator in 2004. It has several brochures within its brand including various beach activity holidays, particularly sailing and also skiing and snowboarding.

My Travel

This tour operator underwent restructuring in 2004. It owns several tour operating brands but only the Cruise Store concentrates only on special interest holidays. The other brands deal with different destinations and different levels of the market. There are two brands trading in short breaks. Skiing is offered by Panorama and Airtours.

Other operators

Cosmos is perhaps the best known independent tour operator in the UK but their main offering in special interest holidays is their dream wedding brochure. They do offer 'Energise' programmes at some hotels but these are the usual sports and activity programmes which most tour operators include in packages.

Holidaybreak claims to be the UK's leading operator of specialist holiday businesses. It has

Tui Brands

American Holidays	Specialising in the US as a destination
Jetsave	Jetsave specialises in the Caribbean and Florida as destinations and offers escorted tours to the US
Simply Travel	Handpicked holiday properties off the beaten track
Headwater Holidays	Holidays to Italy, Spain and Portugal
Crystal International Travel	Offers ski and snowboarding, active, lakes and mountains, Italy, France, cities, Grand Prix and Croatia
Thomson Ski and Snowboarding	Ski and snowboarding holidays

invested heavily in acquiring adventure holiday companies. Each of these trades under its original name, Explore, Regal Dive and Djoser (a Dutch company). Explore operates in the UK and offers a range of cycling, walking and trekking holidays as well as adventure short breaks and escorted tours. In 2003/4, 41,800 holidays were sold by Explore. The company strategy is to create holidays which

CASE STUDY

EXPLORE

Explore was founded in 1981 by three travelling companions who had breathed, eaten and slept travel for as long as they could remember. From the relatively tame overland to Kathmandu, to venturing beyond dubious frontiers, from ferrying Land Rovers across the Ubange on hand-built rafts, to close encounters with unlikely creatures – they had a few stories to share.

Whatever the case, their blend of idealism, practicality, skills and culture soon translated into a very simple and successful formula. They called it Explore and the menu was short but inventive: across Iraq overland, Lima to Rio, the Nile by felucca...

Many miles down the road, and now offering the most diverse recipes in over 100 countries, the ingredients remain exactly the same:

- travel in small diverse groups of like-minded people
- get 'further and closer', with no frills
- do things the local way as much as possible, and respect the local culture
- invest in responsible tourism
- be 100% organised and professional - but also adaptable and always offer good value.

One or two things may have changed since the heady days of two phones plus telex machine: we now operate over 300 trips and the Explore family has multiplied to over 120 staff based in Aldershot plus over 150 Tour Leaders.

In March 2000, we became part of Holidaybreak plc, the UK's leading specialist holiday business.

Source: © Explore Worldwide Ltd 2006

1. **Why was Explore acquired by Holidaybreak?**
2. **Summarise Explore's product offering.**
3. **Who are Explore's competitors?**
4. **Choose one Explore holiday (visit the website rather than contacting the company and requesting a brochure) and explain why the destination is suitable for the specific type of special interest holiday.**

Extension Task: Find out who are Explore's major competitors. Compare their range of products and destinations with Explore and produce a comparative chart with explanatory notes.

Theory into practice

Go through this unit and note the names of all the operators mentioned. Make a table and try to categorise the operators. An example has been given to start you off.

NAME	PARENT COMPANY/INDEPENDENT	SPECIALISM
Headwater	First Choice	Cycling and activity holidays

a customer booking elements independently would find hard to replicate, thus ensuring that customers depend on the tour operator. The company has acknowledged and benefited from the trend to special interest holidays.

Many specialist interest holidays are by their very nature, more suited to being offered by specialist operators than by mass market operators. We have seen that First Choice has made great inroads into the market but the other big four tour operators still have a long way to go to capitalise on the trend towards special interest holidays. There are great opportunities for niche operators to capitalise on demand for special interest holidays. Throughout this unit so far you have been introduced to examples of specialists who deliver each type of holiday. Most of these are small independent companies with great experience in their field.

Specialists in tailor made holidays

Special interest holidays lend themselves well to being tailor made. The specific needs and interests of the customer can be better met by finding a destination that offers all the activities and features they would like and matching it with appropriate transport and accommodation.

A list of tour operators offering tailor made special interest holidays can be found at www.travel-quest.co.uk/tqtailor.htm. There are numerous operators offering stag and hen party weekends. Roving Romania offers nature tours and hiking and The Killing Game offers murder mystery parties. The big four operators are also aware of the trend towards tailor made holidays and First Choice has a brand in its activity division called FlexiSki which specialises in tailor made ski holidays, including weekend breaks.

Specialists in one destination or market segment

Tour operators who specialise in one destination are not always offering special interest holidays. They are often small, independent operators who have built up a knowledge and expertise of a specific resort or country. The four major tour operators have always had separate brands for specific destinations such as First Choice's 'Citalia' brand with holidays to Italy. Some of these brands were once independent tour operators who have been acquired by the big four. Another example is 'Magic Travel' in Thomson's portfolio.

Tour operators specialising in one market segment are usually niche marketers. They have built up expertise in one market area which is often an area of special interest. It is relatively easy for small independents to start up in niche markets as long as they have the relevant knowledge and some start-up capital.

Of course, some specialist operators have developed into large businesses whilst retaining their specialism. There are several examples within this unit. You have met:

* Tours for Churches
* Burleigh Travel
* BTCV
* Exodus
* Headwater
* Cellar Tours
* Orient Express
* Oasis Overland
* Kumuka.

PGL is an example of a large specialist tour operator dealing in activity holidays for young people and children. In 2005 PGL Travel was bought out by its management in a deal worth £42 million. The company is 50 years old and was founded in order to provide canoe and camping trips for teenagers. Now, it sends 250,000 youngsters a year on school trips and activity holidays in the UK and in France and Spain. The company was expected to make £5 million in profit in 2005.

Transport principals

Sometimes transport principals act as tour operators and organise trips. Coach operators are particularly well placed to offer special interest

NAME	OPERATOR	INDEPENDENT/PARENT
cultural		
religious		
heritage		
sporting		
dancing		
health and fitness		
weddings		
working		
conservation		
trekking		
cycling		
cruising		
rail journeys		
wine tasting		
overland adventure		
safaris		
backpacking		

tours. Shearings, Wallace Arnold and Leger have dedicated brochures for special interest breaks. They usually term these themed breaks and expect increased interest from customers in the next few years as people enjoy a holiday whilst participating in their hobby.

An example from Cosmos Tourama is given below.

ABOUT YOUR TOUR

Delve into American Music and the life of the international King of Rock 'n' Roll – Elvis Presley – on this exciting behind the scenes tour of America's musical landmark cities.

INCLUDED HIGHLIGHTS

Memphis Behind the scenes guided sightseeing **Stay at the Heartbreak Hotel Graceland** Guided tour **Sun Studio** Visit **Tupelo** Visit to Elvis Presley's birthplace and museum **Rock 'n' Soul Museum** Visit **Grand Ole Opry** Country music show **Nashville** Guided city sightseeing **Country Music Hall of Fame** Visit

Holiday price includes

- **Flights:** UK – Memphis; Nashville – UK
- **Accommodation on tour** in twin room with private facilities

- **Porterage** at hotels during tour (for one suitcase per person)
- **Professional tour director** on tour and local representative in resort
- **Transfers** between overseas airport and hotels
- **All local and airport taxes/service charges**
- **Single share option** (on tour only) no supplement to pay (see page 7 for full details)

The Elvis Presley Tour

Source: Travel Corporation

CASE STUDY

Crystal Active

CRYSTAL HOLIDAYS is axing its destination brochures – Crystal France, Crystal Italy and Crystal Croatia – and focusing on becoming an experience-based operator.

The Tui-owned specialist, known mainly for its ski and winter sports programme, will expand its Crystal Active programme and retain Lakes and Mountains and Grand Prix.

It will also produce a new Crystal Families brochure featuring the best options for customers travelling with children from the entire Crystal portfolio, including summer and winter options.

Crystal will also launch a new Crystal Active Beach brochure in September featuring the Beach Club resort on the west coast of France added for 2005, plus two new Beach Clubs in Turkey and Corsica. A separate

Crystal Active Alpine brochure, containing much of the current programme will be released in December.

Managing director Stuart McLeod said: 'We are in the position of being able to make a specialist product that offers slightly more than the mainstream.

'We'll make these activities accessible for people who want to give them a whirl.'

New brochure for Crystal Active

Source: *Travel Trade Gazette* 15th July 2005

1. **Who is the parent company of Crystal Active?**
2. **Why are the destination brochures being axed?**
3. **Why do Lakes and Mountains and Grand Prix fit in with the current portfolio?**

Extension Task: Why is the entire programme being restructured?

This assessment provides evidence for Unit 11.1. It covers assessment objective:

1. Demonstration of knowledge, understanding and skills

   To succeed in this assessment you must consider all types of special interest holidays from the range given in the text and produce a description and an explanation of the geographical distribution and providers of a range of special interest holidays.

   Your evidence will include:

   * maps showing the geographical distribution of different types of special interest holidays

   * a description and explanation of the geographical distribution and providers of a range of special interest holidays.

On completion of this assignment, you will be awarded a number of marks. These will contribute towards the marks for this unit. The quality of your work will determine the marks awarded. Your work will be assessed against the following criteria:

1–6 marks
Location of destinations for a limited range of special interest holidays will be described with little reference to the geographical distribution. A limited range will be provided. Some maps may have inaccuracies in selection of destination and location although some appropriate destinations are located. The explanation of geographical distribution will be mainly descriptive. Some providers of special interest holidays are stated but their link to different types of special interest holidays may be limited.

7–9 marks
The locations of a range of special interest holidays are described in some detail with clear reference to their geographical distribution. Maps are presented for appropriate destinations that are located accurately. There will be some detail. There is an explanation of the geographical distribution of a range of special interest holidays that makes reference to key features. A range of different types of providers of special interest holidays are identified, some of them exemplified.

10–12 marks
The locations of a wide range of special interest holidays are described in detail with clear reference to their geographical distribution. Maps show the appropriate worldwide destinations for a wide range of special interest holidays and their location and key features. Maps are detailed, fully labelled and accurate. A clear and comprehensive explanation is given of the geographical distribution of a wide range of special interest holidays that makes clear links between key features and the geographical distribution. A wide range of providers of a wide range of special interest holidays is stated with examples of specific named products.

On the Edge is a special interest holiday company, a subsidiary of a major tour operator, Global Travel. The company was started 20 years ago by a married couple, Stephen and Violet Brown, who had spent years travelling and gaining knowledge of destinations that were off the beaten track. In 2001 they sold their company to Global but remained as directors ensuring the original spirit of the company was kept. The company offers a very broad range of special interest holidays across the world. These are usually presented in separate brochures. For example, there is a cycling brochure and a weddings brochure. You are working in the marketing department and have been assigned to a team who are preparing an insert for Sunday newspapers. The insert will have several pages and will be printed in full colour. The purpose of the insert is to give a summary of On the Edge's product portfolio and to bring the company to the attention of a larger audience. There will be a sample itinerary and examples of holidays in the insert.

Your first assignment is to prepare material that gives the reader a good idea of the kinds of special interest holidays that the company offers. You should prepare several pages which include:

✳ Maps showing the geographical distribution of different types of special interest holidays: The maps should have notes which show the key features of the destination. Consider including notes on climate, landscape, transport routes and accessibility, accommodation, local services, attractions, special events and other facilities.

✳ Text which gives a description and explanation of the geographical distribution of special interest holidays.

Stephen and Violet have asked you to provide examples of providers of comprehensive special interest holidays as they wish to provide a database of competitors. This will be very useful in enabling them to carry out competitive research on prices and destinations. Present these notes separately as they will not form part of the insert.

11.2 Itineraries for special interest holidays

In this section you will learn how to put together an itinerary for a special interest holiday that takes place in one destination.

> ### Key term
>
> An *itinerary* is a detailed plan for a journey.

At its most basic the itinerary gives details of the journey to be undertaken, in order to arrive at and return from the destination. However, for a special interest holiday the itinerary may be much more complex as it must give details of times and locations for each activity that is to take place. An itinerary for a tour must have departure times and details of journeys and activities for each day of the tour. We will consider some examples before you make up your own itineraries.

A basic itinerary for a journey to a destination includes:

✳ departure date

✳ departure time

✳ departure point, e.g. airport

✳ mode of transport, e.g. airline

✳ arrival point

✳ arrival time

✳ contact details in case of enquiry.

Here is an example of a basic itinerary:

Holiday Reference number: 5947832

Your Flight Details

Departure Date:	Fri 17 Nov 2006	Flight Number:	Departing:	Arriving:
Departure Airport:	Heathrow to Prague	CZ409	12:30	15:30
Airline:	Czech Airways			
Return Date:	Thu 23 Nov 2006			
Return Airport:	Prague to Heathrow	CZ649	17:35	18:35
Airline:	Czech Airways			
Your Accomodation:	St. Wenceslas Hotel			
	Coach transport to hotel provided			
Contact number:	0227 1234567			

Here you can see a schedule of activities for one particular day of a cruise. It isn't an itinerary as no-one would be able to do all the activities even if they wanted to! Imagine you are the entertainments officer on the ship and you have been asked by one family to help plan their day's itineraries. There are three members of the family Mr. and Mrs. Jones are in their sixties. Mr. Jones is a history professor and very interested in the arts and culture. He hates exercise of any kind and he also hates shopping. Mrs. Jones likes gentle exercise and wants to make lots of new friends on ship. Their daughter Miss Jones (32) also wants to make new friends, particularly males. She has been on a strict diet and exercise regime and has lost a stone. She is determined not to put it back on whilst on the cruise. Plan an individual itinerary for each member of the family for 1st November. For the full holiday you would have to do this for each day!

TODAY AT A GLANCE
Monday 1 November

MORNING/AFTERNOON

8.00 AM	**Total Step and Abs** Greenhouse Spa, 9
8.00 AM	**Catholic Mass** Queen's Lounge, 2
8.00 AM	**Protestant Morning Devotional** Hudson Room, 3
9:00 AM	**Yoga for Relaxation (nominal fee)** Greenhouse Spa, 9
9:00 AM	**PORT TALK: Dubrovnik** Queen's Lounge, 2
9:30 AM	**Scattergories** Piano Bar, 2
9:30 AM	**Explore the Westerdam: Ship Tour** Northern Lights Nightclub, 2
10:00 AM	**SHOPPING TALK: Valletta & Dubrovnik** Queen's Lounge, 2
10:00 AM	**Bridge Lecture** Hudson Room, 3
10:00 AM	**Casino Gaming Lessons** Casino, 2
10:15 AM	**Art Preview** auction begins at 11.00am Ocean Bar, 3
10:15 AM	**Mixed Ping Pong Tournament** Lido Deck, 9
10:30 AM	**ENRICHMENT LECTURE** Vista Lounge, 2
10:30 AM-12:00 NN	**Bloody Mary Bar is open** Lido Bar, 9
11:00 AM	**Honeymooners Registration** Windstar Café, 2
11:00 AM	**SHORE EXCURSION TALK** on all upcoming ports Queens Lounge, 2
11:00 AM	**Magic Make Up & Hair Care Seminar** Oak Room, 10
11:45 AM	**SNOWBALL JACKPOT BINGO – 2 for 1 Drinks** – cards on sale at 11:30am Vista Lounge, 2
12:00 NN	**Ship Building Signups** Lido Poolside, 9
12:00 NN	**Team Trivia** Queens Lounge, 2
12:00 NN 2:30 PM	**The Wine Desk is Open** Lido Poolside, 9
12:30 PM	**Singles & Solos Lunch** Vista Dining Room, 2

AFTERNOON/EVENING

1:00 PM	**Floral Demonstration** Explorer's Lounge, 2
1:15 PM	**Art Preview** auction begins at 2:00pm Ocean Bar, 3
1:30 PM	**PORT TALK: Messina & Naples** Queen's Lounge, 2
1:30 PM	**Golf Chipping Tournament** Lido, 9 midship
2:00 PM	**Bridge Play** Stuyvesant Room, 3
2:00 PM	**Wine Testing Seminar (nominal fee)** Vista Dining Room, 3
2:00 PM	**Firming, Toning, Inch Loss & Detox** Oak Room, 10
2:15 PM	**Line Dancing Class** Northern Lights Nightclub, 2
2:30 PM	**Holland America A to Z** Queen's Lounge, 2
3:00 PM	**Groovy Group Cycling (nominal fee)** Greenhouse Spa, 9
3:00 PM	**Cruise Crafts** Piano Bar, 2
3:15 PM-4:00 PM	**Afternoon Tea Time** Vista Dining Room, 3
3:30 PM	**SNOWBALL JACKPOT BINGO – 2 for 1 Drinks** – cards on sale at 3:15pm Crow's Nest, 10
3:30 PM	**Service Club Meeting** Explorer's Lounge, 2
4:00 PM	**Pilate's Perfection (nominal fee)** Greenhouse Spa, 9
4:45 PM	**Friends of "Bill W"** Oak Room, 10
4:45 PM & 7:00 PM	**Captain's Champagne Reception** Vista Lounge, 2
5:00 PM	**Basic Stretch** Greenhouse Spa, 9
7:00 PM-11:00 PM	**Holland America Flaming Stromboli Coffees** Explorer's Lounge, 2
8:30 PM & 10:30 PM	**SHOWTIME: Tommy Tune's** *Paparazzi* Vista Lounge, 2 & 3
9:00 PM-12MN	**Cigars Under the Stars** Oak Room, 10
9:30 PM-12 MN	**BABY BOOMERS PARTY** Northern Lights Nightclub, 2

One day's cruise schedule

Source: Holland America Line

Airlines can also issue very simple itineraries which only contain flight details. It only serves to get the customer to their destination. A tour operator adds other details to this or a travel agent would use it as part of a fuller itinerary.

Someone going on a special interest holiday is going to need more details than just journey information. They are going to need information about accommodation and specific details of all the activities they have chosen.

Below is an extract from a sample itinerary for a special interest holiday based on salsa dancing in Cuba. Note that this extract contains details of the activities and the full itinerary would also have journey details:

Our final example is that of a full itinerary for a cycling tour. This is more difficult to produce because of the amount of detail needed and the complexity of planning to ensure that everything goes smoothly for the customers.

In the example you will note the following details:

* departure date and time
* departure point
* arrival details
* arrival point
* mode of transport including change of aircraft in Madrid
* accommodation for each night
* board basis.

In addition to this the customers require details of each day's tour to complete their itinerary.

Thursday 29 December

The production team will be waiting at Arrivals for you with an ice-cold Cuba Libre and refreshments for a very warm Cuban welcome to Cuba!! The coach will then whisk us to our 5* hotel with its impressive five star accommodation, swimming pools, balconies and two in-house Salsa clubs, one of which is on the 24th floor where the ceiling opens up at midnight to reveal the Havana skies. Hotel check-in is arranged for you in advance, so enjoy your welcome cocktail and meet even more dancers. We will get together for fun and relaxation around the pool, meeting later for dinner before moving on to a huge welcome party at a salsa club by the sea.

Friday 30 December

After breakfast, classes begin with the first hour concentrating on a warm up and body movement. After one hour together, the group is joined by the Rueda team and the classes split into four levels. All the male and female ratios are evened up and everyone has a further two hours of classes and fun. The teachers will help you decide which class is best suited to you so that everybody will be working at the right level.

Afternoon: Hit the salsa matinee with all the dancers and practise what you've learned in class. We always have the best table reserved in a prime location to see the top bands. After salsa-ing the afternoon away, we'll go for dinner at a local palador (a restaurant in a Cuban's home).

Evening: Meet in the top floor salsa club for drinks and a late night boogie.

Saturday 31 December

Morning: Breakfast followed by classes. The first hour will concentrate on understanding Cuban rhythms and the differences between son/rumba and salsa followed by two hours of rueda, partner work and warm down stretches.

Afternoon: Free afternoon to chill out around the pool, visit the museums or pamper yourself for the evening with a massage, pedicure or manicure.

Evening: Meet for the cocktails before heading off to the Gala Dinner. Live music from Cuba's top two bands followed by dancing at one of three salsa clubs until 5am with all the dancers joining us.

Sample itinerary

Source: www.salsafever.co.uk, www.KeyZemba.com

Thursday 28th July 2005
Highlights of La Rioja Cycling – Air
Basic Price

Thursday 28th July 2005

Depart	LONDON HEATHROW	1055 hours
Arrive	MADRID	1415 hours
On	IBERIA IB3163 Economy class	
Check-in	2 hours prior to departure	
Baggage allowed	20k per person	

Thursday 28th July 2005

Depart	MADRID	1610 hours
Arrive	BILBAO	1705 hours
On	IBERIA IB438 Economy class	
Check-in	2 hours prior to departure	
Baggage allowed	20K per person	

Thursday 28th July 2005

Transfer   Transfer from Airport to Hotel

Thursday 28th July 2005
Hotel Los Augustinos for 1 night

Room type	1 x standard double
Board basis	Half board

Friday 29th July 2005
Hotel Cladad de Ceni for 2 nights

Room type	1 x standard double
Board basis	Half board

Sunday 31st July 2005
Hosteria M de San Mi for 2 nights

Room type	1 x standard double
Board basis	Half board

Tuesday 2nd August 2005
Hospederia de Casala for 2 nights

Room type	1 x standard double
Board basis	Bed and Breakfast

Evening meals are taken at a local restaurant.

Thursday 4th August 2005
Hotel Los Augustinos for 1 night

Room type	1 x standard double
Board basis	Bed and Breakfast

Friday 5th August 2005
Transfer   Transfer from Hotel to Airport

Friday 5th August 2005

Depart	BILBAO	0955 hours
Arrive	LONDON HEATHROW	1045 hours
On	IBERIA IB4120 Economy class	
Check-in	2 hours prior to departure	
Baggage Allowed	20K per person	

Cycling itinerary

Source: www.headwater.com

These run to several pages and give explicit directions as well as information on interesting sights along the route. An extract is given here:

> Today your route takes you across valleys, through vineyards, market gardens and agricultural plains to the intriguing town of Najera, set on the banks of the River Najerilla. Here you'll probably see pilgrims taking a rest on the grassy banks before continuing their route to Santiago de Compostelo. Your route, however, continues out of town into undulating open countryside, before arriving at the UNESCO site of San Millan de la Cogollo.
>
> Najera is quite a substantial town, and this would make an ideal lunch break. Alternately there is a lot of off road cycling today so there are plenty of good places to stop for a picnic. Remember to take plenty of water.
>
> **Hotel Urunela**
> **9.5km**
> Leave the hotel, turn left along the main road and cross the bridge. Then turn left after the Iber Caja following this road up and out of town. At the four-way junction, take the middle-left road keeping the fence to your left. You then go under the main road and the road bends to the left. Carry straight on following the signs to 'Huercanos'. You cross and then go under the motorway. You start to climb and, in the distance, you can see the mountains (snow-capped in May). After about 3km of climbing the road levels off and you soon begin to descend into the village of Huercanos.

A detailed route description

Source: www.headwater.com

This type of itinerary needs a lot of work. Although the cycle tour will remain more or less the same for each customer (so the directions remain the same), different clients may request specific hotels or longer durations in a hotel so the itinerary is tailor made according to their wishes. Bookings must be made in each hotel, meal arrangements have to be made and then the necessary flight bookings and transfers added. In this case bicycles and the services of the tour rep must also be organised.

A good itinerary for a special interest holiday is one that is accurate and detailed and manages to accommodate the individual needs of the customer. All tourists have basic needs of transport, accommodation and food. In addition they have needs relating to their special interest, whatever that may be, but also to their needs for relaxation, special facilities, extra quality such as five star accommodation, or alternative activities for different members of the party.

Think it over...

The Patel family goes skiing every February half term. The three children and their mother Ella love skiing and spend every day on the slopes. Joe Patel dislikes skiing ever since he broke his collar bone two years ago. He would prefer not to go at all but is reluctant to dip out of the family holiday. You are organising their trip and you need to find some alternative activities for Joe whilst his family is skiing. Bear in mind that he does not drink and does not want to spend all day reading his book. Discuss your ideas with your colleagues.

Assessment guidance

This assessment provides evidence for Unit 11.2. It covers assessment objective:

2. Demonstration of knowledge, understanding and skills.

   To succeed in this assessment you must produce an itinerary for a special interest holiday based at one destination and an explanation of how the itinerary meets the needs of tourists. Pen portraits of the tourists are given.

On completion of this task, you will be awarded a number of marks. These will contribute towards the marks for this unit. The quality of your work will determine the marks awarded. Your work will be assessed against the following criteria:

1–7 marks
An itinerary is submitted that may have some inaccuracies or omissions and limited detail. It is appropriate to tourists' needs as provided

in the pen portrait. There may be evidence to suggest that an existing itinerary or package has been used. The style of presentation may lead to information lacking clarity. The explanation about appeal will be mainly descriptive and make limited links to tourists' needs. Emphasis will be on their basic needs.

8–12 marks

The itinerary will be realistic and appropriate to tourist's needs. Itinerary will include all appropriate information, much of it described in detail. The itinerary will include many original elements. The itinerary will be presented in a style that is clear and easy to interpret. There is an explanation of how the itinerary meets the needs of the tourist with clear links to specified needs, many of which are complex.

13–15 marks

The itinerary will be realistic and clearly appropriate to tourists' needs. There will be no inaccuracies or omissions. Information provided will be detailed and specific. The itinerary will be original. It will be presented clearly and in a style that is appropriate for the task. There is a comprehensive explanation of how the entire itinerary meets the needs of the tourist with clear links to their complex needs.

Assessment practice

On the Edge marketing team is continuing work on their insert for the Sunday newspapers. They are planning a sample itinerary to include in the insert. Stephen is keen to make sure that the reader can see how the itinerary is tailor made to meet the particular needs of each customer. Therefore, he has prepared a description of customers and their needs based on a request that was received by the company last season.

A group of four friends in their mid twenties wish to arrange a special interest holiday. They are two couples, Marsha and Frederik, Carla and Pedro. They are all working in the UK, in London. Frederik and Pedro are both archaeology graduates although they now both work in the city. Marsha and Carla are lecturers at a college of further education. Marsha lectures in communications and Carla in art.

The four have decided that they want to visit South America. All have very busy lives and they need to incorporate some relaxation and rest into their holiday, so they want to stay in one hotel in one destination for the duration of their holiday. They are high earners so they can afford luxurious surroundings but they do want to have the opportunity to visit historical sites and the men would like to pursue their interest in archaeology. Carla would like to look at local arts and crafts and may want to buy some pieces to bring home. All are agreed that they want some time to rest on a beach in the sun and to wine and dine in the evenings but it is also important to them that they get to know the local culture.

They can travel in March or April – around Easter time – for two or three weeks.

Tasks

1. Produce an itinerary for the four friends based in one destination. The itinerary should be in appropriate format and include all essential information.

2. Produce an explanation of how the itinerary meets the needs of the customers. This can be a presentation for Stephen and Violet or a feature article for the insert.

11.3 Appeal and popularity of special interest holidays

This part of the unit looks at information on the popularity and appeal of special interest holidays. You will have the opportunity to examine and interpret statistics and to do your own research into popularity and appeal.

Sources of information on the popularity and appeal of special interest holidays

There is no one source of information on special interest holidays as the range of holidays is so diverse. However it is possible to find information on the different kinds of special interest holidays. The most useful reports are market reports compiled by market research organisations like Mintel and Keynotes. These are not easily accessible as Mintel and Keynotes are commercial organisations and sell the reports to interested businesses. However, many academic institutions subscribe to the reports so you may be able to access them through a college library or online, if you have an Athens password.

Mintel and Keynotes reports include Activity Holidays and Backpacking and general travel and tourism reports.

A recent Mintel report on activity holidays showed that the overseas activity holiday sector increased by about 37% between 2000 and 2005. One of the reasons for this increase is that people are becoming more adventurous in their choice of holiday.

A useful reference source is 'Insights', the tourism marketing intelligence publication produced by VisitBritain. Insights may be available in your library. Again it is available by subscription only. It offers in depth analysis of particular markets including recent reports on cycling holidays and golf tourism.

The International Passenger Survey, from VisitBritain, includes inbound and domestic tourism statistics for the UK and the regions and includes occupancy figures, visitor travel patterns and visitor spend figures. Special interest holidays are not specifically covered but you will find useful and free general information.

The United Kingdom Tourism Survey is a source of information about domestic tourism. Part of the data produced concerns activities pursued on holiday. This information is available in the public domain and gives us useful information about activities which can be and are undertaken in the UK.

CASE STUDY
United Kingdom tourism survey

TABLE 11.1

This section contains information about any activities pursued by UK residents on holiday trips in the United Kingdom.

	2203 TRIPS MILLIONS	2002 TRIPS MILLIONS	2001 TRIPS MILLIONS	2000 TRIPS MILLIONS
Total Holiday Trips	91	101.7	101.2	106.0
Swimming	22.2	22.2	23.2	23.2
– indoor swimming	15.7	16.6	17.4	17.5
– outdoor swimming	9.5	8.2	8.5	8.2

	2203 TRIPS MILLIONS	2002 TRIPS MILLIONS	2001 TRIPS MILLIONS	2000 TRIPS MILLIONS
Scuba diving	0.4	0.4	0.3	0.5
Motor boat cruising	2.3	2.5	2.6	2.4
Other sailing*	4.1	5.3	5.3	5.3
Water-skiing or power boating	0.9	1.0	0.8	0.8
Fishing	3.9	4.9	4.3	4.7
– sea angling	1.9	2.3	2.3	2.2
– coarse or game	2	2.6	2.0	2.5
Walking	92.4	91.3	84.6	88.0
Cycling	6.8	6.8	6.9	7.8
Field study*	**	17.4	15.6	5.7
Mountaineering*	2.7	2.5	1.7	2.9
Horse riding*	**	2.2	2.3	2.5
Shooting*	**	1.0	0.9	0.9
Snow skiing	0.2	0.2	0.2	0.2
Adrenaline sports*	1	0.8	0.7	0.9
Golfing*	3.8	4.9	4.6	4.8
Tennis	2.5	2.9	3.1	2.9
Any other sport*	5.5	5.3	5.6	5.8
Visiting heritage sites*	27.5	29.1	28.5	29.0
Visiting artistic exhibits*	21.3	22.0	21.4	20.2
Visiting a theme park*	11	13.5	12.0	12.7
Visiting Millennium attractions	**	4.0	3.2	3.6
Watching performing arts*	15.5	19.0	17.7	18.2
– theatre/concert	**	9.6	9.0	9.3
– traditional music event*	4.1	4.9	4.3	4.8
– cinema	9	11.5	10.8	10.9
Watching any sport*	5.1	5.6	4.5	5.3
Health/fitness activities*	6.8	6.2	5.6	5.1
Hobby/special interest	13.8	16.6	16.9	17.1

Note: Data on activities undertaken by overseas residents on holidays to the UK is not available.

*UKTS *Activity Category Definitions*.

** – Activity not measured in 2003.

Last Updated: 13 December 2004

Source: *United Kingdom Tourism Survey*

Assessment guidance

The assessment guidance provides evidence for Unit 11.3 and 11.4. It covers assessment of objectives:
3. Research and analysis.
4. Evaluations.

On completion of this assessment, you will be awarded a number of marks. These will contribute towards the marks for this unit. The quality of your work will determine the marks awarded. Your work will be assessed against the following criteria.

1–9 marks
Some research has been undertaken and evidence may be provided in a bibliography. The appeal and popularity of two different types of special interest holidays have been included but there is limited comparison. The conclusions are mainly subjective with little use of information or statistical data used in support. There is an assessment of the factors affecting the popularity and appeal of two different types of special interest holidays. This will be mainly subjective and descriptive with little supporting evidence and detail.

8–14 marks
Research has been undertaken using different sources, some of which are referenced. The appeal and popularity of two different types of special interest holidays have been compared. Conclusions are drawn from information and statistical data. Some findings are substantiated. An assessment is made that considers a range of factors influencing the popularity of two types of special interest holidays. Evidence obtained through research is used to support the assessments made, some of which are in depth.

13–15 marks
Independent research is evident and there is evidence from a range of courses of information, which are referenced. There is a comprehensive comparison of the appeal and popularity of two different types of special interest holidays that draws on information and statistical data obtained as a result of research undertaken. Findings are substantiated.

15–18 marks
A detailed assessment is made of a wide range of factors influencing the popularity of two types of special interest holiday. Statistical data and other evidence is used to substantiate assessments made.

Assessment practice

Part of the On the Edge insert will be an article in two parts, one comparing the features, tourist types and popularity of two special interest holidays, the second an assessment of the factors influencing the popularity of two types of special interest holidays.

Your task is to write the article. You must select two special interest holidays to compare, one must involve the tour and one must be based in a single destination.

In the article compare the features, tourist types and popularity of the chosen holidays.

11.4 Factors that influence the popularity of special interest holidays

Here, you will find out about the factors that have affected the popularity of special interest holidays and assess those which have had the most significant impact.

Life work changes

In today's society people are put under a lot of pressure at work as modern communication systems increase the pace of work and mean people find it difficult to escape from their work, even on holiday. Most of us can be contacted by mobile phone wherever we happen to be, and whether we are on holiday or not. This makes it difficult to ignore work problems. In the UK people work some of the longest hours in Europe

CASE STUDY

In the lap of the Gods – Culture on a weekend break

Have you got a weekend to spare? Looking for more than lying on a beach? The ultimate weekend break is to visit one of the ancient wonders of the world – the Pyramids at Giza. These are the best preserved and largest pyramids in the world. Three are easily accessible to visitors. These are the Great Pyramid of Cheops, the oldest, thought to have been built between 2589BC and 2566BC, Chephren's Pyramid and the Pyramid of Mycerinus.

Once you have toured the pyramids, consider taking in the Egyptian Museum in

Cairo. However, you may not manage to see all of it in a weekend; it has 107 halls, where you can find collections of mummies and artefacts excavated from sites including the renowned Tutankhamen.

Adapted from The Independent 3rd July 2005

1. What are the factorss of this or a similar break that make it suitable for a weekend trip?
2. What are the drawbacks of taking this trip rather than a longer break?

Extension Task: Carry out some research and find out what factors may have deterred tourists from visiting Egypt over the past few years. What advice would you give someone travelling to Egypt in terms of safety and security?

and many professionals find it difficult to take extended breaks from their work. Once away from work people are looking for ways of relaxing and filling their leisure time. Special interest holidays help fulfil these needs. In addition there is greater demand for short breaks which allow people to have a short period of relaxation or indulgence in an interest and then to return to work.

Changing holiday patterns

Many people now consider holidays to be a necessity not a luxury, so there has been an increase in the number of holidays taken. Personal disposable income has steadily increased so people can afford to take more holidays, particularly short breaks. Some people take several holidays a year. These 'extra' holidays are more likely to be special interest holidays. People demand more flexibility which has led to an increase in bookings for the independent sector and a decrease in the numbers of package holidays taken. This trend is aided by the ease of online booking. There has been a steady increase in the average age of the UK population and we have noted the particular needs of this growing 'grey' market. Also there are more single person households, due to more people get divorced. These single people may be interested in activity holidays as they can also offer an opportunity to meet new people. Another trend is the interest in new destinations from the UK such as Eastern Europe and long haul destinations.

Accessibility

Time, cost and convenience are factors which may constrain the distance that people will travel to go on holiday. However, developments in air travel routes have led to an increase in long haul travel and if your special interest lies in seeing elephants in their natural habitat then you will take the trouble to travel to do it. Tourists choosing to travel long distances, for example, to Australia from the UK, make that trip infrequently and tend to go for a longer period of time.

Travellers will also take into consideration how much further they have to travel to the destination having arrived at the gateway airport or port. Skiers have to carefully consider access to the resort when deciding how to travel. Even if they fly to a gateway airport such as Geneva or Lyon, they will still be faced with a lengthy drive or rail journey into the mountains. In general terms, access to worldwide destinations has become easier and cheaper. Direct links by plane and rail are increasingly available. High speed trains provide easy access between European cities including London via Eurotunnel.

Access is not just about transport links. Politics and economics also affect it. Only fifteen years ago Eastern Europeans were not free to travel to their relatives and friends in the west and vice versa. Even when they received their political freedom with the fall of the Berlin wall and the dissolution of the Soviet Union, the people of those developing nations could hardly afford to travel. However, Western Europeans could benefit from visiting new destinations which they could easily afford. Prague is a good example, now in the top ten of city breaks from the UK.

Availability of attractions and other tourist facilities

This factor relates closely to access. People taking a special interest holiday will require all the usual tourist facilities besides being able to participate in their chosen activity. They need accommodation, food and local transport. In remote areas even basic facilities may not be available.

Changing attitudes

Increased awareness of cultural, environmental and health issues

Those who visit a destination to study the architecture, the arts and music are motivated by a desire to experience culture. In its wider sense many tourists want to experience the language, lifestyle, food and drink offered by another culture. Cultural events attract tourists, for example the Olympics in Athens or the Euro 2004 football in Portugal. Many holidaymakers are environmentally aware and expect the tour operator and hotels they choose to act responsibly in terms of the environment. Many companies publish environmental policies to reassure guests. Health awareness has had a great impact on special interest holidays. Concern about too much sunbathing means people look for other ways to spend their holiday time. Those who take care of themselves and exercise regularly at home, often want to incorporate some physical activity into their holiday. Awareness of health issues may have a negative effect on some destinations, as if they are perceived as being less healthy, they will be avoided. An increase in awareness of health

issues is leading to an increase in sales of all kinds of activity holidays and in visits to spas and 'wellness' centres.

Increased health, wealth and fitness of retirees

One of the most important markets in travel and tourism is the 'grey' market. This refers to older people who have plenty of time and available funds and want to travel. Older people these days are usually in good health due to the success of our National Health Service and availability of good nutrition throughout life. Contributing to private pension schemes over their working years has led to a good income in retirement for many people. If the mortgage has been paid and the children have left home, older people can afford to travel and enjoy themselves. Saga is the most famous tour operator catering for older people but all tour operators are aware of and marketing to this group. They are aware also that these people by no means consider themselves old and wish to pursue special interest holidays, including adventure holidays. However, they must recognise that this group has particular needs, for example an expectation of high quality products, good customer care, demand in off peak periods and single person holidays.

Increased interest in national sports, education and adventure

Many special interest tour operators have grown up around the demand for people to travel to watch or participate in sport. Some examples were given earlier in this unit. The 2012 Olympics in London will attract many international tourists and give a boost to our economy. Adventure holidays are increasing in popularity although this does not necessarily mean extreme sports and physical challenge. Soft adventure holidays provide tourists with a sense of fun or enjoyment without great risk.

In the article you wrote for the On the Edge insert, add a second section.

In this section assess the factors influencing the popularity of the two chosen holidays including:

- life-work changes and changing holiday patterns
- accessibility
- availability of attractions and other tourist facilities

- changing attitudes
- increased awareness of cultural, environmental and health issues
- increased health, wealth and fitness of retirees
- increased interest in national sports, education, adventure.

Knowledge check

1. What is meant by the term 'special interest holidays'?

2. Give two examples of health and fitness holidays.

3. How many people get married abroad?

4. Give two reasons why people get married abroad.

5. Give two sources of information on working holidays.

6. What kinds of adventure holidays are most popular?

7. What kind of people go backpacking?

8. Give an example of a specialist operator offering overland tours.

9. What is horizontal integration?

10. Which adventure holiday operators are part of the Holidaybreak group?

11. What is a tailor made holiday?

12. What is a management buyout?

13. Give examples of sources of statistical information on activity holidays.

14. Why are holiday patterns changing?

15. How does accessibility affect special interest holidays?

16. What is meant by the grey market?

Travel organisations

This unit covers the following sections:

12.1 Sectors of the travel and tourism industry

12.2 Legal and regulatory requirements of organisations in a selected sector of the travel and tourism industry

12.3 A travel organisation, its operation and how it meets the needs of customers

This unit will give you the opportunity to investigate a particular sector of the travel and tourism industry. Sectors include travel agents, tour operators, transport providers, accommodation providers and tourist boards. You will choose a sector and explore its connections with other sectors in the industry. You will also examine the legal and regulatory requirements of the organisations in your chosen sector and how these have affected their operations.

Within your chosen sector, you will select a specific organisation to study in depth, considering its operations, products and services and how they can be adapted to meet the needs of customers.

If you are taking up a work placement or have a part time job in travel and tourism, you will be able to carry out much of your research at your place of work.

How you will be assessed

This unit is internally assessed by your tutor and externally moderated by Edexcel. A variety of activities and case studies is provided in this unit to help you understand how travel organisations operate, what type of influence they have in the industry and how legislation and regulations impact on them. These activities will help you prepare for the assessment.

Your assessment evidence must include:

* a description of a selected organisation from within a specific sector of the industry. The description should include the type, scale and structure of your organisation, as well as a description of its products and services. You should explain how the products and services meet the needs of the organisation's customers, identifying gaps in provision.

* a proposal for a new or adapted product, service or facility for the selected organisation to fill the identified gaps in provision. There should be a detailed description of your proposal and an explanation of how it meets customer needs.

* research undertaken to complete all tasks and an analysis of the extent to which legal and regulatory requirements have affected the operation of the chosen sector of the industry

* an evaluation of the degree of influence held by key organisations in the sector and the connections between the sector and others in the travel and tourism industry.

12.1 Sectors of the travel and tourism industry

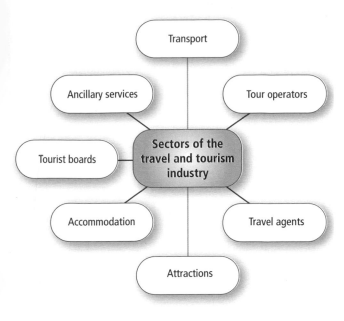

FIGURE 12.1 *The sectors of the travel and tourism industry*

Travel agents

There are different types of travel agents. The main categories are:

* multiples
* miniples
* independents
* e-agents
* homeworkers.

> **Key term**
>
> *A travel agent* is a person carrying on business, in whole or in part, as agent for a principal remunerated by commission or otherwise, in respect of the sale or offer for sale of travel arrangements. Travel agents are not in contract with the client. (Adapted from ABTA definition).
>
> Source: Association of British Travel Agents

Multiples

These are large chains, some of which have hundreds of branches. By definition they should have more than 100 branches. The branches are to be found on almost every High Street. They are usually part of Public Limited Companies who prefer, and can afford, prime locations. The three largest groups are Thomson, Going Places and Thomas Cook Retail. Note that these are all part of major travel groups which include tour operation, airlines and hotels.

These large groups sell holidays and other services under different brand names as the chart below illustrates.

TABLE 12.1 *Travel brands*

PARENT COMPANY	RETAIL TRAVEL BRANDS	NO OF RETAIL OUTLETS	E BRANDS
Tui UK	Thomson Travel House	700+ 100	Travel House Austravel Callers Pegasus Sibbald Travel Skydeals Team Lincoln
Thomas Cook AG	Thomas Cook	600+	Thomascook.co.uk JMC brand website
First Choice	First Choice Travelshops First Choice Holiday Hypermarkets	270	First Choice and websites for each tour operating brand
My Travel	Going Places Travelworld	650	goingplaces.co.uk fly cheap, late escapes and websites for each tour operating brand

Remember that these companies operate internationally and therefore have retail travel operations in other countries also. In 2005 MyTravel announced the closure of 110 of its Going Places shops as customers turned increasingly to online booking.

Miniples

These are chains too, but they are smaller and less powerful than the multiples. They tend to be located in one region where they may

be well known and have developed a good reputation. They are often large enough to need a head office as well as retail outlets. They are often independent companies. An example is Cambridge based Premier Travel with 14 retail travel shops throughout East Anglia.

Independents

An independent travel agent is often owned by a family or partnership. These outlets are more likely to be found in smaller towns as it

---

CASE STUDY

ENTREPRENEUR BUYS BACK 21 SHOPS

Travel entrepreneur Martin Morgan is buying back almost half of the Travel House agencies he sold to TUI five years ago – for a fraction of the price.

Sources believe he is paying 'significantly less than half' the £40 million he received for the chain – capitalising on Lunn Poly's declared intention to shrink its costly retail network. Morgan's purchase of the 21 shops in the Bristol and south Wales area will boost morale in the independent sector, as the multiples continue to close shops. His plan to mix independent-style service with dynamically packaged tailor made holidays is indicative of a wider trend: while the multiples are closing shops – TUI has admitted branches in southern England are most at risk and Thomas Cook is telling under-performing outlets to buck up or be axed – the independent sector is flourishing.

Chains such as Flight Centre and STA Travel, and miniples including Lets Go Travel, Hays Travel and Global Independent Travel, continue to expand their horizons. Morgan said: 'High-street agents have a future, as long as they adapt.' Although it appears TUI cannot make the Travel House shops profitable, he added: 'These shops have a £1 million turnover, are in great positions and still viable businesses.'

Morgan would not be drawn on specific plans, but earlier this year he said: 'No one is dominating dynamic packaging – certainly not in the retail sector. There is a niche for an agent who can pull together low-cost flights with villa accommodation – perhaps in a coffee shop environment.' He is due to meet managers and frontline staff of the Travel House branches he is buying to gauge their opinions. Sources believe he may build up his network to make it indispensable to Cardiff and Bristol airports. Morgan added: 'We have to look at all options. Call centres and websites are increasing in popularity.

Agents have to have a multi-channel presence; you have to diversify.' By contrast, TUI is homogenising its retail estate further by rebranding more than half of the stores in the Travel House Group – which also includes Sibbald Travel in Scotland and Callers-Pegasus in the north-east – to Lunn Poly. It is also shutting seven units because of duplication: three Callers-Pegasus outlets, two Travel House branches and two Sibbald shops.

NB: Lunn Poly has now been rebranded as Thomson.

Source: *Travel Trade Gazette*, 29th October 2005

1. **Why did Lunn Poly (now Thomson) decide to sell some of the Travelstore shops?**
2. **Why did Martin Morgan want to buy them back?**
3. **Summarise the marketing objectives of Martin Morgan's Travel Stores.**

Extension task: What market factors have affected the multiple travel agency business? Explain them. What measures should travel agents be taking to remain successsful? Report on your findings.

This company is one of ABTA's largest independent travel agents. It is based in Sunderland and has 31 branches mostly in the North East. Its operations include a call centre. The company profile is taken from www.hays-travel.co.uk.

Company Profile

As ABTA's largest independently owned travel agency, Hays Travel employs over 600 people and generates a turnover in excess of £200 million.

Since being established in 1980, the company has expanded steadily and now maintains an enviable position as a front-runner within the travel industry.

Hays Travel currently has 32 retail branches and four call centres based in the North East, as well as 150 homeworkers across the UK and more than 100 independent agents operating under licence to the company. For further information regarding the Independence Group please see www.independence-group.co.uk.

1. Visit the Hays website and find out what services they provide. Describe them.
2. Research the services offered by the Independence Group to members and describe them.

Extension task: Explain the differences and similarities between an independent travel agent and a branch of a multiple chain.

is difficult for them to afford the high rents of prime locations. The independent travel agents tend to be more flexible than multiples and can quickly adapt to changing markets. The market for package holidays is in decline so those travel agents who remain successful are those which adapt their services, for example providing tailor made holidays or specialist products, finding niches in the market or providing excellent customer service.

E-agents

Many of the major tour operators have set up travel agents online. They recognise that Internet access and use is growing and that they have to be part of the Internet revolution rather than be overtaken by it. There are also companies that have set up trade as online travel agencies without any retail shop presence. They sell packages, flights or accommodation. The most successful examples include Expedia and Lastminute.com. These are constantly in the top 20 travel sites as measured by Hitwise, a company which researches online marketing.

Lastminute.com

The idea for a website selling holidays at the last minute at cheap prices came from Brent Hoberman. Martha Lane Fox was a colleague of his and became involved in the idea. The two of them worked together on the company's business plan for eight months. Ms Lane Fox and Mr Hoberman bought the lastminute.com domain for £5,000 in 1998. They needed to raise capital to start their business and this proved to be difficult as, at that time, people didn't fully understand the Internet and its potential. Hoberman and Fox had to reassure investors that the Internet would take off. It did and the company now offers customers everything to do with going away, going out and staying in, including package holidays, short breaks, hotels, flights, trains, going out, theatre tickets, restaurants and sports events. They also offer home food delivery, DVD rentals and personalised TV listings. Everything is at the last minute which is defined as about three months.

Martha Lane Fox attracted a lot of publicity and was interviewed in papers and magazines, gaining a lot of interest in the new venture. In March 2000, it was the height of the dot. com boom and Lastminute.com was floated on the stock market. The company's share price rose to a high of 487.5p. Lastminute shares rose 28% on the first day of trading, representing a valuation of £732m and earning the company £113.5m. Martha Lane Fox was personally worth £40 million. However, in 2001, the dotcom bubble burst, and Lastminute.com's share price fell to an all-time low of 18.75p. Lane Fox's fortune was now only £9 million.

At this point many dot.com businesses went bust but Lastminute.com staged a strong recovery.

In 2003 Lastminute.com announced its first full-year profit, £200,000 against losses of £16.2 million a year earlier. Martha Lane Fox decided to resign from her post as managing director. She was only 30 years old. Her 3.6 per cent stake in the company was then worth about £26 million. In July 2005, Sabre Holdings Corporation announced that the acquisition of lastminute.com plc ('lastminute') by Travelocity Europe Limited had been completed. Travelocity is another hugely successful Internet company.

Lastminute.com also trades in Sweden, Netherlands, Belgium, Italy and France and has joint ventures in Japan, Australia, South Africa and Spain.

1. **What is the likely impact of the Travelocity takeover on Lastminute's business?**
2. **Lastminute.com is a middleman. What do you think will happen to it as more and more suppliers, such as airlines, sell their product direct on the Internet? Write notes on your ideas.**

Extension task: Carry out Internet research to find out about the extent of Lastminute's operations and their turnover and profit figures. Give details of your reference sources.

Homeworkers

Many people enjoy the flexibility of working from home, especially those with family commitments. They can work full time or part time as they choose. There are several companies operating in this market with a network of home workers. Examples include Travel Counsellors and Holidays by Phone. Holidays by Phone is a fairly small business with about 40 homeworkers in the UK in addition to its own call centre staff whereas Travel Counsellors has about 400 agents.

Most travel agents belong to the Association of British Travel Agents (ABTA). ABTA had a total Membership of 1,787 (February 2005). Of these 1468 are travel agents and 866 are tour operators. Of these, 547 are dual Members (both travel agents and tour operators). According to ABTA its members sell about 80% of all package holidays sold in the UK.

Read the following two extracts from Travelmole and discuss with your colleagues the possible reasons for the demise of these agents.

Third agency this week goes under

HULL-BASED agency QP Travel has become the third ABTA member company to collapse this week.

QP Travel also traded as Cheap Online Flights and Travelworld. ABTA said the company was unable to meet its liabilities and ceased trading today.

Agency Allan Watson Travel, based in Banchory near Aberdeen, and operator and agent London Air Travel in Slough, which also traded as A Travel, ceased trading earlier this week.

Source: www.travelmole.com 18th November 2005

Scottish miniple goes bust

Seven-branch Perrin (Goods & Services Glasgow), trading as Prentice Travel and Sunsavers, has become the fourth ABTA member to fail in less than a week.

ABTA said the company, which traded as an agent and operator, was unable to meet its liabilities and had ceased trading on Friday.

Source: www.travelmole.com, 19th November 2005

Tourist boards

Tourist boards form part of the public sector in travel and tourism. As they are not commercial organisations they do not compete for market share to try and make a profit but they do work as part of an overall national structure to promote tourism within the UK, that is to domestic tourists, and to inbound tourists.

Government departments set policy and provide funds for implementation of policy.

The Department for Culture, Media and Sport (DCMS) has responsibility for tourism policy in the UK. This policy was determined and published in 'Tomorrow's Tourism' in 1999. In 2004 the policy was updated in 'Tomorrow's Tourism Today'. The department determines the responsibilities and actions of public and private sector organisations in key areas such as marketing and quality. DCMS has greater control over public sector organisations in tourism than over the private sector. This is because the department provides much of the funding for tourism organisations. For example, the grant for 2004/05 to VisitBritain for promoting Britain overseas was £35.5 million. Further money was granted for domestic marketing and for the specific marketing of England as a destination.

The responsibility for the development of Scottish tourism lies with The Scottish Executive. Tourism comes under the remit of the Department for Education and the policy is published in 'Tourism Framework for Action'. In Wales it is the Welsh Assembly who has responsibility for tourism. In Northern Ireland the government Department for Enterprise, Trade and Investment (DETI) develops the tourism strategy. Each of these government departments funds its national tourism offices.

National tourist offices

In the UK, these are VisitBritain, VisitScotland, Wales Tourist Board and the Northern Ireland Tourist Board.

They are responsible for attracting incoming and domestic tourists, marketing of destinations, developing new products, research projects and providing information both to tourists and to the travel trade.

VisitBritain

VisitBritain is the statutory organisation for tourism for the whole of the UK. It does not concern itself with outbound tourism but seeks to market Britain to the rest of the world and

England to the British. Note that in terms of domestic tourism VisitBritain markets England and not Scotland, Wales and Northern Ireland. It has to work very closely with the national tourist offices of these countries in order to achieve its aims of promoting the whole of Britain to the rest of the world and to persuade the Scottish, Welsh and Irish peoples to take holidays in England.

Here are the aims of VisitBritain as laid out in its website.

Overseas Customer: To promote Britain overseas as a tourist destination, generating additional tourism revenue throughout Britain and throughout the year.

Domestic Customer: To grow the value of the domestic market by encouraging British residents to take additional and/or longer breaks in England.

Tourism Industry: To help the British tourism industry address international and domestic markets more effectively.

Government: To provide advice to Government and devolved administrations on matters affecting tourism and contribute to wider Government objectives.

Strategic Partners: To work in partnership with the devolved administrations and the national and regional tourist boards to build the British tourism industry.

Staff: To achieve all goals by making efficient and effective use of resources and by being open, accessible, professional, accountable and responsive.

Source: VisitBritain

To promote Britain abroad, VisitBritain has 25 offices covering 31 different markets. It also employs staff overseas in these offices. They have to work with the travel trade in their area to promote the UK. They are in competition with other countries vying for the tourism trade. Besides the funding given to VisitBritain by the DCMS, the organisation raises money itself through partnerships and activities.

VisitEngland

The role of VisitEngland is to promote England to the rest of the UK and to overseas visitors. It is part of VisitBritain but has its own website, 'Enjoy England'.

Wales Tourist Board

The Wales Tourist Board is the national tourist organisation for Wales. It reports to the Minister for Economic Development of the Welsh Assembly Government. It also receives funding from the Assembly. The role of the Wales Tourist Board is to:

'support the tourism industry and to provide the appropriate strategic framework within which private enterprise can achieve sustainable growth and success, so improving the social and economic well being of Wales.'

Source: Wales Tourist Board

To assist in marketing Wales is divided into 12 marketing areas. Examples include the Isle of Anglesey, Snowdonia and Pembrokeshire.

The Northern Ireland Tourist Board

Northern Ireland also has its own national tourist office, the Northern Ireland Tourist Board. This is the body responsible for the development, promotion and marketing of Northern Ireland as a tourist destination. It also advises the government on the formulation of policy on tourism in Northern Ireland.

VisitScotland

VisitScotland is the national tourist organisation for Scotland, supported and funded by the Scottish Executive. The Scottish Executive recognises the importance of promoting tourism in Scotland and has funded extra marketing activities.

Regional tourist boards

Tourist boards were set up to carry out the development and promotion of tourism in the regions. Traditionally they represented the public sector and implemented national policy. They aim to attract both incoming and domestic visitors to their region as this extract from the VisitLondon website illustrates:

'VisiLondon is the official visitor organisation for the capital. Our aim is to promote London as the world's most exciting city by marketing to domestic and overseas leisure and business visitors, as well as Londoners themselves. VisitLondon is a partnership organisation which also acts as a voice for the London tourism industry.'

Source: VisitLondon

The role of tourist boards has changed a great deal in recent years and now they have a key role in bringing together public and private sector parties in the tourism business. This role is summarised in this extract from the Tourism South East website:

'Tourism South East is the only organisation with a specific interest and responsibility for tourism across the Region and it plays a key role in building understanding and support between the different sectors.

Part of this key role is to liaise with and lobby government departments, local authorities and other tourism bodies. Tourism South East works closely with VisitBritain and the South East England Development Agency, and consults extensively with our members, either in meetings or via a membership magazine. '

Source: www.tourismsoutheast.com

The Internet has changed the way that the tourist boards present themselves to the public. Many of the boards now have two websites. One is aimed at consumers with lots of information about destinations and attractions in their region. Some of the tourist boards have changed their names on their consumer websites to make them more attractive in marketing terms and easy for overseas visitors to understand, e.g., VisitLondon rather than the London Tourist Board. Technology has been a benefit to the boards as it means potential visitors can find out information from the Internet wherever they are in the world. This enables them to research and plan their visit. The second website is generally aimed at businesses and tourism trade partners with information about how to market their products and take advantage of the tourist boards' services.

The activities of regional tourist boards are wide ranging and also cover:

* **Training** – many of the courses provided are under the 'Welcome to Excellence' brand. The courses are available to all tourism employees at a reasonable fee (usually paid by the employer). There is a specific course 'Welcome International' for welcoming international visitors.

* **Research** – research services may be surveys carried out on behalf of tourism businesses or mystery shopper services covering TICs

* **Quality** – inspecting accommodation and determining quality grades

* **Development** – the tourist boards employ business advisers who will give advice to tourism businesses and also inform them of any grants they may be eligible for.

Scotland has fourteen Area Tourist Boards which have been established since 1996. These Tourist Boards are responsible for Tourist Information Centres at local level. They also undertake marketing activities at local level and work with partners in the private sector. They aim to bring together the public and private sector and to link national and local tourism policy. Wales has three regional tourist boards. These are North Wales Tourism, Mid Wales Tourism and Southern Wales.

Regional development agencies

Regional development agencies have responsibility for tourism in their regions and usually work closely with regional tourist boards. Between 2003 and 2006, the RDAs are to receive £3.6 million per annum from the DCMS specifically for tourism. This money is to be passed on to regional tourist boards until the end of 2005. The RDAs will determine what objectives and targets the RTBs should meet in return for the funds. After this the money will still be earmarked for tourism but not necessarily through the tourist boards. This is because there has been overlap between the role of RDAs in tourism and the tourist boards.

Therefore, in some regions the regional tourist boards have disappeared as separate bodies and have been subsumed under the RDAs. In other regions the role of the tourist board has been altered to that of 'Destination Management Organisation' set up and monitored by the RDA.

Some examples of the regional organisations are given here:

* Tourism South East (www.tourismsoutheast. com).

* VisitLondon (www.londontouristboard.com).

* North West Tourist Board (www. northwesttourism.net).

* The Mersey Partnership (www.visitliverpool. com).

* Marketing Manchester (www. destinationmanchester.com).

The organisations are not totally dependent on government funding. Funds can be raised from business membership fees and from the provision of training courses to tourism organisations and employees.

Tourist information centres

A network of tourist information centres covers most towns and cities in the UK. Their role is to provide information and services at a local level. They are funded from the regional tourist board and by the local authority. Most TICs have had cuts in funding in recent years and have had to become more enterprising to be, to some extent, self financing. They can make money by selling souvenirs in their shop, by charging for maps, etc., by selling tours and by organising conferences as a separate arm to their business.

Theory into practice

Find out the following information about your own regional tourist board:

* The name

* The location

* Examples of partner organisations

* The stated aims

* Funding

* Examples of specific campaigns.

Produce a leaflet about the regional tourist board with the information presented under appropriate headings.

Attractions

The Visitor Attractions sector is an important component of the travel and tourism industry. It's the sector that provides the interest, excitement and activity for tourists when they visit a destination or when they venture out on a day trip.

The Visitor Attractions sector covers many different categories of attraction. They include museums, art galleries, historic houses and castles, churches and cathedrals, gardens, wildlife sites, leisure parks and other recreational facilities.

A 'Survey of Visits to Visitor Attractions' is conducted annually by the national tourist boards of England, Northern Ireland, Scotland and Wales

CASE STUDY
Marketing Manchester

Marketing Manchester is The Tourist Board for Greater Manchester. Its strategic aims are stated on its website www.marketingmanchester.com

Top line aim
To develop Greater Manchester into a leading leisure, learning and business tourist destination for domestic and international visitors, enhance the national and international reputation of the city-region and promote sustainable economic development and growth.

Image
Develop the Manchester brand through promotion of the city to focus on the temporary and traditional strengths of the city-region's culture.

Events
Increase the interest in, and visitors to the city, through the creation of a world-class events programme that builds on the success of the Commonwealth Games and strengthens the Manchester brand.

International destination
Position Manchester as a vibrant international destination, which also acts as a gateway to the Northwest and represents an alternative gateway to Britain.

Business destination
Ensure that Manchester is further established as one of Europe's leading business destinations.

Infrastructure
Support the enhancement of the tourism product in Greater Manchester through the development of tourism infrastructure.

Source: Marketing Manchester

1. Visit the website and find an example of a campaign that is helping to achieve each of the strategic aims, that is:
   * developing the image of Manchester
   * an example of a specific event which helps promote the city
   * a campaign aimed at international visitors
   * a campaign aimed at business people
   * the development of infrastructure.

Extension task: Choose one of the strategic aims and deign a marketing activity which would help achieve that aim in Manchester. If you like you can use examples of good practice elsewhere to help you.

---

to monitor visitor and other trends. According to the survey, there are an estimated 6,400 visitor attractions in the United Kingdom.

This is an extract from the definition of a visitor attraction according to the survey.

'An attraction where it is feasible to charge admission for the sole purpose of sightseeing. The attraction must be a permanently established excursion destination, a primary purpose of which is to allow public access for entertainment, interest, or education; rather than being primarily a retail outlet or a venue for sporting, theatrical, or film performances. It must be open to the public without prior booking, for published periods each year, and should be capable of attracting day visitors or tourists, as well as local residents.'

Note the main points of the definition:

* It must be feasible for the attraction to charge admission – but many are free.

* It must be permanently established – thus for the purposes of the survey, events such as the Notting Hill Carnival would be excluded.

* It must have a primary purpose of interest, entertainment or education – thus shopping centres are excluded even though they attract tourists.

* It must be open to the public for at least part of the year.

* It must attract tourists not just locals.

The top five paid admission visitor attractions in 2004 were:

1. British Airways London Eye.
2. Tower of London.
3. Pleasureland Theme Park.
4. Pleasure Beach.
5. Flamingo Land Theme Park and Zoo.

Note that theme parks are very popular. Euromonitor research published in May 2005 showed that some 49.7 million tourists visited UK theme parks in 2003, up by 3% on the year before.

A growing number of theme parks also now have hotels attached. A survey by Pricewaterhouse Coopers in April 2004, found that, of 29 theme parks in Europe, 14 offered accommodation, totalling 29 hotels and 10,015 rooms.

The top five free admission visitor attractions in 2004 were:

1. Blackpool Pleasure Beach
2. Albert Dock
3. National Gallery, London
4. British Museum
5. Tate Modern

Note that Blackpool Pleasure Beach tops the list of free admission attractions but of course it is not free unless you choose not to go on any of the rides. Each ride is paid for individually.

Although all of the top five paying and free admission attractions are in England, each national tourist board compiles its own separate figures. You can find out what these are by visiting the website of each national tourist board.

Many visitor attractions have large revenues and make a healthy profit – but not all. Many are in the public sector and owned by the nation. Consider all the national museums, many of which are in London. Examples include the British Museum, the National Gallery, the Victoria and Albert and the Science Museum. Many are free to enter and so the museum has to find other ways of making money from visitors. The intention is to bring in some revenue to help with running costs but government funding will provide the main source of revenue.

Attractions in the heritage sector may not make huge profits or may not make profits at all. However, it is important that they are conserved as they represent our history as a nation and form our heritage. There are two key organisations in this sector that you should be aware of as their role is to take care of heritage attractions. The two key organisations in this sector that are essential to note because of their role in looking after heritage attractions are English Heritage and the National Trust. You were introduced to these organisations in Unit 7.

English Heritage

English Heritage is best known for its role in preserving heritage but the organisation also aims to encourage diverse groups to appreciate and enjoy their heritage. To help achieve this aim an Outreach Department was set up in 2003. The Outreach Department works with local communities on creative projects. The purpose of the projects is to encourage people to be aware of English history and build a sense of community and identity.

Examples of projects are community archaeology digs, collection of oral histories and the creation of local heritage gardens. The projects are run in co-operation with local organisations and are open to all members of the public but particularly targeted groups are people from ethnic minorities, people on lower incomes, young people, and people with disabilities.

In 2000/01 public funding was worth £115m, and income from other sources was £30.5m. By 2004 the government had decided to cut English Heritage's funding by 5%. However, the Heritage Lottery Fund has given £3bn in grants in its 10-year life, including £1bn on historic buildings.

The National Trust introduced a similar project in 2003. Known as 'The Untold Story', its aim was to engage new audiences and community groups with heritage. Part of the National Trust's mission is to be 'for ever, for everyone' and the project was a means of working towards that aim. The National Trust acquired a grant from the Heritage Lottery Fund which enabled a group of community artists to be employed. The artists worked at various National Trust sites, using theatre and other forms of art to attract local community groups to sites to discover for themselves the heritage of these special places.

Tour operators

A tour operator designs and puts together package holidays and tours for sale to customers. These products and services are sold through travel agencies or directly to the customer through call centres, websites and television channels. To put the package together, the tour operator must contract the services of airlines, accommodation providers and transport organisations.

There are three main types of tour operators catering for the different categories of tourism:

* Outbound

* Inbound

* Domestic.

CASE STUDY
London Eye

In November 2005 British Airways sold its stake in the London Eye to the Tussauds group for £95 million . In addition Tussauds assumed responsibility for the £175 million debt that the Eye owed the airline. In 1998, British Airways advanced £48 million towards the construction of the Eye. British Airways could never hope to recoup the loan as it was charging 25% interest on it. This meant, for example, that in 2004 the Eye had a revenue of £38.6 million but its large interest bill of £34 million, alongside other costs, resulted in a loss of £24.5 million. In fact the Eye has never made a profit even though it is London's most popular tourist attraction. Tussauds was already a one third stakeholder in the Eye along with British Airways and Marks Barfield Architects (designers of the Eye). The Tussauds group are owners of several theme parks and the famous waxworks in London. Marks Barfield has been offered a similar amount of money to sell its third stake to Tussauds. The Tussauds group is in turn owned by Dubai International Capital who bought the group for £800 million in March 2005. The Tussauds group has agreed to invest £50 million over the next five years on improvements to the Eye and services for visitors.

1. Explain in your own words why the British Airways London Eye has never made a profit.
2. Find out how many visitors the London Eye received in the last four years and make a graph of the data.
3. Find out about one of the other attractions owned in the UK by the Tussauds group. Find out the number of visitors last year and its revenue and profit figures. Visit the website of the attraction to help you and see if you can access the annual report.

Extension task: The London Eye has a landlord, the South Bank Centre to whom rent is payable. In 2005 British Airways were in dispute with their landlord about a proposed rent increase. Research the background to this dispute and find out what the outcome was. Prepare some notes and explain this dispute to one of your colleagues.

✱ REMEMBER!

Four major tour operators dominate the outbound market. These are often referred to as the 'big four'. They are Tui, My Travel, First Choice and Thomas Cook.

Outbound tour operators

There are many other tour operators in the market. Some specialise in particular destinations, for example, Simply Spain, or in a product, for example, diving holidays.

Cosmos is the UK's largest independent tour operator and part of the Globus group of companies, a family run organisation established in 1928 which encompasses Cosmos Tourama, Avro, Monarch Airlines and Archers Direct along with Cosmos. The market shares of the tour operators are given in the chart overleaf.

FIGURE 12.2 *Market share*

	2002 000	2003 000
TUI UK (formerly Thomson Travel Group)	4,547	4,698
MyTravel (formely Airtours)	3,655	3,128
First Choice	2,996	2,759
Thomas Cook Company	2,565	2,629
Cosmos*	1,112	1,096
Virgin Travel	327	297
Other	9,728	10,196
TOTAL	24,930	24,803
*consolidated group figures.		

Source: Mintel *Short Breaks Abroad* UK June 2004

Theory into practice

Create a pie chart from the figures given for market share of the major UK tour operators in 2003.

We will examine the big four operators in more detail.

Tui UK

Tui is the UK's largest holiday company. Tui is the largest tourism and services group in the world consisting of 500 companies, including airlines, tour operators and travel agents. The major brand in the Tui UK portfolio is Thomson. The Thomson head office is in London. The company has 3000 employees, many of whom work in destinations abroad. Many of the company's holidays are served by the charter airline Thomsonfly, also part of the Tui UK group. The retail travel agency, Thomson, formerly Lunn Poly, forms part of the group. Other brands within the group are:

* Team Lincoln is a teletext and Internet specialist selling in excess of 250,000 holidays a year throughout the UK and is based in the North East where it operates four call centres.

* Callers-Pegasus is one of the UK's leading Regional Retailers based in the North East with about 20 shops.

* Manchester Flights is a teletext and Internet specialist selling in excess of 300,000 flights a year with a call centre operation based in Bury.

The Specialist Holidays Group was established in Spring 2000 and comprises a portfolio of specialist tour operating businesses including the following brands; American Holidays, Jetsave & Jersey Travel, Tropical Places, Something Special, Villadeals, OSL, Simply Travel, Headwater Holidays, Magic Travel Group, Crystal International Travel Group, Thomson Breakaway, and Thomson Ski and Snowboarding/Lakes and Mountains.

In 2003, the Northern Europe division of Tui had a turnover of £4306 million but made an overall loss of £385 million. The Northern Europe countries in the division are UK, Ireland, and Scandinavian countries.

Think it over...

What factors do you think contributed to this loss in 2003? Think back to what was happening at the time or look at some news archives. Consider issues such as the weather in the UK in the summer of 2002, international relations and wars.

My Travel

Another large tour operator, My Travel divides its operations into three markets, the UK and Ireland, Northern Europe and North America. It serves over ten million consumers a year. Within the UK, brands include several tour operators. These are Airtours, Aspro, Direct Holidays, Manos, Panorama and Tradewinds. City break tour operators are Bridge Travel and Cresta. Airlines are branded My Travel and My Travelite. Travel agents are branded Going Places. One hundred and ten Going Places shops were closed in November 2005 saving an estimated £10 million as a result. Website agents are lateescapes.com and mytravel.com.

Interim results for 2005 showed a loss for the group of £87.8 million. However, this was an improvement on previous years. At the end of November 2003, the losses had reached £911 million. Widespread cost cutting was undertaken including 2000 job losses. Some subsidiaries were sold. The group also estimates that the Indian Ocean tsunami resulted in a loss of £11.5 million and fuel cost increases cost £17.5 million in 2005.

Think it over...

www.mytravelgroup.com is a source of news about this company and will give you up to date financial information.

First Choice Holidays

Like the others in the big four First Choice is a vertically integrated group with tour operation brands, travel agents and an airline in its portfolio. Tour operator brands include:

* Sovereign
* Hayes and Jarvis
* Meon Villas
* Villapool.com
* Exodux
* Flexiski
* Flexi Conference and Incentive
* Sunsail
* Island Cruises
* Platinum
* Crown Blue Line
* Connoisseur
* In Ireland First Choice has JWT Holidays and Falcon.

Theory into practice

First Choice has more specialist brands than the other major tour operators and its success is attributed to this. Choose one of the brands listed and find out more about that brand. Explain the types of products and services it provides and at whom they are targeted. Evaluate the success of the brand in today's holiday market.

CASE STUDY
First Choice holidays

Trading Report in Summer 2005

All of the Group's four Sectors have performed strongly in the year.

In the Mainstream Holidays Sector, our strategy of remixing the business away from the commoditised short-haul market, which now represents less than thirty per cent of Mainstream Holidays revenues, and continuing to develop differentiated product has proved successful. We have seen strong rates of sale on our long-haul offering (+18%) and exclusive products. Accordingly, we have achieved excellent top line growth of 13% at margins that are better than last year.

In the Specialist Holidays Sector another year of strong double-digit top line growth (+13%) has been achieved. Trading across Europe (+14%) and in Canada (+9%) has been particularly pleasing in light of certain of the businesses' key destinations being impacted by the Egypt bombings, the tsunami and hurricanes in the Caribbean.

Our Activity Holidays Sector has performed well (+4%) with improved asset utilisation in the Marine business (+5%) and strong organic growth in the Activity Adventure division (+15%). The 2003/04 and current year acquisitions in this division have also made strong contributions.

The rapid growth of our Online Destination Services Sector has continued in 2004/05 with online bednights sold increasing by 86%. The Hotelopia business-to-consumer online business has now been trading for just one year and now serves eight source markets.

Source: First Choice

1. Explain the following terms:
   * **Commoditised short haul**
   * **Mainstream holidays**
   * **Specialist holidays**
   * **Online destination services**
   * **Source markets**
   * **Asset utilisation**
   * **Differentiated products**

y-o-y variation %	Summer 05		
		Sales	Customers
Mainstream holidays*	Short haul	+6	–2
	Medium haul	+16	+6
	Long haul	+18	+17
TOTAL AVERAGE INCREASE		**+13**	**+4**
Specialist holidays	Europe	+14	+15
	North America	+9	+5
TOTAL AVERAGE INCREASE		**+13**	**+14**
Activity holidays	Marine	+5	n/a
	Adventure	+15	n/a
	Lake and Mountains	–55	n/a
TOTAL AVERAGE INCREASE		**+4**	**n/a**
Online distribution services		Sales	Bednights
Online	Hotelbeds	+44	+45
	Bedsonline	+128	+117
	Hotelopia	+1500	+1370
TOTAL AVERAGE INCREASE		**+95**	**+86**
Island Cruises		**+13**	

Notes
These figures are up to 15 October 2005
*These statistics reflect inclusive tour statistics only

TABLE 12.3 *Trading report*

Source: First Choice

2. **Where has the greatest growth occurred in the mainstream sector? Give reasons for this growth.**
3. **Sales in Lakes and Mountains holidays have fallen dramatically. Give possible reasons for this decline.**
4. **Account for the large increase in sales through Hotelopia.**

Extension tasks: Find out more about Hotelopia. Describe its products and services and identify the target market. Find out the current trading figures for First Choice Holidays and comment on the company's performance.

Thomas Cook

This company was formed in 1841. Today it is the fourth largest travel group in the UK and the third largest in the world operating across more than 1000 locations. Brands in its portfolio include:

* Club 18-30
* Flexibletrips.com
* JMC
* Neilson
* Style
* Sunset Holidays
* Signature
* Latitude
* Flythomascook.com
* Thomas Cook Sport
* Thomas Cook airlines.

Theory into practice

Find out the difference between Thomas Cook Airlines and Flythomascook. Write some key bullet points and check them against those of a colleague.

In 2004 Thomas Cook made profits of £51 million and expected to expand on these in 2005. Their focus for growth was to be on making better use of their customer database to encourage repeat customers and on getting more Internet bookings.

Think it over...

Thomas Cook provides a student pack on their website. You can download it at www. thomascook.com/corporate

✱ REMEMBER!

The big four operators are all vertically integrated companies. This means they own companies at every stage of the chain of distribution from airlines to travel agents.

CASE STUDY

Go West

Go West is a **medium-sized incoming tour operator based in Leicestershire in the UK,** close to the major centres of London, Birmingham, Leicester, Coventry and Nottingham and to touristic gems such as Oxford, Cambridge, Stratford-upon-Avon and Warwick.

Go West provides a **whole range of inbound services to the UK and Ireland and Mainland Europe:**

✳ **Accommodation** in all categories, from hostels and 'homestay' right up to 5 star hotels and castles
✳ **Sightseeing** and **touring**
✳ **Rail and coach tickets**
✳ **Meals** – from the simple to the exquisite
✳ **Guides** – for sightseeing, tour management or translation
✳ **Entrances** to attractions
✳ **Tickets** for theatres, shows and events
✳ Special deals with **ferry** companies and **Eurotunnel** for coach parties

In addition, Go West specializes in areas such as arranging **incentives, corporate and business travel,** often organising **meetings and specialist visits.** We also place students and business people on **language** courses, helped by our knowledge of the language school 'scene'.

As well as the UK head office, Go West also has a **European Sales Office in Budapest** (Hungary), **representation arrangements in Prague** (Czech Republic) and **Poland** and a planned office in **China.**

Together with English, **linguistic skills** of our experienced staff include the following: French, German, Italian, Russian,, Hungarian, Czech, Slovak and Chinese.

Our **core market is Central and Eastern Europe,** the market we began to target in 1990 and have remained leaders in since then. The demands of this market are many and varied, and this has ensured that we have built up a wide product range within the UK and Ireland, and have first-class buying power with our suppliers, including allocations at numerous hotels.

Go West also works with partners in the **Baltics, Russia, the CIS, and most recently China** (please visit our Chinese website: www.go-west.cn), **Australia, Malaysia and Singapore,** and has business links with no fewer than 40 nations.

First and foremost we work with the **local travel trade** in each of our partner countries, which is why you will find special 'trade pages' on our website. These contain an exciting array of programmes, tours and innovative ideas.

Source: GoWest

Answer the following:
1. **What type of organisation is Go West?**
2. **What types of partners does Go West work with?**
3. **What role does each partner have in helping Go West meet the needs of its clients?**
4. **Why does Go West have offices in Prague and Budapest?**
5. **Go West has recently employed a Chinese member of staff in its marketing department. Why do you think this is?**

   You can find further information at www. gowest.co.uk

Extension task: Suggest possible marketing objectives for Go West. Suggest ways of implementing these objectives. Use the VisitBritain website to help you identify

Inbound tour operators

Inbound tour operators cater for the needs of overseas visitors to the UK. You will not be as aware of them as you are of outbound tour operators as their promotional activities are directed at overseas customers. Their interests are represented in the UK by Ukinbound, a trade organisation. It has over 260 members in all sectors of tourism.

Domestic tour operators

Domestic tour operators package holidays in the UK for UK residents. Some of them are coach companies who place advertisements in the local newspapers. Like outbound operators, they offer beach, city, touring and special interest holidays.

CASE STUDY

Big four to become big three?

ABTA Convention special report: The big four vertically integrated tour operating groups will shrink to three in the future - or the big four will only be the same size as three are now.

The prediction came from former TUI UK boss Chris Mottershead at the ABTA Travel Convention.

He warned: 'Whilst the new entrants are growing apace, the big four are just scrapping over the same size pot.

'In the 1990s these were the boys dominating and moulding the market and growing aggressively. Now they have become inward-looking as they try to respond to the pace of change wrought by the Internet.'

Mottershead, now chief executive of Travelzest, claimed the majors – TUI UK, Thomas Cook, First Choice and MyTravel – 'can't reinvent themselves fast enough to compete, so they can only get better at what they do'.

He added: 'They are admittedly investing millions in the Internet but what else are they doing? Cutting shops, cutting staff, cutting commission, cutting capacity, cutting down hotel guarantees and on top of that trying to change people's perception of what they really are.'

The continued growth of US firms such as Expedia and Sabre with their deep pockets and expansion of no-frills carriers Ryanair and easyJet will put the major operators under even more pressure.

Mottershead went on: 'I believe the big four will be the big three or certainly no bigger than three of the big four are today.

'Cendant and Sabre will still be struggling to make returns and will be heavily focused on re-organising and re-structuring themselves and Expedia will still be struggling to grab a share of the sun market unless they acquire a mainstream operator.'

Report by Phil Davies

Source: Travelmole 26th November 2005

1. Why does Mottershead predict that the Big four's market will shrink?
2. Why does the expansion of Easyjet and Ryanair impact on tour operators?
3. Find out who these organisations are and what they offer:
   * Cendant
   * Sabre
   * Expedia
   * Travelzest.

Extension task: What do you think the future holds for the big four? We have noted, at the time of writing, that most are operating at a loss and are undertaking restructuring and cost cutting measures. Find out what the current trading position is for the big four. Analyse which of their markets are in decline and which areas are growing. Give recommendations for products or services they should be offering.

Transport providers

This sector includes airlines, ferry and cross channel providers, car hire companies, coach companies and rail companies.

Airlines

The chart compares airline capacity between the major UK carriers in 2000 and 2004.

	2000 SEAT KM AVAILABLE 000	2000 % OF ALL AIRLINES	2004 SEAT KM AVAILABLE 000	2004 % OF ALL AIRLINES	% CHANGE 2000–04
British Airways*	172,524	50.9	130,892	39.2	−24.1
Virgin Atlantic	39,228	11.6	38,820	11.6	−1.0
easyJet	5,801	1.7	25,176	7.5	+334.0
Britannia Airways (Thomsonfly)	22,236	6.6	23,768	7.1	6.9
MyTravel Airways**	20,317	6.0	21,141	6.3	4.1
First Choice Airways***	19,939	5.9	17,199	5.1	−13.7
Thomas Cook Airlines****	15,598	4.6	15,563	4.7	−0.2
Monarch Airways	15,427	4.6	15,098	4.5	−2.1
Bmi Group	9,376	2.8	12,547	3.8	+33.8
Flybe#	2,060	0.6	2,923	0.9	+41.9
Other airlines	16,289	4.8	30,914	9.3	+90.9
Total	338,795	100	334,041	100.0	−1.4

* includes franchises   ** previously known as Airtours International Airways
*** previously known as Air 2000   **** previously known as jmc airlines and before this Flying Colours Airlines
\# previously known as British European
\# \# On this table BMI British Midland and BMI Regional are combined for 2000, not 2004. BMIBaby also included.

TABLE 12.4 *Airline capacity*

Source: CAA UK Airline Statistics

The chart on page 222 is interesting as it lists all the UK's major airlines and shows the change in capacity over four years. We see that easyJet has experienced massive growth and other low cost carriers have also experienced growth at the expense of British Airways. You will note that Ryanair is not included in the chart and this is because Ryanair is registered in Ireland.

British Airways

British Airways is one of the largest airlines in Europe with about 290 aircraft in its fleet. After the events of 9/11 the airline suffered financial losses but managed to turn its fortunes around with a series of cost cutting exercises and computerisation of operations. Thus in 2003/04 the company achieved profits of over £230 million. The airline was one of the first to introduce self service check in kiosks at 39 airports around the world.

Theory into practice

Produce a description of British Airways or Virgin Atlantic including the scale and structure of the operation and its products and services. Explain how its products and services meet the needs of three different types of customers.

YEAR ENDED 31 MARCH	2000/01 £M	2001/02 £M	2002/03 £M	2003/04 £M	2004/05 £M	% CHANGE 2000–05
Turnover	9,278	8,340	7,688	7,560	7,813	−15.8
Operating Profit (Loss)	380	(110)	295	405	540	+42.1
Net Profit (Loss)	150	(200)	135	415		+176.7

TABLE 12.5 *British Airways*

Source: www.mintel.com

Virgin Atlantic

This is the UK's second largest airline with a fleet of 31 aircraft, mainly A340s. The airline flies to 22 long haul destinations in the US, the Caribbean, the Far East, India and Africa. Like British Airways, the airline suffered a downturn in passengers following 9/11, reflected in the group profit figures for 2002, but passenger numbers, and profits have now recovered. Virgin is the first British airline to place orders for the new Airbus A380.

✱ REMEMBER!

The Airbus A380 is a super plane, introduced in 2005. It can seat 555–800.

YEAR ENDED 30 APRIL	2000 £M	2001 £M	2002 £M	2003 £M	2004 £M	% CHANGE
Turnover	1,268	1,518	1,500	1,401	1,272	+0.3
Group profit before tax (loss)	4	46	(93)	16	21	+425.0
*10 months to 204						

TABLE 12.6 *Virgin Atlantic*

Source: www.mintel.com

	UK	EUROPE
2004	Due Airways	SkyNet, JetGreen, JetMagic (all Ireland); Sobelair (Belgium); V-Bird (Netherlands); Volare (Italy); Air Polonia (Poland)
2003	Euroceltic	Aero Lloyd (Germany); Air Lib (France)
2002	British World Airways, HC Airlines	
2001	Gill Airways	Sabena (Belgium); Swissair (Switzerland)
2000	Debonair AB Airlines	

TABLE 12.7 *Airline collapses failures since 2000*

Source: *Travel Trade Gazette* 10th June 2005

Low cost airlines

The principle of low cost airlines is to cut costs as much as possible so that low prices can be charged. If costs are cut then services are either cut or paid for as extras. Sometimes flights are free to promote custom and the airline makes its profits from add-on sales. Low cost airlines sell food and drinks on board. They charge a lot for excess baggage. In common with other airlines they sell gifts and perfumes on board. They also make revenue through commission on selling insurance, hotel accommodation and car hire through their websites.

These are the services that passengers on low cost airlines can expect to be excluded from their fare:

* Allocated seats
* Food and drink
* Headrest covers
* Blankets
* Entertainment
* Hotel accommodation if a flight is delayed or cancelled.

In addition, they should expect lower baggage allowances (Ryanair has 15kg).

New low cost airlines are constantly emerging but many go out of business very quickly. An important issue is that passengers booking flights only are not protected if the airline goes bust whereas people who book package holidays are covered by bonding schemes and will be offered refunds or alternative flights if the tour operator goes out of business.

easyJet

easyJet is a major low cost airline that has enjoyed huge growth and success over the last ten years since it commenced operations in 1995. It has a fleet of 98 aircraft flying on 193 routes within Europe all, therefore, short haul. It has two types of aircraft, Airbus A319s and Boeing 737s. In 2004 the airline carried 24.3 million passengers.

The revenue and profits of this airline have risen incredibly over the last few years as the chart demonstrates.

TABLE 12.8 *easyJet revenue and profit*

YEAR ENDED 30 SEPTEMBER	2000 £M	2001 £M	2002 £M	2003 £M	2004 £M	% CHANGE 2000–04
Turnover	263.7	356.9	551.8	931.8	109.1	+313.7
Group profit before tax	22.1	40.1	71.6	51.5	62.2	+181.4

Source: www.mintel.com

Charter Airlines

You saw earlier that the big four tour operators each have their own airline. An example is First Choice Holidays whose airline is First Choice Airways. The airline has a fleet of 32 aircraft. First Choice runs this airline as part of its vertically integrated operations. The purpose is to serve the package holidays which First Choice Holidays organise. Thomsonfly, My Travel Airways and Thomas Cook Airlines are all of a similar size to First Choice Airways and similarly serve the package tours of their parent companies.

Sea travel

As we live on an island, sea travel has always been an important part of our travel and tourism industry. The main mode of transport to the continent was sea travel across the English

Source: P & O Ferries

P&O offers a number of additional features, as well as price, to compete within the crowded market.

Channel. In addition we have important sea routes to Ireland across the North Sea and to Holland from Eastern ports. In the north, particularly from Newcastle, there are routes to

Scandinavia. The largest companies operating across the Channel are P&O, Brittany Ferries and SeaFrance. SeaFrance operates on the Dover to Calais route and is the only French operator carrying about three million passengers a year. In May 2004 SpeedFerries started a single fast catamaran between Dover and Boulogne, claiming to be the first low cost ferry operator. The market is extremely competitive as competition is not only between ferry operators but from the Eurotunnel services and low cost airlines.

CASE STUDY

Eurotunnel

Eurotunnel manages the infrastructure of the Channel Tunnel and operates accompanied truck shuttle and passenger (car and coach) services between Folkestone, UK and Calais/Coquelles, France. Eurotunnel also earns toll revenue from train operators (Eurostar for rail passengers, and EWS and SNCF for rail freight) which use the Tunnel.

Eurotunnel is open 24 hours a day, seven days a week, 365 days a year. In 2004, Eurotunnel carried 1.3 million trucks, 2.1 million cars and 63,500 coaches on its shuttle services. It also provided access through the Tunnel for 7.3 million Eurostar passengers and 1.9 million tonnes of rail freight.

Eurotunnel is quoted on the London, Paris and Brussels Stock Exchanges. Eurotunnel has 2,546,097,327 shares in issue. As of 31 December 2004, the capital is split between individuals (68%) and institutions (32%).

Eurotunnel's operating revenue in 2004 was £538 million. Transport activities account for 96% of revenue, from Eurotunnel's own shuttle services (53%) and from the railways (43%). The remaining 4% of revenue is derived from non-transport activities including retail, telecoms and property development.

As of 31 December 2004, Eurotunnel employed 3,205 people split between the UK (1,278) and France (1,927).

	2004	2003	2002	2001	2000	1999
In £M	1.466	1.435	1.573	1.631	1.630	1.546
Total turnover	555	584	581	564	600	654
Operating margin	294	316	334	322	345	355
Operating profit	171	170	194	183	208	210
Net interest	(298)	(318)	(299)	(330)	(332)	(349)
Underlying loss	(127)	(148)	(105)	(147)	(124)	(139)
Net profit/(loss)	(570*)	(1,334)*	302	(132)	(124)	202

(*after impairment charges)

Source: Eurotunnel

TABLE 12.9 *Summary financial information*

1. Draw a graph illustrating the revenues and profits/losses of Eurotunnel between 1999 and 2004.
2. Explain why Eurotunnel is making losses in spite of extensive revenue.
3. Find out what is meant by 'the capital is split between individuals and institutions'?
4. Find someone who has travelled through the Channel tunnel and report on their experience.

Extension task: Carry out further research and find out who are the institutional shareholders of Eurotunnel. Find out also what the stated marketing objectives of Eurotunnel are.

Road travel

Travel by car is very important in the UK. We have extensive motorway networks and good road systems and most people own a car. However, it is the car hire market that is important in terms of organisations in the travel and tourism industry. Domestic car hire is a growing and vibrant market. According to a 2005 Euromonitor report the market size for car rentals in the UK had grown to a value of £1.16 billion by 2004, a rise of 2.2% on the previous year. More than half of car hire sales are for business use. Major car hire companies in the UK are Hertz, Avis, National, Europcar and Enterprise. Hertz is the market leader with a market share of 19.2% in 2004. The major companies control 64.9% of the market.

CASE STUDY

Hertz and travel agents

Hertz restructures travel agency remuneration to reflect industry changes

London, 29 October, 2004. Hertz, the world's largest car rental firm, today confirmed that starting April 2005, bookings made by travel agents on behalf of corporate clients on specifically negotiated contract rates only, will no longer be eligible for commission and bonus payments. This policy will apply to reservations made from all sources for rentals in the key European markets. All other commission programmes will remain unchanged.

Bill Jones, Vice President, Marketing and Sales said: 'To help the Company remain cost competitive, Hertz will no longer make commission or bonus payments on negotiated contract rates, but all other programmes sold by agents remain commissionable and we believe that significant opportunities remain for agents to earn significant revenue in the still growing discretionary segment of the car rental business.'

Hertz is already talking to its travel agent partners across Europe to make them aware of the new arrangements and to discuss ways in which they can implement this new policy and work collaboratively to help agents grow their business aggressively.

Source: Hertz

Q. How important is the trade to Budget and what prompted the new scheme?

A. Since Budget was bought out of administration by Avis Europe in 2003, we have been concentrating on restructuring the business. We are now in a position to re-establish a relationship with the trade, which is a fundamental part of our turnaround strategy.

Research suggests that only about 10% of agents offer car hire to clients without being prompted, so we hope the launch of 1-2-3 will encourage agents to book Budget – and receive suitable rewards for doing so. We want to make agents a key part of our strategy of expanding our independent traveller business.

Agents can often secure more commission by selling car rental than selling a flight, and we want to educate them on how to maximise this opportunity by suggesting car hire to every customer and selling up to larger vehicles. The 1-2-3 scheme is a simple, easily accessible tool for the trade to get the rewards they deserve for booking Budget.

We will also be making point-of-sale material, such as leaflets, available to help agents boost their sales.

Source: *Travel Trade Gazette* Budget Rent-a-Car Q & A, 14th October 2005

The extract from the Hertz press release and the piece about Budget illustrate the relationship between hire car companies and travel agents. Answer the following:

1. How do you think travel agents responded to the Hertz announcement?
2. Why do you think Hertz made this decision?
3. Why does Hertz work with travel agents?
4. What is Budget's approach to travel agents?
5. Visit the Budget 1-2-3 website and find out more about their commission structure.

Coach operators

There are around 650 coach operators in the UK. Wallace Arnold and Shearings are the largest companies and hold about 15% of the market between them. Other examples include Eurolines, Cosmos, Titan and Travelsphere. All these coach operators offer package holidays not just coach transport. The market for coach tours tends to be older – 50 plus. Singles are an important market and the fastest growing in this sector. Travelsphere is the market leader for this type of holiday for single travellers. The larger operators like Shearings also own hotels and so are vertically integrated companies.

Rail travel

Network Rail owns and operates the national rail network in the UK. Their role is to maintain the infrastructure and renew tracks as necessary. In addition there are train operating companies (TOCs) who lease trains from rolling stock companies. There are 26 train operating companies in the UK and they compete for franchises to run each service.

The Strategic Rail Authority issues the franchises. This body also monitors the train operating companies to make sure the interests of rail passengers are protected. They are able to fine the TOCs if they fail to meet agreed standards. The TOCs are commercial companies and aim to make a profit but they do receive government grants. Freight services are run by specialist operators.

Network Rail

Network Rail is the operator of Britain's rail infrastructure. They have to ensure railway safety. They do this by maintaining or upgrading the 21,000 miles of track owned by the company. They are also responsible for the signalling operations on the railways. Control rooms monitor traffic on the rail network at all times. Network Rail has over 40,000 bridges which must be maintained. Existing railway tunnels, over 600 of them, have to be looked after and sometimes new tunnels have to be built.

Network Rail also owns 2500 railway stations. They are not responsible for running all these stations but lease most of them to the train operating companies who then run them. The 17 largest stations are run by Network Rail themselves and they are known as Major Stations.

Network Rail states that its key objectives are to:

* improve safety
* produce higher service performance
* improve customer relations-customers are passenger and freight operating companies, community groups, government agencies and local authorities
* improve financial control – all profits are reinvested into the railway infrastructure, there are no payments to shareholders
* achieve organisational effectiveness and management of assets.

As there are 26 train operating companies, they need to have a common voice to represent their interests and provide advice and support. This is provided by the Association of Train Operating Companies (ATOC), an incorporated association owned by its members. It was set up by the train operators formed during privatisation of the railways under the Railways Act 1993.

As well as being the official voice of the passenger rail industry, it also provides its members with a range of services that enable them to comply with conditions laid on them in their franchise agreements and operating licences. These include:

* revenue allocation and settlement
* National Rail Enquiries
* railcard marketing
* staff travel arrangements
* international products
* the relationship with London Regional Transport
* travel agent licensing.

Theory into practice

Choose one of the 26 train operating companies and research its activities. Find out its main objectives, how it relates to Network Rail, other train operating companies and the ATOC. Find out also what legal and regulatory requirements apply specifically to rail companies. Produce a set of notes on your findings which you can discuss with your group.

Eurostar

Eurostar is the passenger train service for the Channel tunnel. It operates from London Waterloo and Ashford, Kent to Paris, Lille and Brussels. Eurostar is owned by London and Continental Railways and run by a management company.

Accommodation providers

These providers include hotels, guesthouses, motels, holiday centres, self-catering establishments and camping and caravan parks. We will take a more detailed look at some of these types of business.

Hotels

A hotel is an establishment that offers accommodation, food and drink to anyone who is fit to receive and is willing to pay. Many hotels also provide leisure facilities, conference and banqueting facilities and business services.

Euromonitor, a market research company estimates that the value of the sector is about £8.8 billion but the British Hospitality Association claims £27 billion per year. The figures are so disparate as the sector is very hard to analyse as it includes hundreds of establishments which are not registered. About 22,000 hotels and guest houses are registered with tourist boards and about 16,000 bed and breakfast establishments. Whitbread in the largest hotel operator, owning Marriott and Premier Travel, but the company announced the transfer of its franchised Marriott hotels business to a newly formed 50:50 joint venture with Marriott International in 2005.

Although these figures were accurate at the time they were compiled, they change quickly

TOP 20 UK HOTEL BRANDS 2003–2004 (BY NUMBER OF BEDROOMS)			
Company	Number of hotels	Brands	Number of rooms
Whitbread Hotel Group	505	Courtyard by Marriott (11), Marriott (51), Premier Travel Inn (443)*	37,148
InterContinental Hotels Group (as at 31/12/03)	204	InterContinental (2), Crowne Plaza, Holiday Inn, Express by Holiday Inn	29,053
Hilton International	78		16,044
Travelodge (Permira)	255		13,300
Accor Hotels	84	Sofitel (1), Novotel (28), Mercure (1), Ibis (42), Etap (2), Formule 1 (10)	11,321
Thistle Hotels	54		10,122
Choice Hotels Europe	88	Quality (53), Comfort (27), Sleep (5), Clarion (3)	7,000
Jarvis Hotels	60	Ramada Jarvis (54), Jarvis (5), Travelodge (1)	6,745
Britannia Hotels	24		5,175
Macdonald Hotels	63		5,022
Queens Moat Houses	33	Moat House (32), Holiday Inn (1)	4,933
Corus Hotels	65		4,863
De Vere Hotels	35	De Vere Hotels (21), Village Leisure (14) *Timeshare Lodges (132)*	4,542
Millennium Copthorne Hotels	17	Millennium (6), Copthorne (11)	4,047
Jurys Doyle Hotel Group	15	Hotels (6), Inns (9)	3,401
Imperial London Hotels	6		2,944
London and Edinburgh Inns Group	64	Inns (36), Swallow (28)	2,916
Marriott International	10	Renaissance (5), Marriott (5)	2,953
Shearings Hotels	36		2,800
Warner Holidays (Bourne Leisure)	13	Historic (6), Character (3), Classic (4)	2,652

*Marriott is now owned by Premier Travel Inn

Source: Information has kindly been supplied by Wordsmith & Company and the British Hospitality Association

TABLE 12.10 *UK hotels*

as companies dispose of assets and buy different ones.

A lot of hotels are run by their owners and the average size of a hotel is 20 rooms. The major groups have a lot of influence on the hotel business. The UK hotel industry is affected by economic issues including exchange rates which impact on tourist arrivals. When the pound is strong against the dollar and euro, tourists are less likely to visit the UK as they find it expensive. Fewer visitors results in rooms being let for lower rates and in lower room occupancy levels.

Budget hotels

A budget hotel is a type of hotel that caters for visitors on short stays and those who are travelling. This type of accommodation has more or less replaced the motel sector. Motels were one storey buildings where guests could park their car outside their room and go directly inside. They were built near major road routes so that they were convenient for travellers. Budget hotels are also often built near major routes but there is an increasing trend to build them in cities. These hotels have fewer facilities than other hotels, for example, there are few staff, perhaps just one person on reception and no room service. There are no luxuries and usually no catering facilities. However, en-suite bathrooms are provided.

This sector is growing because customers realise that the budget hotel sector gives excellent value for money in convenient locations.

There are several companies offering budget hotels. The chart shows the number of budget hotels and their ownership in 2004.

Budget hotels are such good value that they enjoy a 90% plus occupancy rate. Travel Inn is the United Kingdom's leading budget hotel brand, totalling more than 230 hotels. There is a Travel Inn at County Hall, London, on the south bank of the Thames near Westminster and the London Eye.

An article from Caterer and Hotelier magazine explains:

The number of branded budget hotel rooms is predicted to rise to 75,000 by the end of 2005 and to 87,000 in 2007, according to a new report from consultants Deloitte.

This will mean adding between 6,000 and 6,300 new bedrooms each year and maintaining the level of growth seen in 2003, when more than 6,000 new budget bedrooms were opened. This represented a 10.6% rise on the 4,500 new rooms that came on stream in 2002.

Since then, the average size of budget hotels has grown from 61 to 64 bedrooms.

Both owner-operated and franchised hotels will fuel the growth, which will be underpinned by an increase in room bookings via the Internet, said the report.

Source: *Caterer & Hotelkeeper magazine*, 25 November 2004

BUDGET HOTELS IN THE UK 31 Aug 2005					
Brand	Company	Hotels 2005	Hotels 2001	Bedrooms 2005	Bedrooms 2001
Premier Travel Inn	Whitbread	460+	405	28,000*	23,302*
Travelodge	Permira	270+	215	15,000	11,590
Express by Holiday Inn	InterContinental Hotels	102	63	10,107	5,907
Ibis	Accor UK	44	37	5,977	4,019
Innkeeper's Lodge	Mitchells & Butlers	79	–	2,300+	–
Comfort Inn	CHE Hotel Group	24	31	1,431	2,042
Campanile	Groupe Envergure	17	15	1,263	1,113
Days Inn	Cendant	23	14	1,242	103
Formule 1	Accor	10	8	746	595
Ramada Encore	Ramada	3	–	353	–
Welcome Lodge	Welcome Break	20	9	1282	569
JDW Lodges	JD Wetherspoon	11	5	314	89
Sleep Inn	CHE Group	6	3	509	226
Tulip Inn	Golden Tulip	5	2	577	199
Etap	Accor	2	2	150	69
Dolby	Dolby Hotels	1	2	4	130
Kyriad	Groupe Envergure	1	2	50	130
Total		1,784	812	69,365	50,818

TABLE 12.11 *UK budget hotels*

Source: Information has kindly been supplied by Wordsmith & Company and the British Hospitality Association

Guest houses and bed and breakfast establishments

Usually the difference between a hotel and a guest house is one of size but also a guest house might not provide food and drink whereas a hotel usually does. Most guest houses are family run and only have a few rooms. They are often situated in large houses that would originally have been intended for families.

Years ago people often went to guest houses, or boarding houses as they were known, for their annual summer holiday. Families sometimes returned to their favourite houses year after year. They would expect to have a bedroom – a large room might be designated a family room – they would not expect to have a private bathroom but would share with all the other guests. Breakfast would be served at a set time and after that families had to go out, whether it was rain or shine, and not return until early evening. Dinner would be served at a set time in the early evening. Afterwards the family might go for a walk along the promenade or go to a show.

The British seaside was full of houses like this and of course there are still thousands. Today the facilities have mostly improved as people's expectations have grown. Many guest houses have rooms with private bathrooms and have lounges for guests to sit in if they wish.

Self-catering apartments and cottages

Many people prefer self-catering accommodation for the extra freedom it allows them in deciding when to eat and controlling the type of food on offer. Self-catering allows a greater level of informality

CASE STUDY

Travelodge

In 2005 Travelodge had 286 properties and more than 15,000 rooms. The company is owned by Permira who bought it for £712 million in 2003.

Since the acquisition many new Travelodges have been built. Many of these have cafes within them whereas the old ones relied on the nearby Little Chef for catering facilities for guests. Older properties have been refurbished and the facilities now on offer are:

* King-sized bed* with cosy duvet
* En-suite bathroom
* Remote-control colour TV
* Tea and coffee-making facilities
* Direct dial phone*
* Internet access*
* In room films*
* Family rooms
* Smoking and non smoking rooms
* Rooms with disabled facilities
* 24 hour reception
* Fast check in – no check out
* Breakfast*
* Drinks and snacks vending.

    *In most hotels

Source: www.travelodge.com

Forty-five per cent of bookings for Travelodge are made through its website which means administrative costs are reduced.

1. **Which types of customers stay in Travelodges?**
2. **Can you suggest any products or services which the customers may need and are not being provided?**
3. **Why is there growth in the budget hotel market?**
4. **Find out more about Permira. What other types of operations are in its portfolio? Why did the company acquire Travelodge? Make detailed notes on your findings.**

Extension task: Find out about other hotel groups in the budget sector. Try to find out which companies are independent and which are parts of other groups. Compare prices and services offered by the different groups.

on holidays. Many tour operators specialise in offering self-catering accommodation holidays. The accommodation may be quite basic, for example in tents on campsites, or it may be luxury villas.

Generally, self-catering properties are suitable for people who want to be independent and do not expect to have the services that would be provided in a hotel such as entertainment, bars and restaurants. However, many resorts have blocks of self-catering accommodation where all the facilities of a hotel are available and yet kitchens and cooking facilities are provided.

Camping and Caravan Parks

The UK Caravan Parks and Campsites Directory shows that there are an incredible 2548 caravan sites, parks and campsites in the UK.

Camping and caravanning have become an important sector of the tourism industry both in the UK and throughout Europe. Camping has changed a lot over the years and campsites have become much more sophisticated and offer many more facilities than they used to.

Customers expect tents to be fixed rather than bring their own, many prefer holiday homes to tents and in fact many campsites now prefer to be known as holiday centres and do not allow any campers bringing their own tents or touring caravans. This enables the campsite owners to exert much greater control over the layout and appearance of the site, increasing its appeal to visitors. Campsite owners have also increased the level of services and hospitality on offer in line with increased customer expectations.

A wide range of accommodation and food services are on offer at some large camping and caravanning sites including a range of luxury accommodation, bars, restaurants, takeaways and supermarkets.

12.2 Legal and regulatory requirements of organisations in a selected sector of the travel and tourism industry

There are regulations and legislation that organisations in the travel and tourism industry must adhere to. They affect the way companies operate and the products and services they provide.

Firstly we will examine legislation specific to travel and tourism.

Package Travel Regulations 1992

As a result of an EC Directive, since 1993 all UK tour operators and travel agents offering package holidays have been subject to the Package Travel Regulations. The regulations set out the tour operators responsibilities to their customers and what they can do if the regulations are breached. If there is a breach the customer has a case against the tour operator not each individual supplier.

A package is defined as:
'the pre-arranged combination of at least two of the following components when sold or offered for sale at an inclusive price and when the service covers a period of more than 24 hours or includes overnight accommodation
(a) Transport;
(b) Accommodation;
(c) Other tourist service not ancillary to (a) or (b) and accounting for a significant proportion of the package.'

The controls lay down terms to be included in every contract for a package. These terms cover:

* the transfer of bookings

* the significant alteration of a package

* the right of withdrawal by a consumer, where there has been a significant alteration to a package

* the failure to provide a significant proportion of services previously contracted for

* the liability of the organiser and/or retailer.

The two principal sections of the Regulations provide financial protection for prepayments and require tour operators to provide what is promised.

The main provisions are:

* tour operators are responsible for the safety of their customers – this means for their safety in the accommodation, on the flight, etc. and must provide assistance in resort

* tour operators must not give inaccurate brochure descriptions

* last minute surcharges cannot be imposed

* if the operator goes bust there must be a guaranteed refund.

There are also regulations about the information that should be provided to the customer and what happens if the contract is altered in any way.

There are requirements for the customer also. If a customer has a complaint they should report it in resort so that the rep has an opportunity to resolve it. If they need to write to the tour operator to complain, this should be done within a reasonable period (usually 28 days).

Tour operators

Compensation and legal redress is available for customers, through the UK courts, when there is a breach of the regulations. Booking conditions are issued by tour operators and explain all requirements for both parties.

The Department of Trade and Industry provides a free booklet 'Looking into the Package Travel Regulations' which fully explains the regulations.

You should also be aware of the following regulatory bodies and their codes of conduct:

* Civil Aviation Authority (CAA)

* Air Travel Organisers' Licensing (ATOL).

All tour operators selling packages must be bonded or protect the prepayments they hold. That means if they go bust before travel, customers should get a refund, or, if they are already abroad, they will be able to get home without any extra payments. Package holidays that include flights must be protected by an ATOL. ATOL is a statutory scheme managed by the Civil Aviation Authority to protect the public from losing money or being stranded abroad because of the failure of air travel firms. All tour operators selling flights and air holidays are required to hold a licence from the CAA. In order to get the licence the company must provide proof or a bond, a financial guarantee provided by a bank or insurance company. If the company goes bust the CAA calls in the bond and uses the money to pay for people abroad to continue their holidays or to make refunds to those who have paid but not travelled.

CASE STUDY

ATOL

In October 2003 the Air Travel Organisers' Licences (ATOL) Regulations were amended so that companies such as travel agents who sold split packages, where the different parts of the package are put together by the agent, now need to hold an ATOL. This would require travel agents to acquire bonding and to complete applications for ATOLs. A small business ATOL has been introduced to help some agents and travel trade associations such as Consortia and the Travel Trust Association have put systems in place to help members affected by the changes.

Find out more about ATOL and the changes in regulations. Look at the websites:

www.caa.co.uk
www.traveltrust.co.uk

1. **What are the implications for travel agents of the changes?**
2. **Write a brief report on your findings.**

Extension task: In 2005 there was a lobby to parliament from various sectors in the travel trade to impose a levy of £1 per passenger on air travel. This levy was to be used to create a fund which could be used to repatriate passengers or refund them in the event of an airline collapse. Find out more about this proposal and analyse the reasons for its rejection by parliament. Give your own views on whether it was a useful idea.

It is the largest travel protection scheme in the UK, covering 28 million people, and the only one for flights and air holidays sold by tour operators. Unfortunately companies collapse very often so the scheme is much needed.

Links between Sectors

Although there are several different sectors in the travel and tourism industry, they are all interdependent, as you noted on page 151 when you studied channels of distribution. For example, tour operators need the services of the accommodation sector and transport sector to put together packages. They rely on the attractions sector to add appeal to destinations. Ancillary services will provide information to holiday makers about their chosen destinations, if required, and travel agents may sell holidays on behalf of the tour operator.

ABTA

The Association of British Travel Agents (ABTA) is the UK's best known trade association for tour operators and travel agents. Eighty-five per cent of UK sold holidays are sold through ABTA agents.

It costs about £1500–2000 to join ABTA initially but it is important for agents to join as the public will look for an ABTA travel agent when booking travel and holidays. It gives them a sense of security, knowing that the travel agency follows ABTA's code of conduct and is bonded. However, membership is not compulsory for travel agents.

The main benefit to consumers of booking through an ABTA travel agent is that in the event of the agent or tour operator going bust, ABTA will ensure that people can continue their holiday arrangements with another operator or be repatriated.

ABTA Code of Conduct

The code itself is too lengthy to reproduce here but is available on the ABTA website. This is an extract from the ABTA website. It includes elements of the code relevant to consumers and travel agents.

Advertising

- ABTA Members must not mislead you with their advertising and must include all compulsory charges in their prices e.g. UK Air Passenger Duty [Code 1.3].

Booking Procedures

- When you book with an ABTA Member they must give you accurate information to help you choose the travel arrangements that are right for you [Code 1.1].

- ABTA Members must follow all the necessary legal requirements such as the ATOL Regulations and must make you aware of the terms and conditions that apply [Code 1.4].

- ABTA Members must also give you guidance about any health requirements and the passport and visa requirements for your travel arrangements [Code 1.6].

- If you have any special requests concerning a disability or other medical condition ABTA Members must ensure that these are dealt with properly and confidentially [Code 1.4 (iii)]. ABTA Members must also give you

information about travel insurance [Code 1.7].

- Before completing a booking, ABTA Members must tell you if the Foreign and Commonwealth Office has issued advice about your destination [Code 1.6 (iii)].

Once the booking is made

- ABTA Members must notify you as soon as possible if it is necessary to change or cancel your travel arrangements. An ABTA Member cannot cancel your booking after the date for payment of the full price unless it is necessary to do so for reasons outside its control. If this happens, the ABTA Member must offer you the choice of having all your money back or choosing alternative travel arrangements [Code 2.1 & 2.2].

- If an ABTA Member makes a significant change to your travel arrangements they must offer you the choice of accepting the changed travel arrangements or having all your money back [Code 2.2].

- If an ABTA Member does cancel your booking or makes a significant change to the travel arrangements

after the date for payment of the full price they must offer you compensation unless the reason for the cancellation or change was outside of their control [Code 2.1 & 2.2].

Building Works

- An ABTA Member must notify you as soon as possible of any serious building works at your destination. If you wish you can transfer to another holiday or cancel and have your money back [Code 2.5].

Complaints

- If you have a complaint about your travel arrangements you should write to the ABTA Member concerned. They must provide you with a full reply within 28 days. If you remain dissatisfied you should write again pointing out the areas of dispute. Again the ABTA Member must respond within 28 days (see 'Complaining') [Code 3.1].

- If you fail to reach a satisfactory position with the ABTA Member you can have the matter resolved through the ABTA Arbitration Scheme (see 'Independent Arbitration') [Code 3.4].

Association of British Travel Agents

Source: Association of British Travel Agents

Any company in breach of the code is reported to a Code of Conduct Committee. If a case is found against the member then disciplinary action may be taken. This could result in a reprimand, a fine or expulsion.

Aviation Security Act 1982 and the Aviation and Maritime Security Act 1990.

These acts cover safety and security at airports and on aircraft. It is an offence to endanger safety at airports or on an aircraft. It is also an offence for an unauthorised person to enter the restricted zone of an airport or an aircraft and to remain there after being asked to leave. The Anti-Terrorism, Crime and Security bill of 2001 extends the Aviation Security Act and gives power of removal of unauthorised persons.

If a passenger gives a false statement when asked questions, for example about their baggage, they can be prosecuted under the Aviation and Maritime Security Act.

Think it over...

In 2004 a woman claimed that there was a bomb on board a flight from Dublin to Stansted. This wasn't true and the woman was accused of making a false accusation which she denied. She was then remanded in custody to await trial by jury. The moral of this tale is never be tempted to make jokes about security matters at airports.

Key term

Denied Boarding Legislation – Regulation (EC) No 261/2004 of the European Parliament and of the Council of 11 February 2004 establishes common rules on compensation and assistance to passengers in the event of 'denied boarding' and of cancellation or long delay of flights.

This extract from the Air Transport Users Council website at www.auc.org.uk gives an example of liability under Denied Boarding regulations:

OVERBOOKING AND DENIED BOARDING COMPENSATION

'Overbooking' is when airlines take more reservations for a flight than there are seats on the plane. This is not illegal. Airlines do it deliberately because they usually expect some of the passengers not to turn up. Usually it works out OK. But occasionally too many people turn up for a flight, so some of them get left behind (or 'bumped').

If you are 'bumped' off a flight at an airport in the EU or at an airport outside the EU when flying to an EU airport on an EU airline, then the airline must pay you compensation. This is called Denied Boarding Compensation (or 'DBC'). The rules for payment of DBC are set out in an EC Regulation (EC Council Regulation 261/2004).

This Regulation says that you will be entitled to compensation provided you can satisfy three conditions. These are:

1. you must have a valid ticket
2. you must have a confirmed reservation
3. you must have checked-in by the deadline given to you by the airline.

The legislation is fairly detailed – full information can be found at the AUC website.

Source: www.auc.org.uk

Domestic and European drivers' hours

Regulations regarding driving hours are very strict and apply across Europe. Drivers of vehicles with more than 18 seats, or only ten, on international journeys are subject to European Union Drivers Hours legislation and must record their hours on a tachograph. There are some exemptions to these rules, for example for journeys under 50 kilometres. However, these drivers are still covered by UK legislation, for example the Transport Act of 1968.

The regulations state that a driver is entitled to a 45 minute break after 4½ hours of driving or 15 minute breaks totalling to at least 45 minutes during a 4½ hour period. There is a maximum of nine hours actual driving per day; this can be increased to ten hours twice a week. A rest period between working days is normally 11 hours but there are variations on this allowing split rest periods. The rules are complicated and can be found in full at www.coach-tours.co.uk. Drivers on tour buses must be aware of, and follow, these rules.

Health and Safety legislation

The Food Safety Act and the Control of Substances Hazardous to Health Regulations are particularly relevant in the hospitality and airline sectors. The Food Safety Act makes it an offence to:

✱ render food injurious to health

✱ sell food which fails to comply with food safety requirements:

- if it has been rendered injurious to health

- if it is unfit for human consumption

- if it is so contaminated that it would not be reasonable to expect it to be used for human consumption in that state

✱ sell any food which is not of the nature or substance or quality demanded by the purchaser

✱ display food for sale with a label which:

- falsely describes the food, or;

- is likely to mislead as to the nature or substance or quality of the food.

The Control of Substances Hazardous to Health Regulations 2002 requires employers to control exposures to hazardous substances to protect both employees and others who may be exposed from work activities. Examples of substances include cleaning agents.

Health and Safety at Work Act

Under the Health and Safety at Work Act 1974 employers are responsible for the health, safety and welfare at work of their employees. Employers are also under a duty to ensure, so far as is reasonably practicable, the health and safety of anyone else on the premises or anyone who may be affected by their activities.

Employers must:

* provide a safe system of work

* provide a safe place of work

* provide safe equipment, plant and machinery

* ensure people are safe and competent at their job including management

* carry out risk assessments as set out in the regulations, and take steps to eliminate or control these risks

* inform employees fully about all potential hazards associated with any work process, chemical substance or activity, including providing instruction, training and supervision

* appoint a 'competent person' responsible for health and safety. Competent persons, such as a head of health and safety, oversee day-to-day safety management, oversee safety inspections, and liaise with staff safety reps

* consult with workplace safety representatives. If a union is recognised, the employer must set up and attend a workplace safety committee

* provide adequate facilities for employees' welfare at work.

The Federation of Tour Operators (FTO) has devised a code of practice which gives advice on health and safety matters including:

* fire safety

* food safety

* pool safety

* general safety

* beach safety

* legionella management

* children's clubs

* incident management.

The FTO also provides a safety training video and courses on health and safety.

Consumer Protection Act 1987

This act makes it an offence to give customers a misleading price indication about goods and services. It lays down rules about use of terms such as 'reduced' and 'bargain'. Price indications given verbally are also covered. In travel and tourism this legislation has most relevance to brochures and advertising.

The Supply of Goods and Services Act 1982 (amended 1994) applies to tour operators as it says contracts should be carried out using 'reasonable skill and care'. This applies to contracts for holidays or other travel services. Also the holiday should comply with any descriptions and be of a satisfactory standard. Some holidaymakers take their holiday brochure with them. This means they can easily check whether the holiday has been described accurately. The operator may also have committed a criminal offence under the Trade Descriptions Act of 1968 if there is a misdescription.

Trades Descriptions Act 1968

This act is one of the most important pieces of consumer legislation and section 14 is the most relevant part for travel and tourism. This section deals with the supply of goods and services. It states that it is an offence to make a statement that is known to be false or to recklessly make a statement which is false. This applies to the provision of services, facilities and accommodation and the location of amenities of any accommodation. An offence can be committed even when there is no intention to deceive the customer.

Unfair Terms in Consumer Contracts Regulations 1999

When a holiday, a hotel room or flight is booked, a contract is entered into with the seller. The seller will publish terms and conditions associated with that contract. You can easily read these in any holiday brochure.

These regulations protect consumers against unfair standard terms in contracts they make with traders. Sometimes terms and conditions are introduced which may reduce the consumer's statutory rights or may impose unfair burdens on the consumer over and above the obligations of ordinary rules of law.

Data Protection Act 1998

This act provides rights for those who have information held about them in 'relevant filing systems'. This may be on computer or in paper files. The act also requires those who record and use personal information to follow sound practice. An individual can have access to information held about them and, if necessary, have it corrected or deleted. Data subjects must have the opportunity to consent to the collection and processing of their data. Personal data must be kept secure, up to date and not longer than actually necessary. The Data Protection Registrar, an independent officer who reports directly to Parliament, administers this act. If you want to have access to information you must make a written request to the holder of the information. This act is very important as so much information is held about us. Travel and tourism companies hold a lot of customer information, which must be revealed if a customer asks for it.

Examples of legislation that affects employment in travel and tourism

Race Relations Act 1976

This makes discrimination on racial grounds unlawful in employment, training, education and the provision of goods, facilities and services. The Act defines two main types of discrimination:

* Direct discrimination occurs when someone is treated less favourably because of their colour, nationality, citizenship or national origin.

* Indirect discrimination occurs when rules which apply to everyone and appear to be fair, in practice put a particular racial group at a disadvantage.

Sex Discrimination Act 1975

This Act makes it unlawful to discriminate against someone on the grounds of their gender, marital status, gender reassignment or sexual orientation.

This Act was updated in 1986 to remove restrictions on women's hours of work. It allows women to take jobs with flexible hours. The Act not only covers discrimination in the workplace but in job advertisements and interviews.

CASE STUDY

Alison is the manager of a retail travel agency. She had a baby, Marcus, and went on maternity leave. When she started back at work, she realised that she didn't want to work full time anymore, she wanted to work part time and have some time with her baby. She was told that she could not work part time and had to come back full time. She was going to resign but got in touch with her union TSSA and explained the situation. An employment rights advisor told her to think about finding a job share partner. She didn't advise resigning without trying to find a solution. Alison did manage to find someone who wanted to job share and the TSSA helped them put a proposal together which was accepted by the employer.

Find out what the TSSA is and what it does.

Was there discrimination in this case and if so why?

Disability Discrimination Act 1995

A disabled person is 'anyone who has a physical or mental impairment which has a substantial or long term adverse effect on his/her ability to carry on normal day to day activities.'

This act makes discrimination against disabled people unlawful in respect of employment, education and access to goods, facilities, services and premises.

Employers are required to make reasonable adjustments to accommodate people with disabilities. Examples include providing specially adapted keyboards for arthritis sufferers, allowing wheelchair access and relocating people with limited mobility to the ground floor.

In travel and tourism it is important that organisations cater for customers with disabilities but it is not always straightforward to do so as our case study shows.

THOMAS COOK TARGETS DISABLED MARKET

In 2004, Enable Holidays was launched, a Birmingham based direct sell operator for those with mobility problems. In 2005 Enable signed a deal with Thomas Cook agencies to sell Enable's holidays. Thomas Cook claims it is the only high street chain with a deal with an operator which audits property in such detail – part of its commitment to responsible tourism.

Every hotel in Enable's portfolio of 60 hotels in 20 destinations is carefully assessed with 150 aspects of accessibility. Cook agencies also offer special assistance teams which can help clients with a range of disabilities. Hearing induction loops have also been installed in shops to help the hard of hearing.

Source: *Travel Trade Gazette*, 17th June 2005

Cook Faces discrimination case

Thomas Cook holidays faces a discrimination case that could shake the industry.

The case is being brought by a Paraolympic athlete who claims he could not book because he is a permanent wheelchair user.

Dean Cavanagh, from Stockport, believes the operator breached the Disability Discrimination Act by giving him a worse standard of service than a non-wheelchair user would have received.

At a preliminary hearing at Manchester County Court, Cavanagh claimed numerous obstacles were put in his way after he went to a Thomas Cook shop in Manchester to book a holiday.

Cavanagh claimed that the web booking service was inaccessible to him, that inaccurate hotel information was given, and that he was told he must go to the shop to research hotels.

His solicitor, Paul Daniels, said: "This was a problem waiting to happen. It will be a red light to people to sort this out."

Cavanagh said: "At one point I was told that there were no hotels with wheelchair access available for the time I wanted to travel to Italy, Egypt and Croatia."

The parties must wait two months for a date for the case. Thomas Cook said it was unable to comment on ongoing legal matters.

Source: *Travel Trade Gazette* 22nd July 2005

1. **Consider which legislation applies in the case of the second article.**
2. **Discuss with your group how two such different reports can occur about the same organisation.**
3. **Suggest methods to prevent the situation described in the second article occurring again.**

Extension task: Find another example of a breach of the Disability Discrimination Act in travel and tourism. Find an example also of good practice. Explain your examples to your colleagues.

Equal Pay Act 1970

This Act allows female employees to claim equal pay for work of equal value in terms of demands made on a female employee, such as effort, skills and decisions made by women. There is also an EU Directive that states that for the same work or work of equal value sex discrimination must be eliminated in all aspects of pay.

Age discrimination

Legislation prohibiting discrimination on the grounds of age is promised in the UK by October 2006. This is in line with a European Employment Directive. This directive also added sexual orientation and religion to discrimination laws and these are already in place. The age legislation is not introduced until 2006 to give the government time to resolve the complex problems associated with its introduction and to allow employers sufficient time to prepare for the changes.

Travel agencies have already increased the number of older staff working in agencies. A Co-op Travel Group manager was quoted as saying 'Mature staff make our customers more comfortable when booking – they are booking with their peers, as most of our customers are 35 plus.' Thomas Cook has been recognised by the government's Age Positive campaign as an 'employer champion' based on its recruitment of older staff for its shops.

✱ REMEMBER!

Note that discrimination is sometimes reasonable and is therefore lawful. At airports female security officers are required to search females.

Discrimination is a very serious issue and can result in paying large amounts in compensation following successful tribunals and bad publicity. Employers need to set up policies to ensure that the workplace is free from discrimination.

Measures to be taken by employers:

✱ Set up a comprehensive equal opportunities policy covering all aspects of discrimination.

✱ Train staff in discrimination legislation and on how to implement the equal opportunities policy.

✱ Set up complaints procedures for instances of discrimination.

✱ Ensure that discriminatory behaviour is never condoned and that action is taken where necessary.

Theory into practice

Find out about the equal opportunities policy at your place of work or education. Is provision made for all aspects of discrimination? What happens if someone feels they are being discriminated against? What training is given to staff or students in equal opportunities? Make notes on your findings and discuss with your group.

Employment Rights Act 1996

When you get a job you can expect to receive a contract of employment. This is a legally binding agreement between the employer and the employee. The employer must give the employee the following information, in writing, within two months of starting work:

✱ Name of employer and employee

✱ Date employment began

✱ Rate of pay and interval of pay

✱ Hours of work

✱ Holiday entitlement and pay

✱ Job title and brief description of duties

✱ Place of work

✱ Notice entitlement and requirements

✱ Sick leave and sick pay

✱ Pension and pension schemes

✱ Disciplinary procedures and grievance procedures

✱ Date of end of employment if fixed term

✱ Additional details about working abroad.

Some terms are 'implied' but still legally binding. For example, the employer has a duty to provide safe systems of work, a safe workplace and to employ competent staff who would not be a danger to themselves or other staff.

EU directives on hours and pay

The European Working Time Directive was enacted in the UK through the Working Time Regulations, 1998. This gives:

* a maximum 48-hour week averaged over 17 weeks

* at least four weeks paid annual leave

* a weekly rest period of at least 24 hours in each seven day period

* a daily rest period of at least 11 consecutive hours between each working day

* an in-work rest break of 20 minutes for those working six hours or more per day.

Some sectors are excluded from the regulations. One of these is transport.

National Minimum Wage Act 1998

This Act provides workers with a floor below which their wages will not fall. Those who work part time benefit most. The Low Pay Commission advises the Secretary of State on the value of the minimum hourly rate. A lower rate applies to 18–21 year olds.

Maternity and paternity leave

The Employment Relations Act 1999 provides for basic rights for maternity leave. There are three periods of maternity leave. Ordinary maternity leave is for a period of 18 weeks which coincides with the period for statutory maternity pay. This applies to all employees.

Compulsory maternity leave extends to a period of two weeks after the birth. The employer must not permit the woman to return to work during this period. Additional maternity leave follows immediately after the original 18 week period and must end within 29 weeks of the birth. Employees with at least one year's service with an employer are eligible for the additional maternity leave.

Under the same Act there are provisions to allow parents three months leave in order to care for a child. This is intended to be before the child is five. It is intended to be available to men and to women, in addition to maternity leave.

Paternity leave is available to men who:

* have, or expect to have, responsibility for the child's upbringing

* are the biological father of the child or the mother's husband or partner

* have worked continuously for their employer for 26 weeks ending with the 15th week before the baby is due.

Statutory Sickness Pay

An employer must pay Statutory Sick Pay to employees who become sick and who normally earn at least £79 per week. After 28 weeks Incapacity Benefit or Income Support must be claimed instead.

12.3 A travel organisation, its operation and how it meets the needs of customers

In this section you will choose one specific organisation from a sector of travel and tourism that is of interest to you. You will carry out research into that organisation to meet the requirements of the assessment evidence.

It is important that you choose an organisation which has sufficient information about its operations in the public arena, particularly financial information, so that you are able to discuss the scale and structure of the company. On the other hand if you choose a multinational organisation which has many subsidiaries you may find there is too much information for you to handle efficiently.

Unit 8 has full details on how to determine whether a research issue is viable and how to go about research. You should refer to pages 41–76 and use this information to help you carry out your research. When choosing your sector, look back through this book to help you choose a sector appropriate to you. Remember to focus as well on customer needs, as explained in Unit 8.

7–9 marks

A description of a selected organisation from within a chosen sector of the industry is given. The description has detail in terms of type, scale and structure of the organisation. A range of products and services provided by the organisation is described in detail. A clear explanation is provided of how the products and services meet the needs of different types of customers. A range of customers is considered and the explanation clearly links to each type of customer. Gaps in provision are described and linked to customers.

10-12 marks

A comprehensive description of a selected organisation from within a chosen sector of the industry is given. The description has detail in terms of type, scale and structure of the organisation. Description is current and accurate. A wide range of products and services provided by the organisation is described in detail. An explanation, with examples, is provided of how the products and services meet the needs of a wide range of different types of customers with explanations clearly linked to the type of customer. Gaps in provision are appropriate and described in detail and clearly linked to customers.

2. Application of knowledge and understanding of the specified content and of related skills in vocationally-related contexts.

1–7 marks

A proposal is submitted for a new or adapted product, service or facility. This may lack detail or is not appropriate to fill identified gaps in provision. An explanation of the proposal is given but this may be limited in terms of its links to customers' needs.

8–12 marks

A proposal is submitted for a new or adapted product, service or facility. The proposal is appropriate to fill identified gaps and meet customer needs. There is a clear description of the proposal. An explanation of the proposal is provided that makes clear links between gaps in provision and customer needs.

13–15 marks

A proposal is submitted for a new or adapted product, service or facility. The proposal is appropriate to fill identified gaps and meet customer needs. There is a clear and comprehensive description of the proposal. A thorough explanation of the proposal is provided that makes clear the link between gaps in provision and how it meets customer needs.

3. Use of appropriate research techniques to obtain information to analyse vocationally-related issues and problems.

1–7 marks

Some research has been undertaken and is evidenced mainly through a bibliography. Sources used were those directed by others. There is some basic analysis of the legal and regulatory requirements that have affected the operation of the chosen sector of the industry but evidence tends to be descriptive. There may be some key legal and regulatory requirements not considered or some are not appropriate to the sector. There is some reference to how the operations in the sector of the industry have been affected but these are not clearly presented.

8–12 marks

Research has been undertaken using different sources, some of which were obtained independently. Some evidence of research is referenced throughout the text, as well as in a bibliography. There is some analysis of the legal and regulatory requirements that have affected the operation of a chosen sector of the industry. An appropriate selection of legal and regulatory requirements has been selected for analysis, most in some depth. The analysis relates to how the legal and regulatory requirements have affected operations within the sector and includes some exemplification. The analysis is mainly clear.

13–15 marks

Research has been undertaken using a range of different sources that have been obtained independently. Much of the evidence of research is referenced throughout the text, as well as in a bibliography. There is clear analysis of a wide range of appropriate legal and regulatory requirements that have affected the operation of the chosen sector of the industry. The analysis relates to how each has affected the operation of a sector of the travel and tourism industry. The analysis is well-exemplified and clearly presented.

4. Evaluation of information to make reasoned judgements, draw conclusions and make recommendations about vocationally-related issues and problems.

1–9 marks

There is an evaluation of the degree of influence held by key organisations in the sector but this is mainly descriptive. Some key organisations may be omitted and some less important organisations included. The evaluation makes some reference to statistical data but this is limited. There is an evaluation of the connections between the sector and other sectors in the travel and tourism industry but this is mainly descriptive. There may be limited reference to some sectors of the industry. Judgements made may lack reasoning and be mainly subjective.

10–14 marks

There is an evaluation of the degree of influence held by key organisations in the sector. Key organisations have been included. The evaluation makes use of statistical data, some of which is current. Data is interpreted mainly accurately. There is an evaluation of the connections between the sector and other sectors in the travel and tourism industry. There are clear references to all key sectors of the industry although some ancillary sectors may not be included. Judgements made show some reasoning and some are substantiated.

15–18 marks

There is a comprehensive evaluation of the degree of influence held by key organisations in the sector. Key organisations have been included. Other organisations are referred to in support of conclusions made. The evaluation makes use of a range of current statistical data.

Data is interpreted accurately and used appropriately. There is comprehensive evaluation of the connections between the sector and other sectors in the travel and tourism industry.

There are clear references to all key sectors of the industry. Judgements made are reasoned and substantiated.

Assessment practice

Travel and tourism organisation

1. Decide which sector of the travel and tourism industry you wish to research and choose an organisation within that sector.

2. Carry out preliminary research to determine whether there is sufficient information available from a variety of sources to enable you to complete your research project.

3. Produce a brief research proposal and confirm it with your tutor.

4. Produce a description of your selected organisation including the following:

   * type, scale and structure of the organisation

   * description of its products and services

   * explanation of how the products and services meet the needs of different types of customers

   * identification of gaps in provision linked to customers.

5. Give a detailed proposal for a new or adapted product, service or facility for your selected organisation to fulfil the identified gaps in provision. Explain how it meets customer needs.

6. Analyse the extent to which legal and regulatory requirements have affected the operation of the chosen sector of the industry.

7. Give an evaluation of the degree of influence held by key organisations in the sector and the connections between the sector and others in the travel and tourism industry.

Make sure you use correct referencing throughout your work and include a bibliography. Consider how you will present your work. You could present it orally, with visual aids, as a written report or as an informative brochure.

Knowledge check

1. What is an e-agent?
2. What is the role of the DCMS in tourism?
3. Explain the difference between the National Trust and English Heritage.
4. What is a regional development agency?
5. Describe the role of a tour operator.
6. Why has the London Eye never made a profit?
7. What is an inbound tour operator?
8. Which airline is the largest in the UK?
9. Where is Ryanair registered?
10. Give two examples of charter airlines.
11. What is an A380?
12. Why did Hoverspeed close its Dover Calais route?
13. Explain the difference between the Shuttle and Eurostar.
14. How does a train operating company work with Network Rail?
15. Give an example of a budget hotel chain.
16. Which legislation is of particular importance to tour operators?
17. Which Act affects food production and service?
18. What is the principle of the Trades Description Act?
19. Which Act affects tour bus drivers?
20. Name two Acts relevant to employment.

Index